FRANCIS FRITH'S
TOWN & CITY
MEMORIES

WISBECH

ROBERT BELL was born in Wisbech in 1964 and for the past fifteen years has worked for the Wisbech and Fenland Museum, where he is now Assistant Curator. Whilst working with the museum's extensive archive he has developed good knowledge of the local history. Other interests include photography and numismatics.

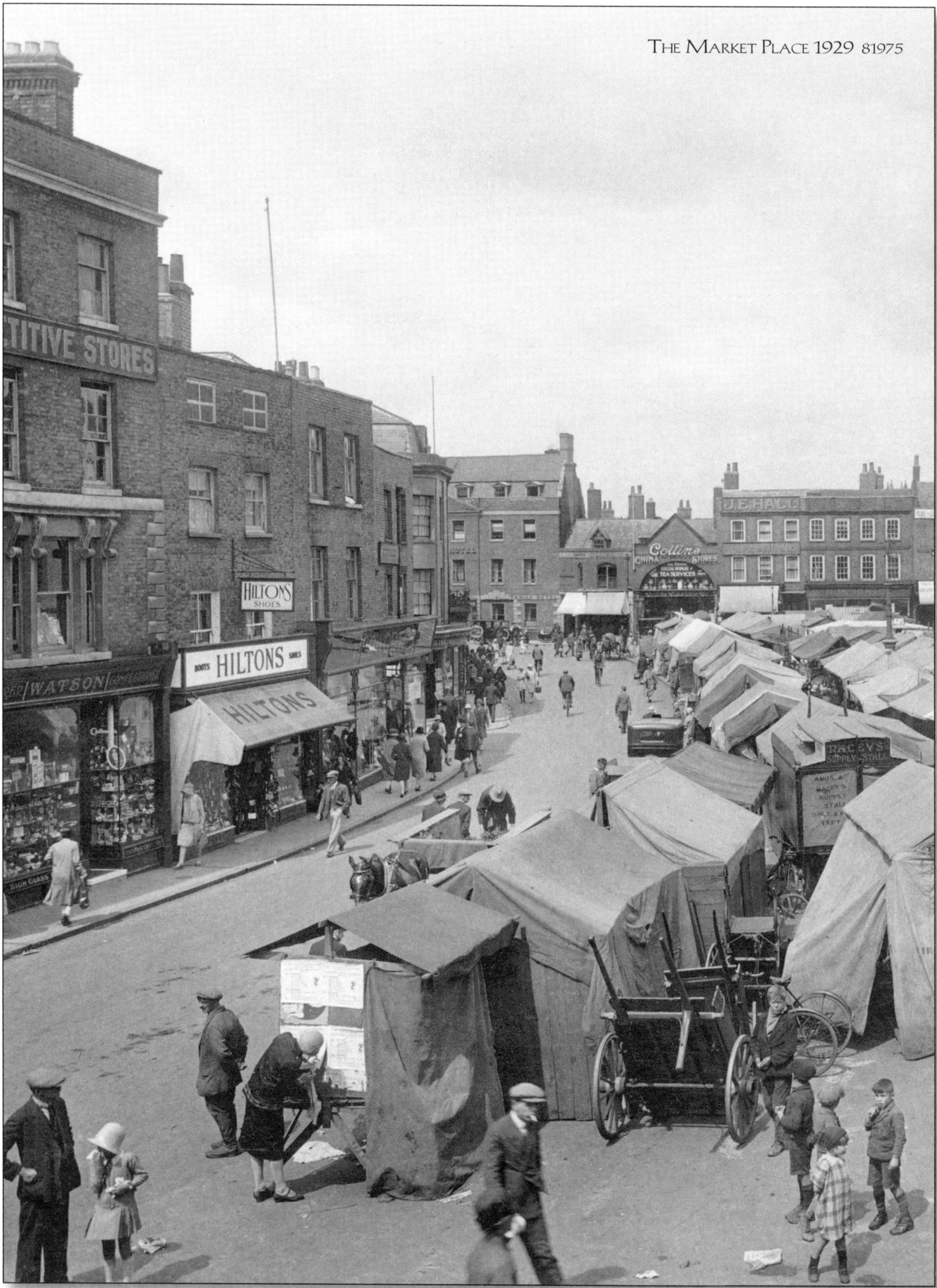

THE MARKET PLACE 1929 81975

FRANCIS FRITH'S
TOWN & CITY
MEMORIES

WISBECH

ROBERT BELL

FRANCIS FRITH'S
TOWN & CITY
MEMORIES

First published as Wisbech, A Photographic History of your Town
in 2001 by Black Horse Books, an imprint of The Francis Frith Collection
Revised edition published in the United Kingdom in 2005 by
The Francis Frith Collection as Wisbech, Town and City Memories
Limited Hardback Edition ISBN 1-84589-060-4
Paperback Edition ISBN 1-84589-031-0

British Library Cataloguing in Publication Data

Wisbech
Town and City Memories
Robert Bell

The Francis Frith Collection®
Frith's Barn, Teffont,
Salisbury, Wiltshire SP3 5QP
Tel: +44 (0) 1722 716 376
Email: info@francisfrith.co.uk
www.francisfrith.co.uk

Aerial photographs reproduced under licence from Simmons Aerofilms Limited
Historical Ordnance Survey maps reproduced under licence from Homecheck.co.uk

Printed and bound in England

Front Cover: **WISBECH, THE MARKET PLACE 1929** 81975t
The colour-tinting in this image is for illustrative purposes only,
and is not intended to be historically accurate

Every attempt has been made to contact copyright holders of illustrative material.
We will be happy to give full acknowledgement in future editions for any items not
credited. Any information should be directed to The Francis Frith Collection.

AS WITH ANY HISTORICAL DATABASE, THE FRANCIS FRITH ARCHIVE IS CONSTANTLY BEING
CORRECTED AND IMPROVED, AND THE PUBLISHERS WOULD WELCOME INFORMATION ON
OMISSIONS OR INACCURACIES

FRANCIS FRITH'S

TOWN & CITY

MEMORIES

CONTENTS

The Making of an Archive 6

Wisbech from the Air 8

Introduction 10

Cambridgeshire's Port 16

The Brinks 24

The Town Bridge and Bridge Street 33

Cambridgeshire County Map 44

Market Place 46

The Castle, Crescent and Church 58

Ordnance Survey Map 70

The Canal, Park and Road to King's Lynn 72

Names of Subscribers 86

Index 89

VOUCHER FOR FREE MOUNTED PRINT 91

The Making of an Archive

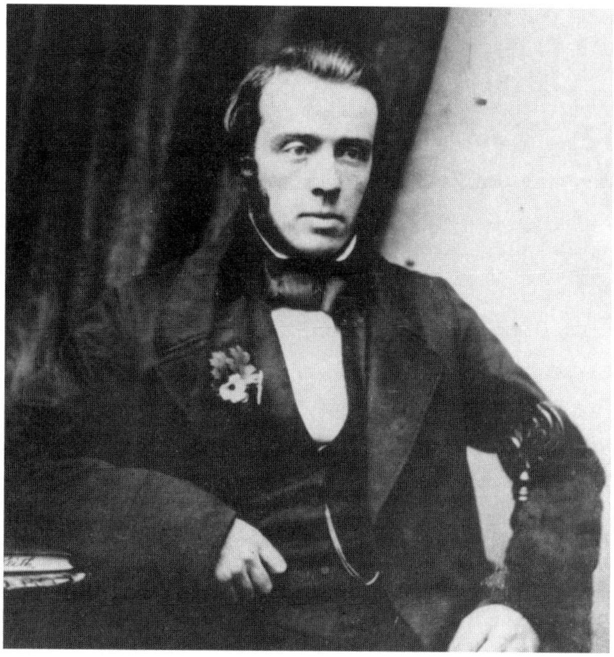

Francis Frith, Victorian founder of the world-famous photographic archive, was a devout Quaker and a highly successful Victorian businessman. By 1860 he was already a multi-millionaire, having established and sold a wholesale grocery business in Liverpool. He had also made a series of pioneering photographic journeys to the Nile region. The images he returned with were the talk of London. An eminent modern historian has likened their impact on the population of the time to that on our own generation of the first photographs taken on the surface of the moon.

Frith had a passion for landscape, and was as equally inspired by the countryside of Britain as he was by the desert regions of the Nile. He resolved to set out on a new career and to use his skills with a camera. He established a business in Reigate as a specialist publisher of topographical photographs.

Frith lived in an era of immense and sometimes violent change. For the poor in the early part of Victoria's reign work was a drudge and the hours long, and ordinary people had precious little free time. Most had not travelled far beyond the boundaries of their own town or village. Mass tourism was in its infancy during the 1860s, but during the next decade the railway network and the establishment of Bank Holidays and half-Saturdays gradually made it possible for the working man and his family to enjoy holidays and to see a little more of the world. With characteristic business acumen, Francis Frith foresaw that these new tourists would enjoy having souvenirs to commemorate their days out. He began selling photo-souvenirs of seaside resorts and beauty spots, which the Victorian public pasted into treasured family albums.

Frith's aim was to photograph every town and village in Britain. For the next thirty years he travelled the country by train and by pony and trap, producing fine photographs of seaside resorts and beauty spots that were keenly bought by millions of Victorians.

The Rise of Frith & Co

Each photograph was taken with tourism in mind, the small team of Frith photographers concentrating on busy shopping streets, beaches, seafronts, picturesque lanes and villages. They also photographed buildings: the Victorian and Edwardian eras were times of huge building activity, and town halls, libraries, post offices, schools and technical colleges were springing up all over the country. They were invariably celebrated by a proud Victorian public, and photo souvenirs – visual records – published by F Frith & Co were sold in their hundreds of thousands. In addition, many new commercial buildings such as hotels, inns and pubs were photographed, often because their owners specifically commissioned Frith postcards or prints of them for re-sale or for publicity purposes.

In order to gain some understanding of the scale of Frith's business one only has to look at the catalogue issued by Frith & Co in 1886: it runs to some 670 pages. By 1890 Frith had created the greatest specialist photographic publishing company in the world, with over 2,000 stockists! The picture on the right shows the Frith & Co display board on the wall of the stockist at Ingleton in the Yorkshire Dales (left of window). Beautifully constructed with a mahogany frame and gilt inserts, it displayed a dozen scenes.

The Making of an Archive

Postcard Bonanza

The ever-popular holiday postcard we know today took many years to appear, and F Frith & Co was in the vanguard of its development. Postcards became a hugely popular means of communication and sold in their millions. Frith's company took full advantage of this boom and soon became the major publisher of photographic view postcards.

Francis Frith died in 1898 at his villa in Cannes, his great project still growing. His sons Eustace and Cyril continued their father's monumental task, expanding the number of views offered to the public and recording more and more places in Britain, as the coasts and countryside were opened up to mass travel. The archive Frith created continued in business for another seventy years. By 1970 it contained over a third of a million pictures of 7,000 cities, towns and villages. The massive photographic record Frith has left to us stands as a living monument to a special and very remarkable man.

This book shows Wisbech as it was photographed by this world-famous archive at various periods in its development over the past 150 years. Every photograph was taken for a specific commercial purpose, which explains why the selection may not show every aspect of the town landscape. However, the photographs, compiled from one of the world's most celebrated archives, provide an important and absorbing record of your town.

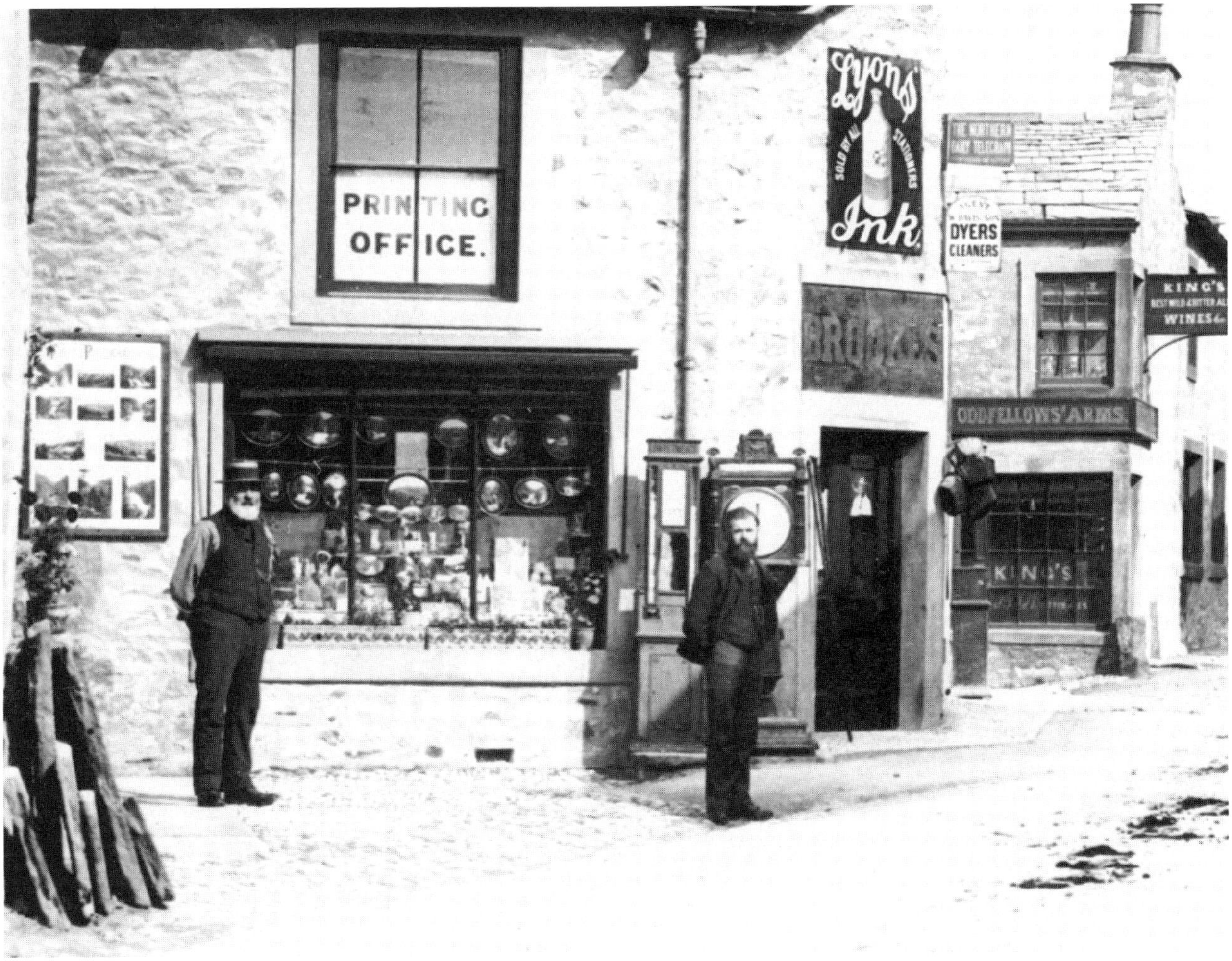

WISBECH

FROM THE AIR

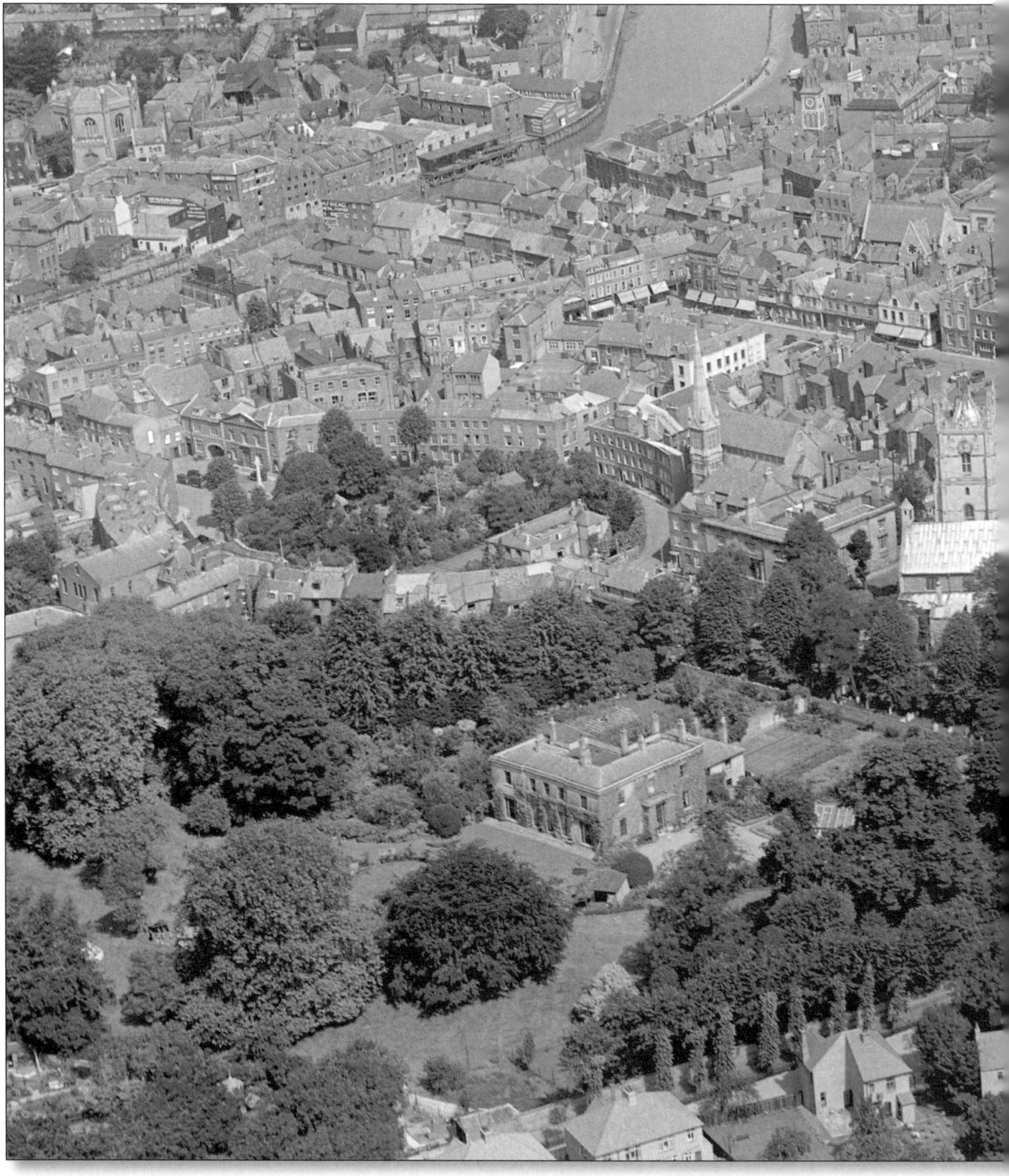

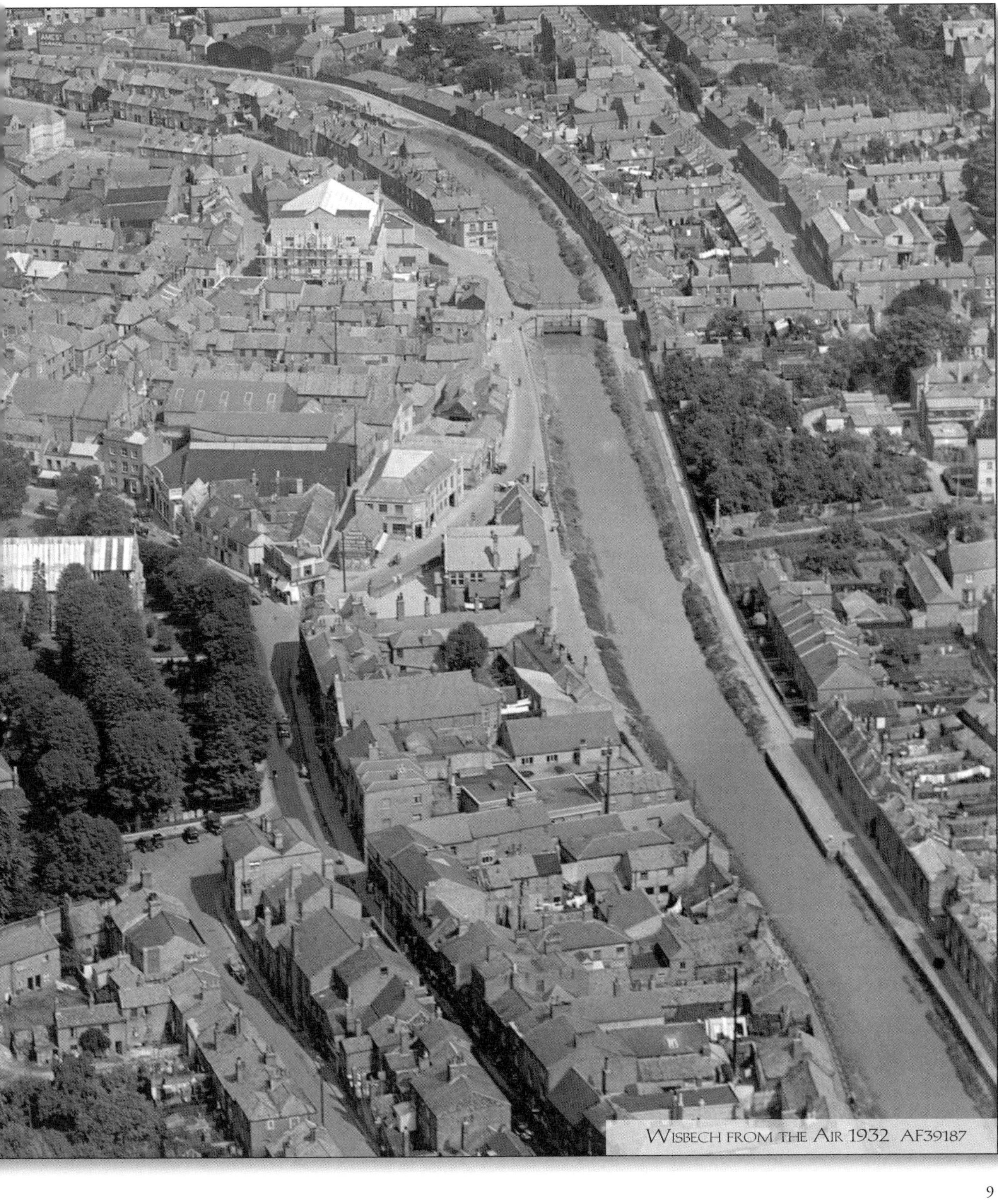

WISBECH FROM THE AIR 1932 AF39187

INTRODUCTION

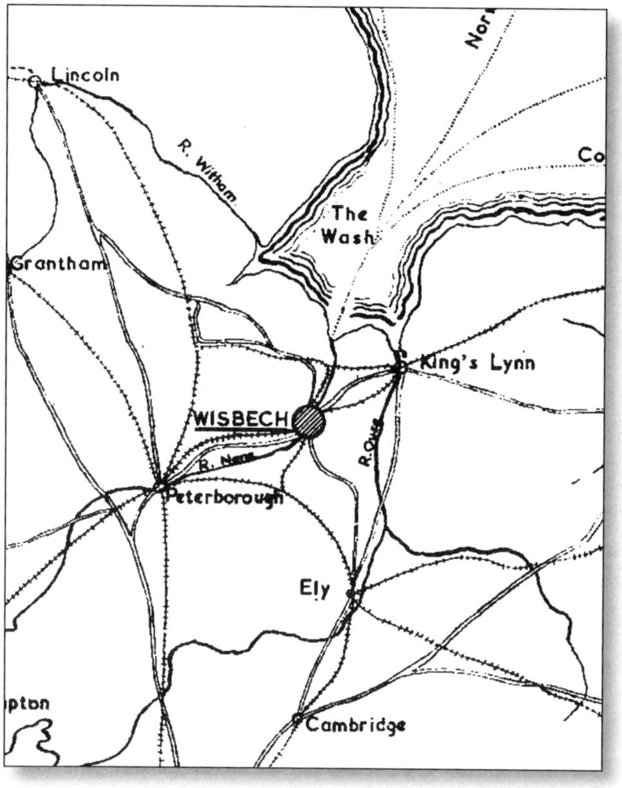

MAP SHOWING THE COMMUNICATIONS TO AND FROM WISBECH c1950

Today there is only a single freight line connecting Wisbech to the railway network.

Wisbech is located around ninety miles to the north of London, at the coming together of the three counties of Cambridgeshire, Norfolk and Lincolnshire. Despite being several miles from the sea, Wisbech is the only seaport in Cambridgeshire. The town's former importance as an administrative and commercial centre is sometimes overlooked, prompting queries as to why the town is referred to as the 'Capital of the Fens'.

The rise of Peterborough over the last hundred years or so, and the relative prosperity of Wisbech's other important neighbour, King's Lynn, as well as the stripping away of most of its municipal powers in the 1970s, has seen a decline in the town's status. The sense of isolation has been compounded by the reduction of the town's rail links to a single freight line.

THE PARISH CHURCH 1923 73580

Parts of the present Parish Church, which is dedicated to St Peter and St Paul, date from just after the construction of Wisbech Castle in the late 11th century. The tower was rebuilt in the 1530s, after its catastrophic collapse during the previous century.

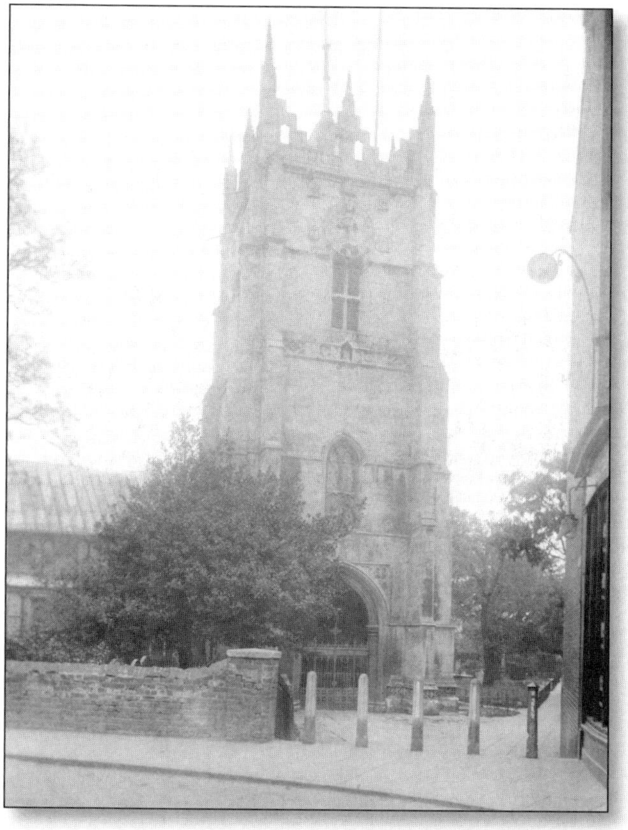

Although there were undoubtedly earlier settlements at Wisbech, the first authenticated mention of the place name occurs in AD 1000: it was one of several manors given by Oswy to the Monastery of Ely, when Oswy's son, Ailwyn, became a monk. There are many theories as to the derivation of the town's name. There is the combination 'Ouze' and 'beck' referring to a beach near the Ouse. Alternatively, you have the 'Wyse' and 'bec' theory: a combination of the river Wissey and the Saxon name for a stream. In the 1660s local tradesmen issued several tokens which had a variety of spellings: Wisbidg, Wisbitch, Wisbich and Wisbech. In more recent years the interest in the town's name has centred

INTRODUCTION

NENE QUAY AND BRIDGE C1955 W115062

It was not until the early 18th century that the benefits of the large-scale drainage schemes of the previous century began to be felt. The subsequent prosperity of the district is praised in the Wisbech entry in the Universal British Directory of Trade and Commerce of the 1790s; this stated that the area had 'been in a most flourishing and productive state, the fields seem to laugh and sing with their superabundant produce'.

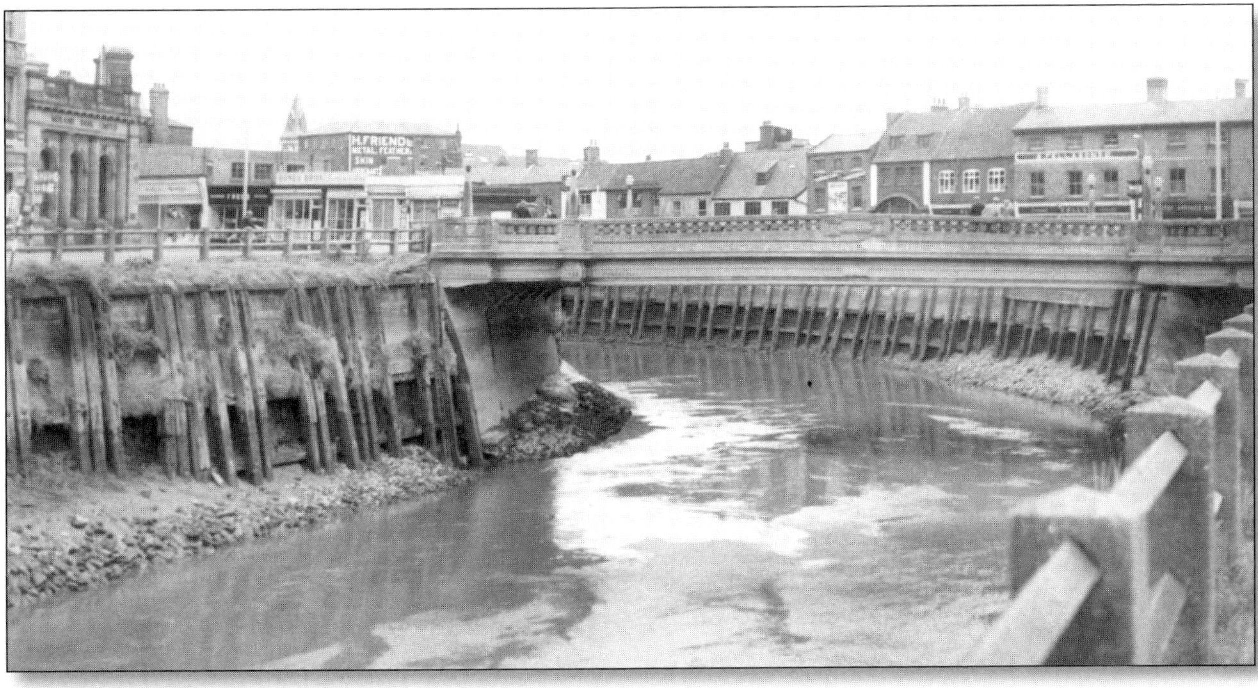

around when it lost its 'a'; the use of the 'Wisbeach' spelling is said to have begun in the 18th century and there seems to have been a dual usage until the 1870s. At this time the Postmaster General and various railway companies were approached for their opinion and it was decided to lose the 'a'. One local wit asked that if the towns of Holbeach, Landbeach and Waterbeach dropped the 'a' would Wisbech restore theirs!

After the conquest of William I, the Fens remained a troublesome problem for the new King and it was not until the betrayal and defeat of Hereward the Wake that the Normans could exercise any measure of control in this inhospitable and dangerous land. William's great survey of 1086, the Domesday Book, records 'Wisbece' as a 'modest vill' (village), although substantial eel fisheries are mentioned. The following year the strategic importance of Wisbech was recognised by the Conqueror with the construction of a stone castle, which probably replaced an earlier timber and earthwork complex.

In October 1216, King John stayed at the castle on his way from King's Lynn to Lincolnshire, and legend has it that he lost part of his baggage-train along with his regalia and treasure! Various theories abound as to the location of this catastrophe: to the north while crossing the broad estuary, or closer to town, as he forded the Well Stream? Despite the best efforts of treasure hunters (including a party of Russian scientists more than 30 years ago), no sign of that unfortunate king's treasure has ever been found.

Wisbech's past wealth has been closely linked to the river; from mediaeval times up to the 18th century, the town enjoyed periods of relative prosperity, punctuated by calamitous floods that set the town's development back on its heels. The port too has seen similar

INTRODUCTION

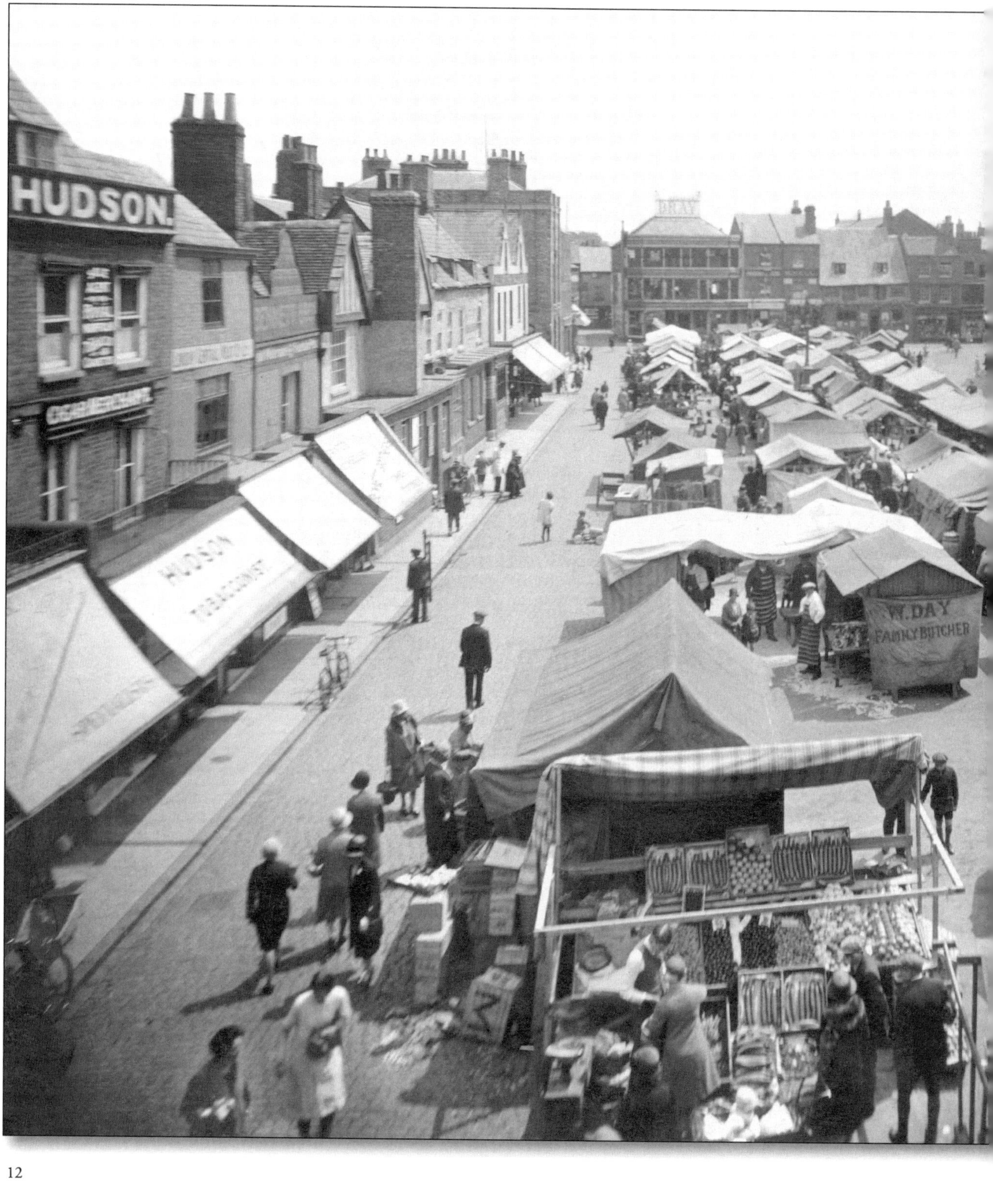

INTRODUCTION

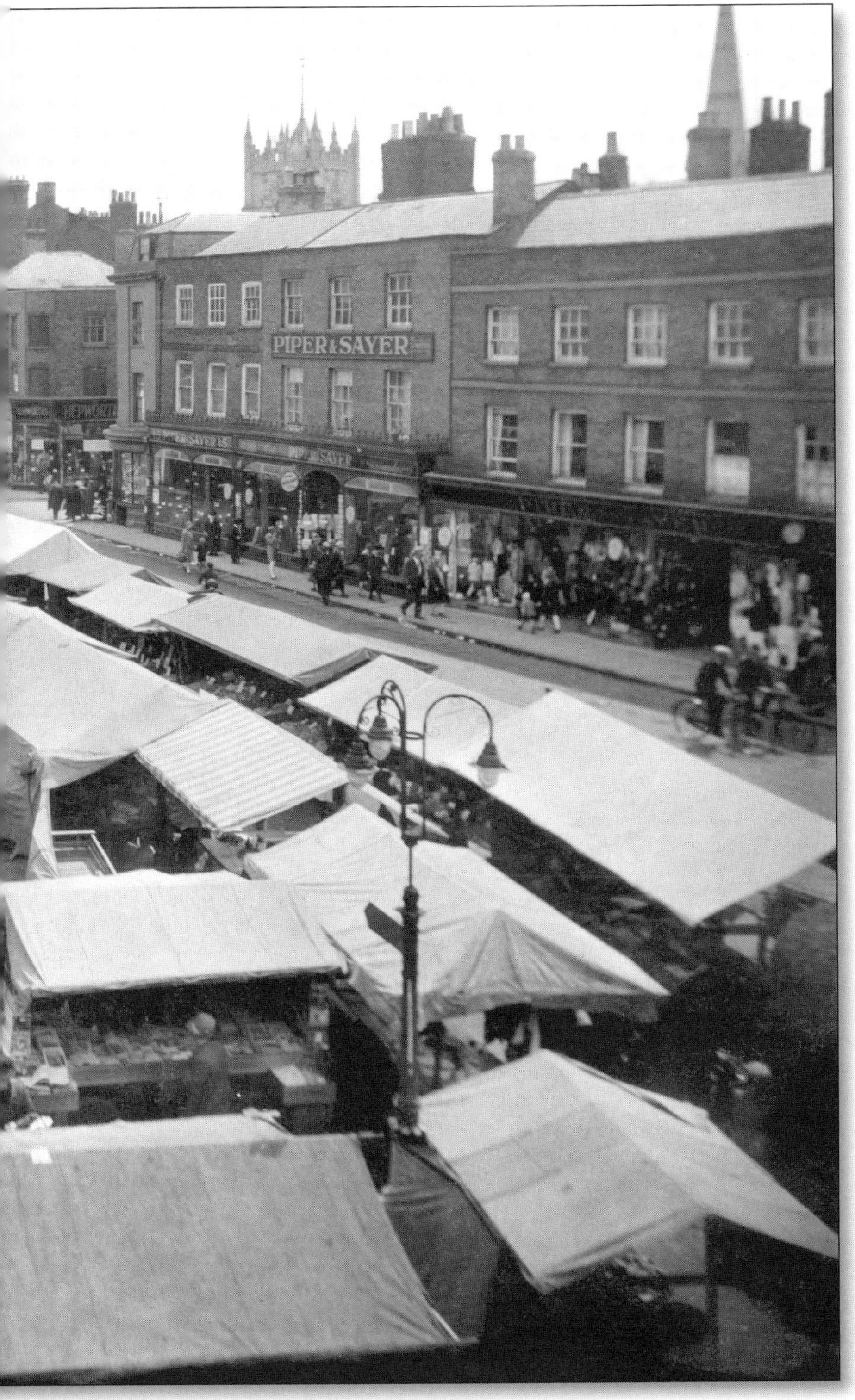

MARKET PLACE 1929 81976

In 1795, the Wisbech Canal was cut along the course of the Well Stream; thus providing communication with Ely, Cambridge and the other local towns, via the network of inland waterways that existed at that time. Within a hundred years, the canal was on its last legs, as the railways and the Wisbech to Upwell Tramway in particular became more popular.

INTRODUCTION

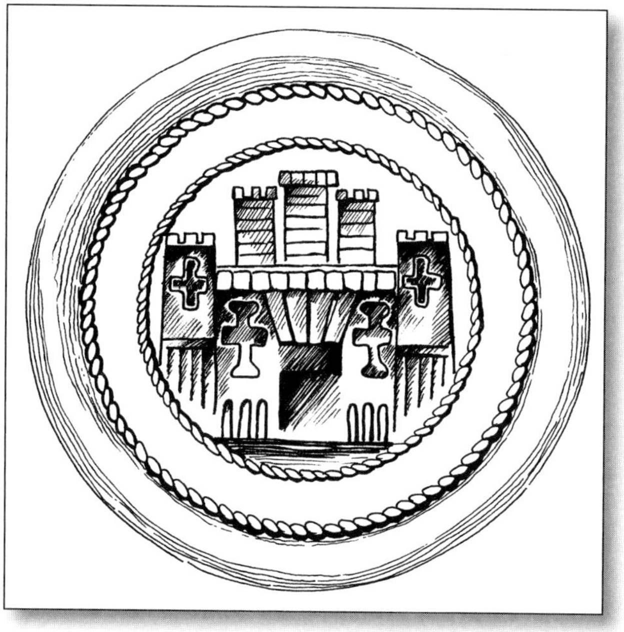

SEAL OF SIR JOHN COLVILE GOVERNOR OF WISBECH CASTLE, 1410

The seal gives a hint of how Wisbech Castle may have looked. Drawn by S Cousins.

ups and downs. When the Great Ouse, which flowed through the Well Stream, was diverted to King's Lynn about 1300, the silting of the estuary at Wisbech became a serious problem. However, with the cutting of Moreton's Leam in 1478, the River Nene became Wisbech's principal artery to the sea and the town enjoyed a revival of its fortunes.

The 18th century saw the building of grand houses by prosperous Wisbech merchants along the brinks, and the laying-out of the Crescent, along with the development of the rest of the Castle estate. During the following century the Victorians used their wealth to construct several public buildings: the gaol (1847), the museum (1847), a public hall (1852), the corn exchange (1858), the Working Men's' Institute (1864) and the cottage hospital (1873). They also built several monuments and memorials, as well as undertaking major engineering projects. It was during this period that Wisbech could justifiably call itself the 'Capital of the Fens'.

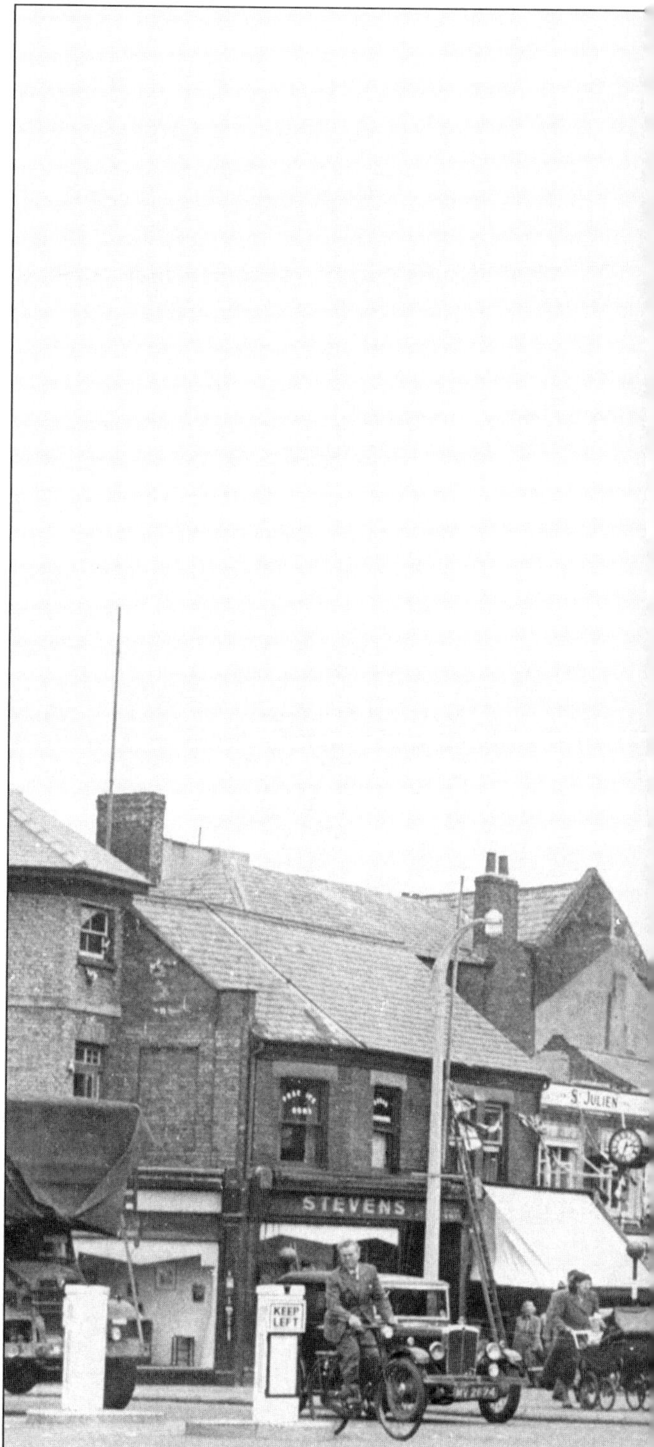

INTRODUCTION

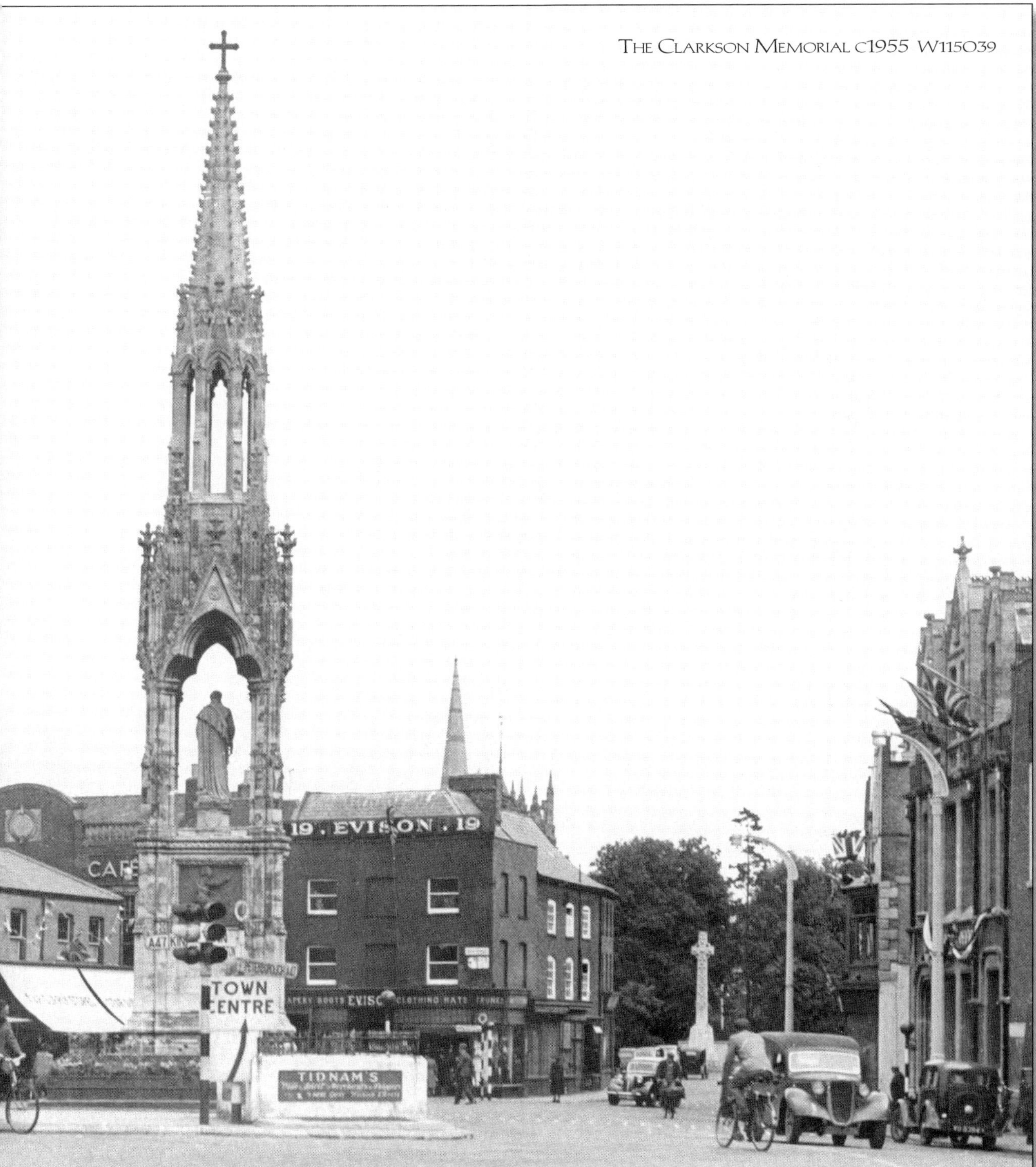

THE CLARKSON MEMORIAL c1955 W115039

WISBECH

CAMBRIDGESHIRE'S PORT

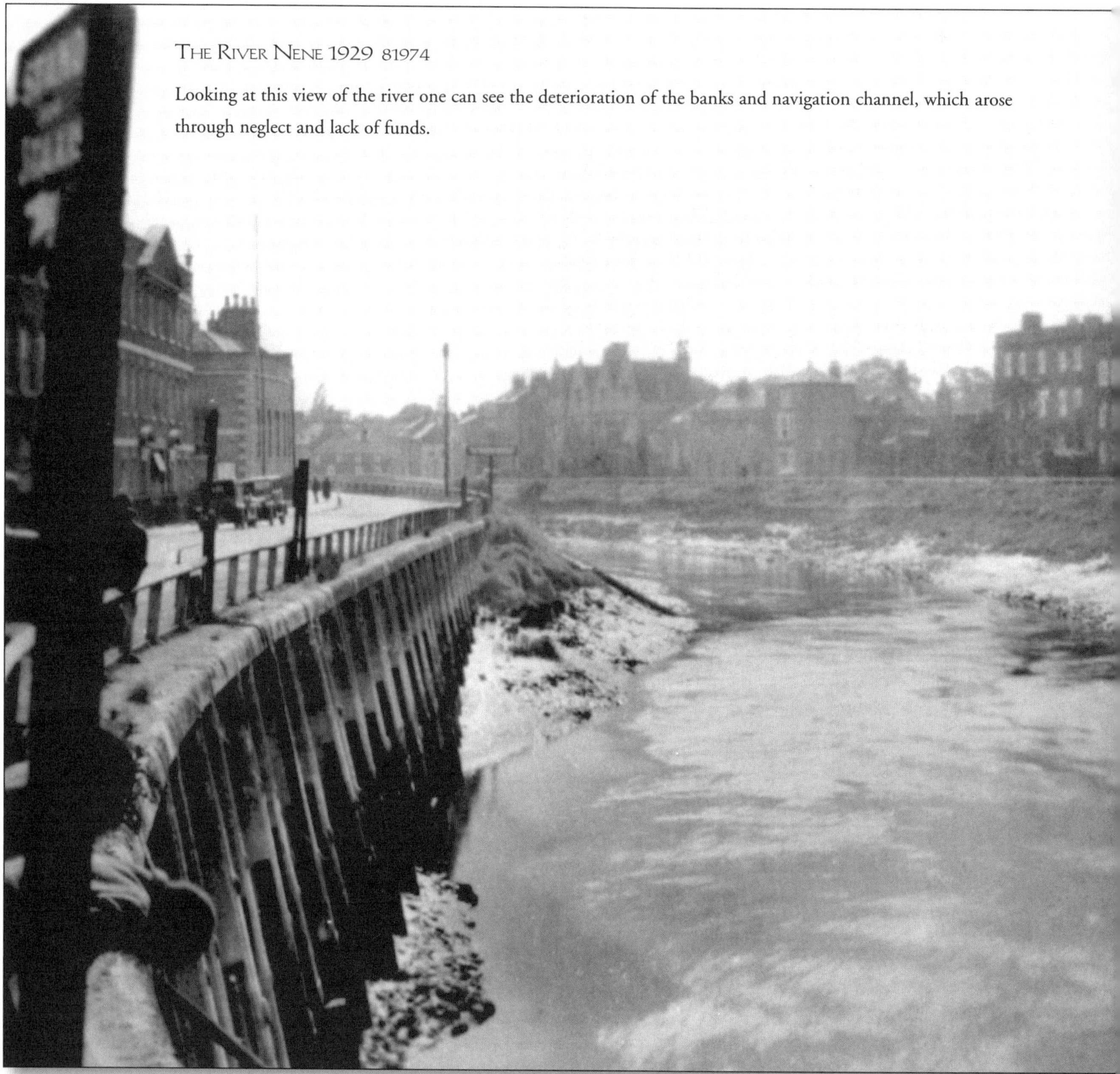

THE RIVER NENE 1929 81974

Looking at this view of the river one can see the deterioration of the banks and navigation channel, which arose through neglect and lack of funds.

Before the coming of the railways, and later motor transport, the source of much of Wisbech's wealth stemmed from its port. Vessels brought in coal from North East England and timber from the Baltic. Ironically, the port's timber trade boomed during the 1840s and 1850s, due to the heavy demand for wood for new railway lines, which were spreading across the country.

Perhaps the greatest engineering work that the Victorians undertook was the construction of the iron swing bridge and the systematic piling of the riverbanks during the 1850s. Made by Armstrong

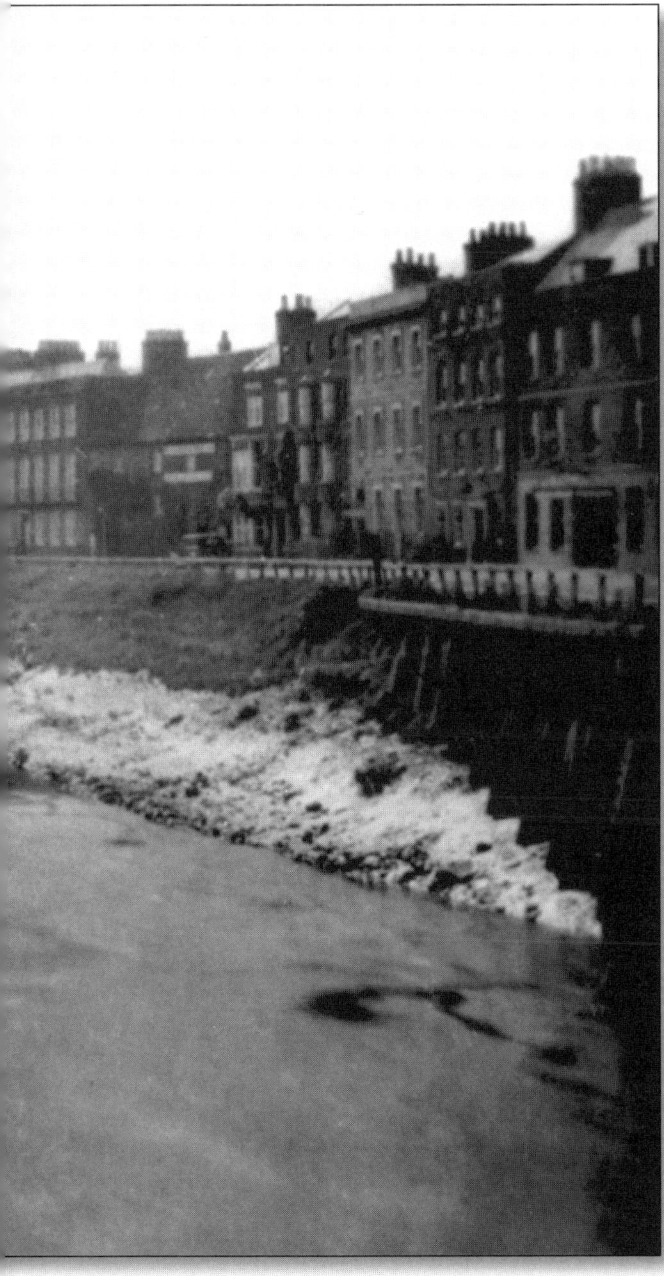

& Co of Newcastle-on-Tyne, at a cost of £15,000, the bridge was only swung once before it was fixed. The bridge may have been more practical in comparison with its predecessor, the stone bridge of 1758; however, it was quite hideous in contrast to the earlier structure with its beautiful semi-elliptical arch.

Extract from Pigot and Co's National Commercial Directory 1830

'Wisbech has for many years been an improving place, as respects its commercial importance and the appearance of the town; and it may be considered now the most flourishing trading town in the Isle of Ely. The inhabitants, duly appreciating the advantages of a fine navigation, are enterprising, and carry on a very considerable trade with London and other ports, in coal, corn, timber, wool, etc.'

With the growth of the timber trade, a series of extensive wood yards were established in the port area along Nene Parade. Before mechanisation, men would carry the planks of wood direct from the boats into the yards, using trestles to walk on. With the reduction in the trade, few of the yards remain, although recently there has been a modest revival in timber imports.

With regards to exports, since the 18th century, the corn trade has been of prime importance to the mercantile health of Wisbech: vast quantities once passed through the town's markets - more than even those of London. Corn was shipped both around the coast of Britain and also to the continent. Large granaries were raised along Nene Quay and the west bank of the river from the bridge to West Parade. Most of the buildings that survived have been converted into flats. H Friend, 'Metal, Feather & Skin Merchant', once occupied one of these.

In the 19th century, it was common to see 30 or more ships in the port at one time. They would moor right up to the town bridge, on the sharp bend in the river, beyond the area that was once known as 'The Throttle' (see photograph W115079, page 22). Even in modern times boats laden with oranges and bananas would come up to the warehouses on the west bank at the rear of the Old Market. However, with the opening of the Freedom Bridge in 1971 this became impossible. Now a busy road, Nene Quay was once an important

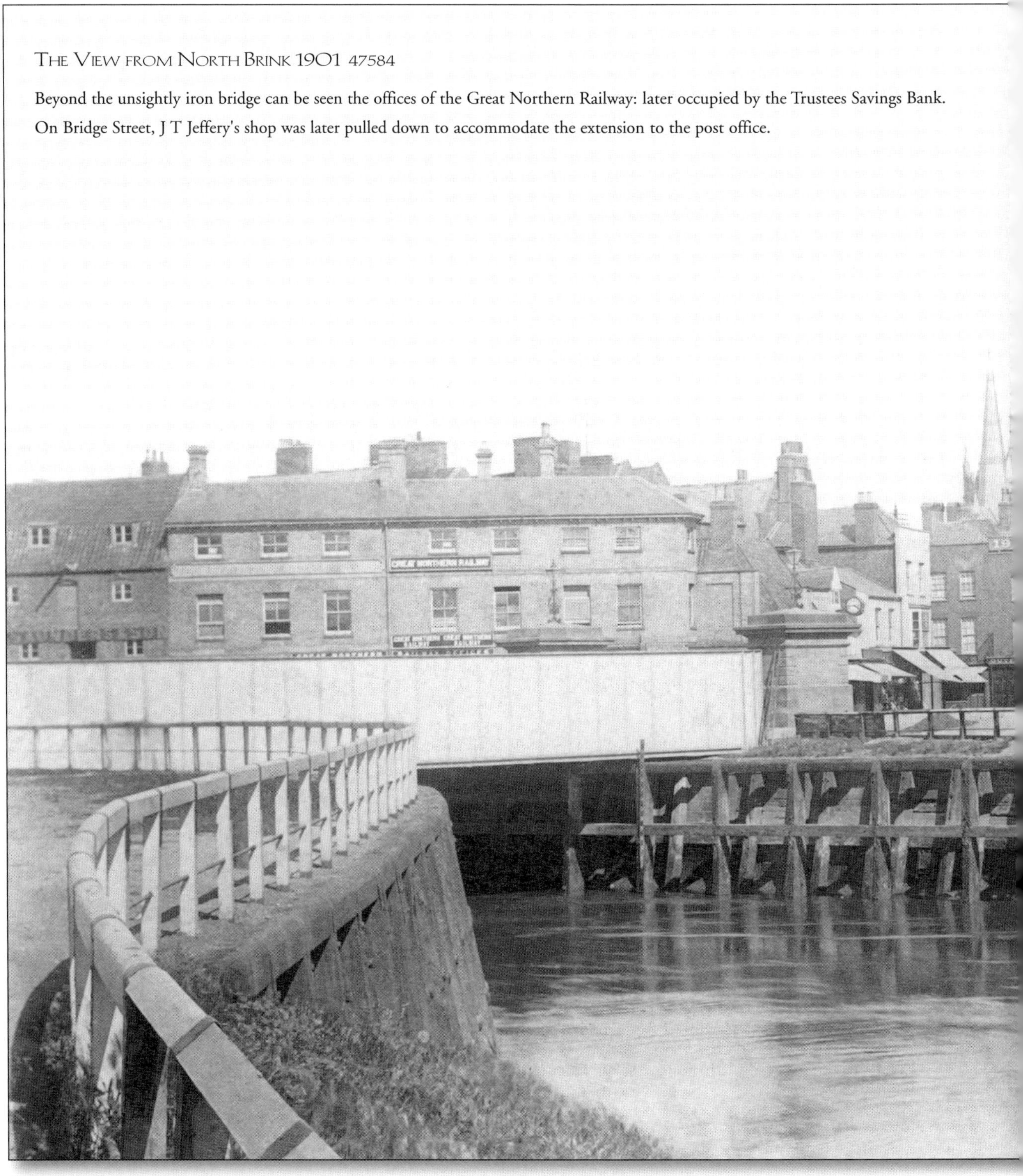

THE VIEW FROM NORTH BRINK 1901 47584

Beyond the unsightly iron bridge can be seen the offices of the Great Northern Railway: later occupied by the Trustees Savings Bank. On Bridge Street, J T Jeffery's shop was later pulled down to accommodate the extension to the post office.

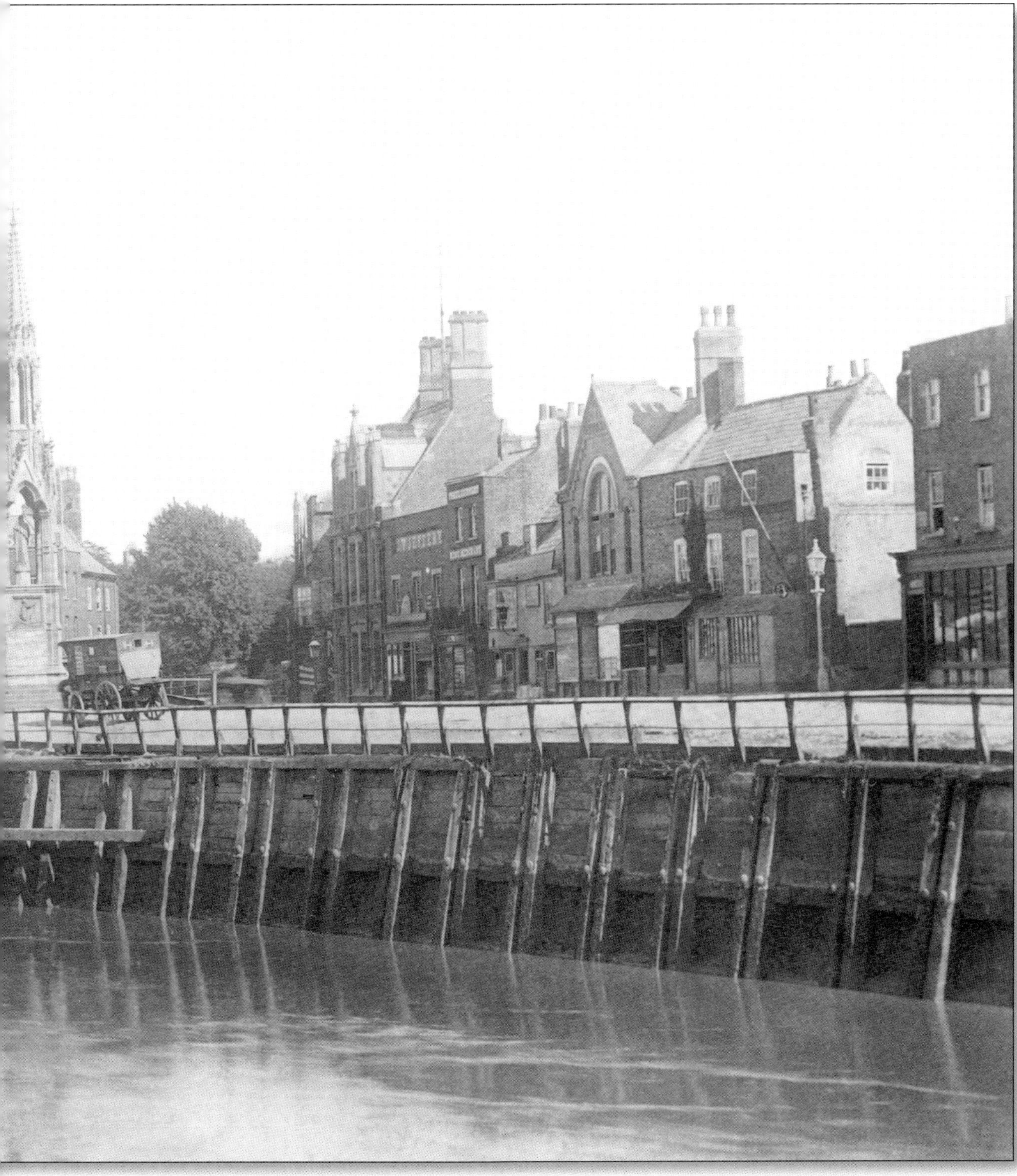

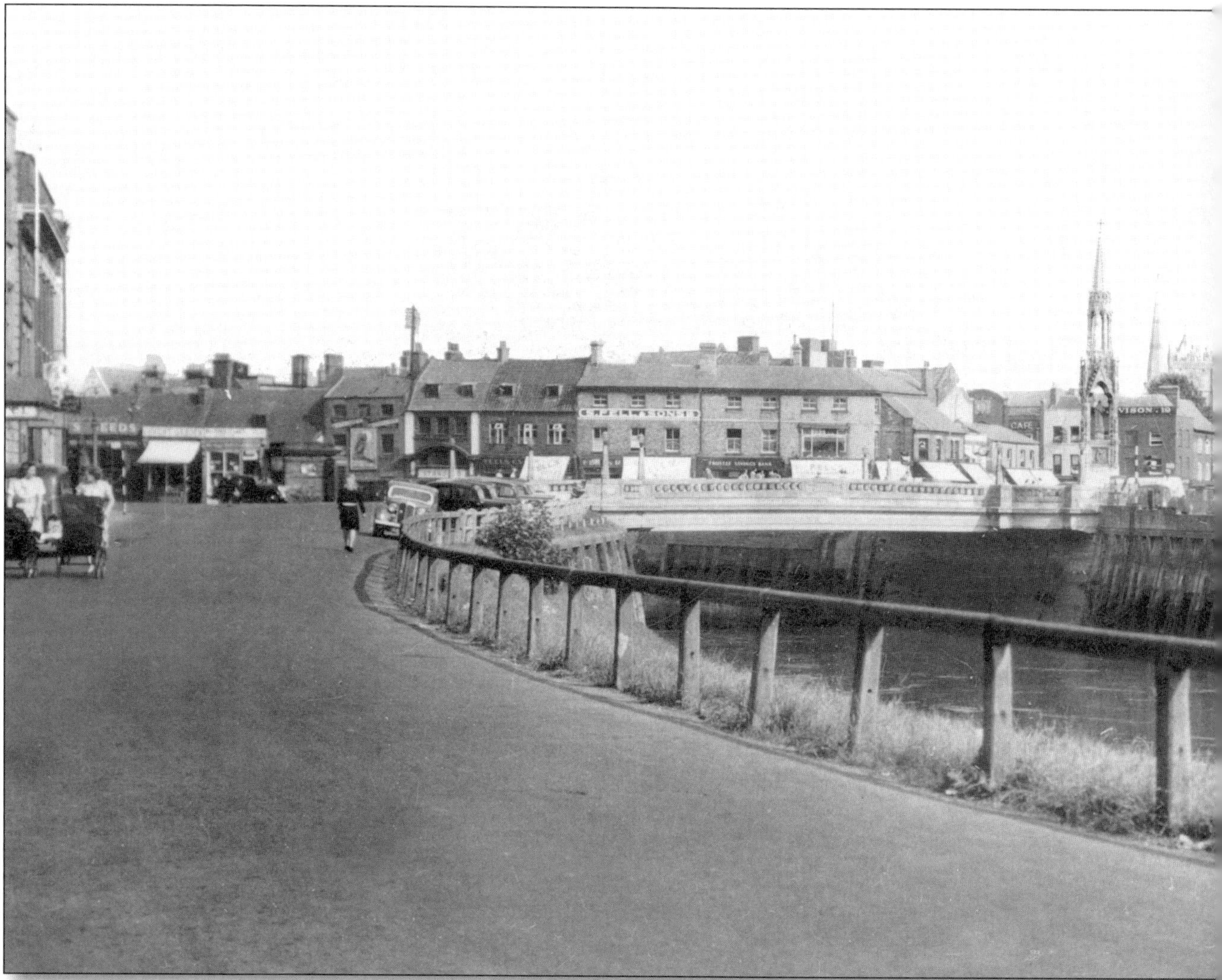

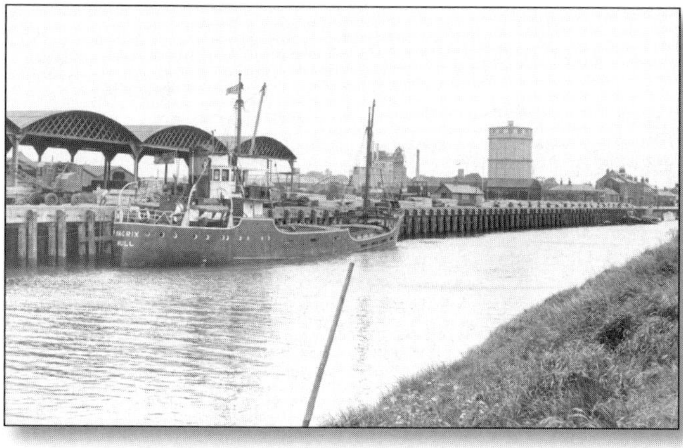

Above:
THE BRIDGE AND THE RIVER c1950 W115005

Right:
THE DOCKS AND TIMBER YARDS c1955 W115047

Beyond the timber yards can be seen the gasholder which stood in Eastfield.

Far Right:
THE BRIDGE AND THE CLARKSON MEMORIAL c1965 W115102

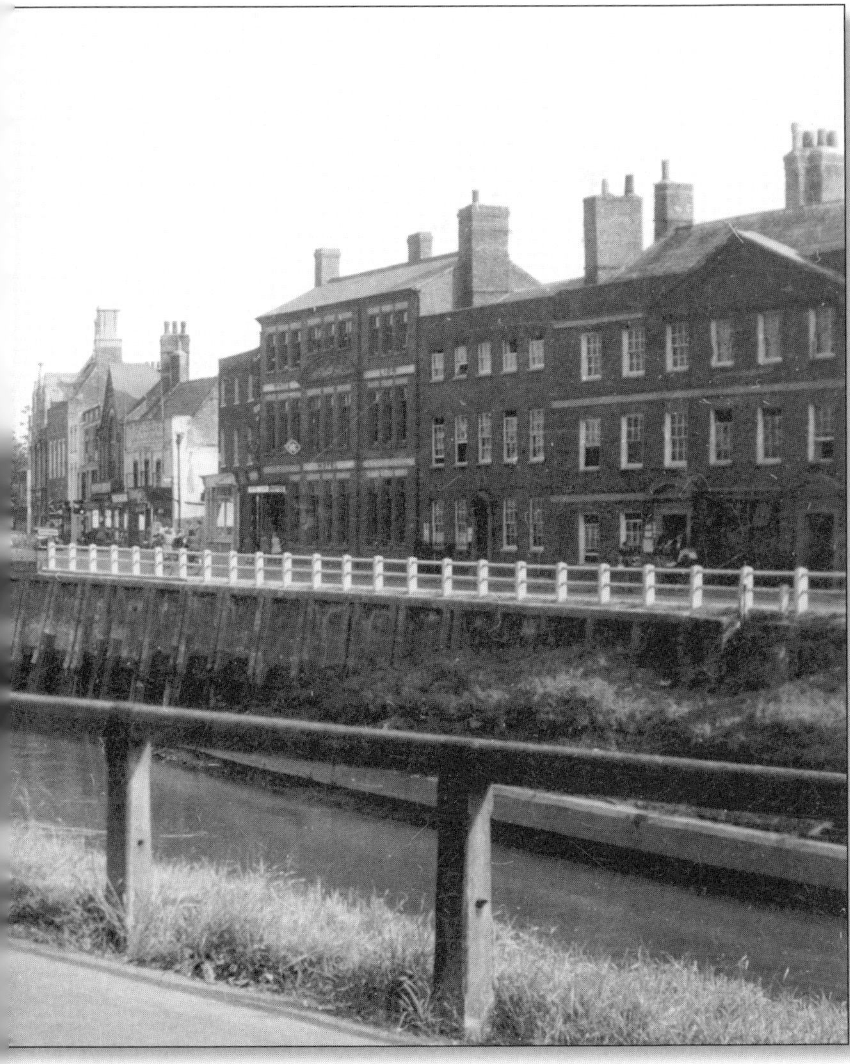

unloading site in the port, the Corporation even going to the expense of constructing a crane and wharf in 1845.

When it opened in 1931, the present town bridge was a welcome replacement for the ugly iron bridge that had spanned the river for over 70 years. The bridge shows just how attractive concrete can be; Tidnam, a local company, made the pre-cast parapets. At the time of completion, the 91-foot span made it the largest portal bridge in the world.

The last 30 years have seen the port decline in trading terms, caused in part by the growth of container shipping for which it is unsuited, but mainly through the rise of Sutton Bridge with its better links with South Lincolnshire and Norfolk.

This decline has led the port authorities, Fenland District Council, to adopt a different strategy. Considerable investment has gone into constructing floating pontoons to provide safe moorings for pleasure crafts. The next phase is hopefully for the development of the land adjacent to the berths, so as to provide superb marina facilities and a further tourist attraction in the town.

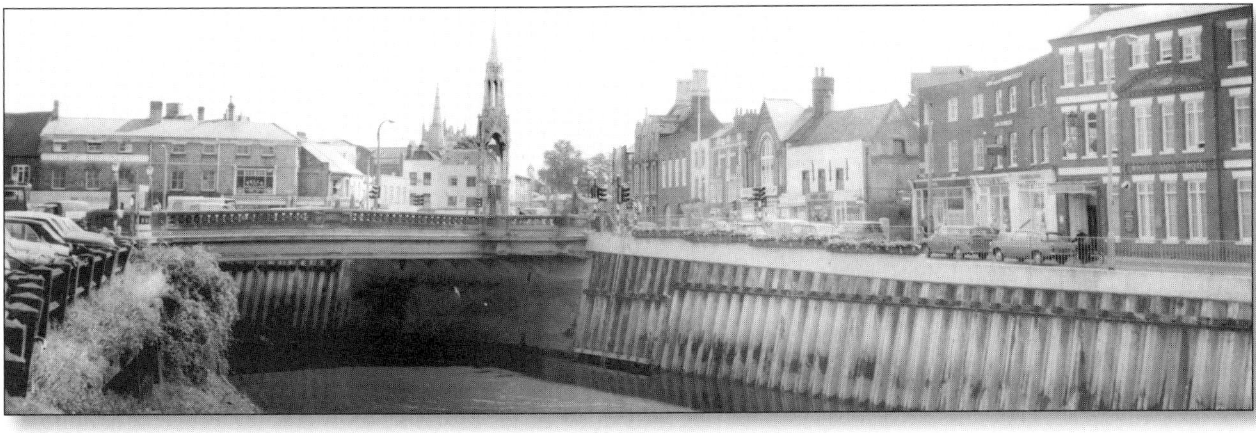

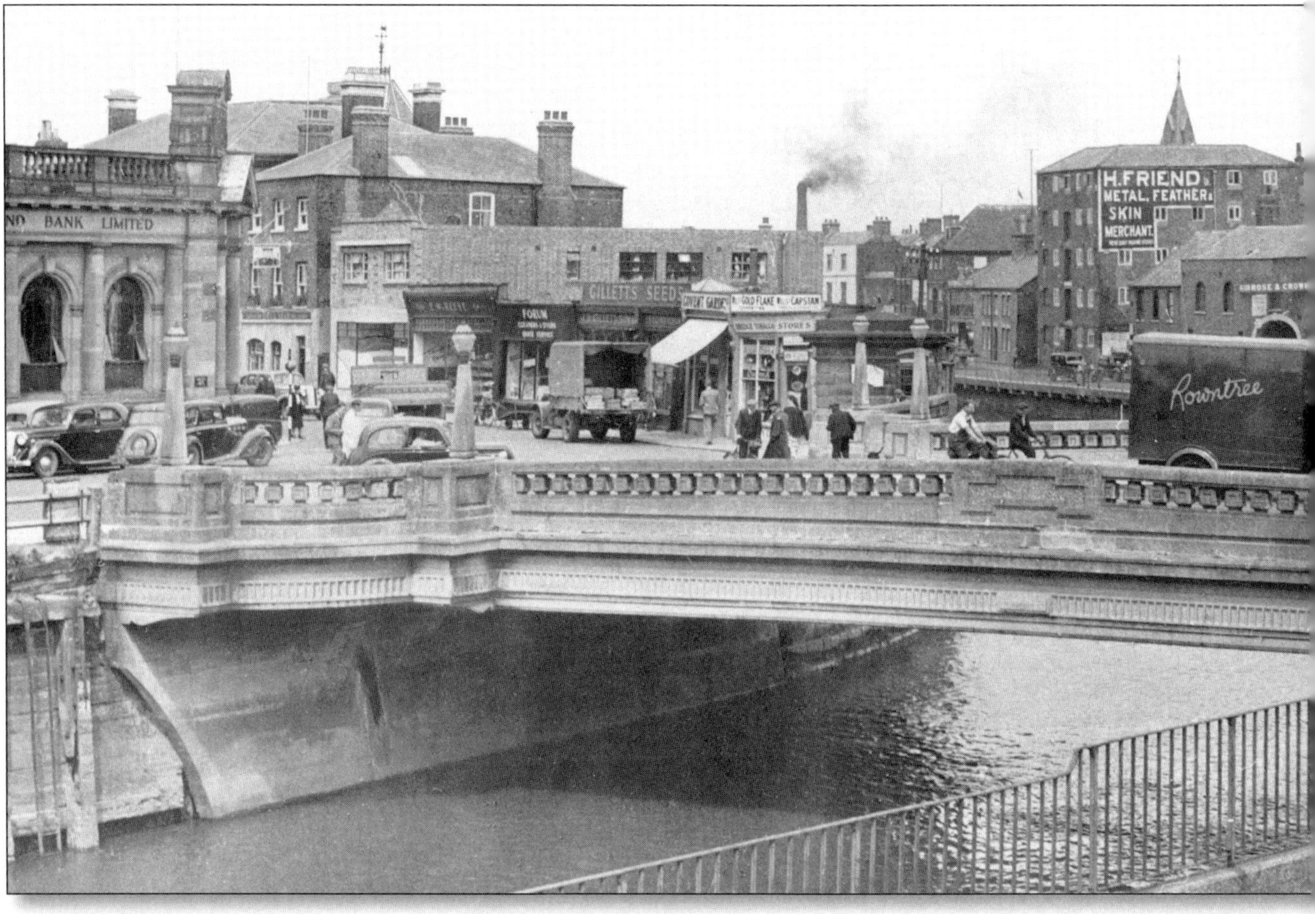
ND BANK LIMITED
H. FRIEND
METAL, FEATHER &
SKIN
MERCHANT
GILLETTS SEEDS
FORUM
CAPSTAN
STORES
Rowntree

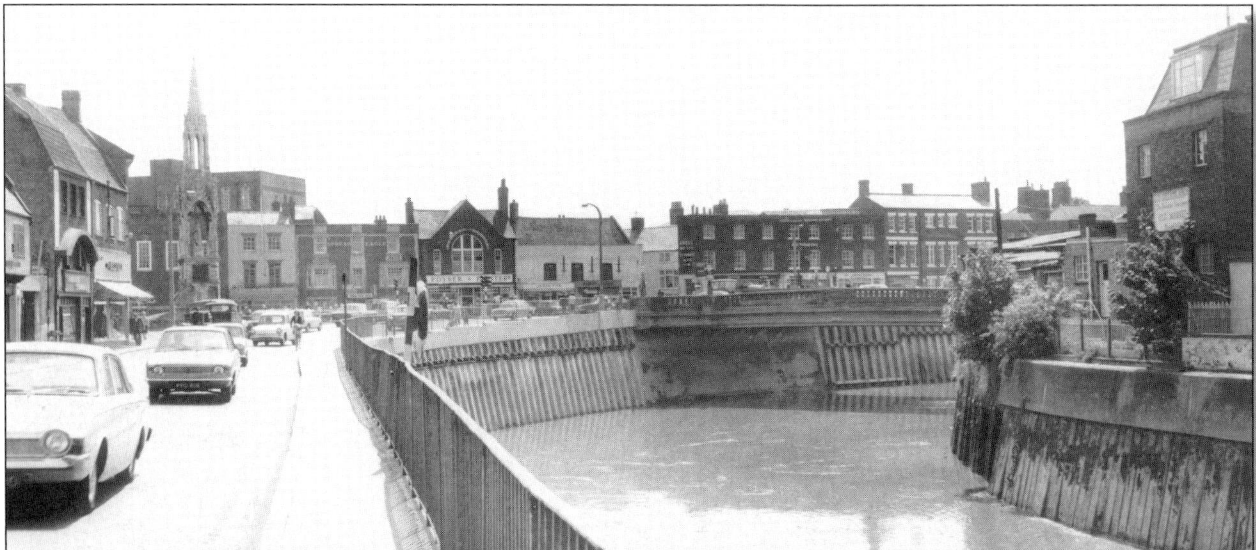

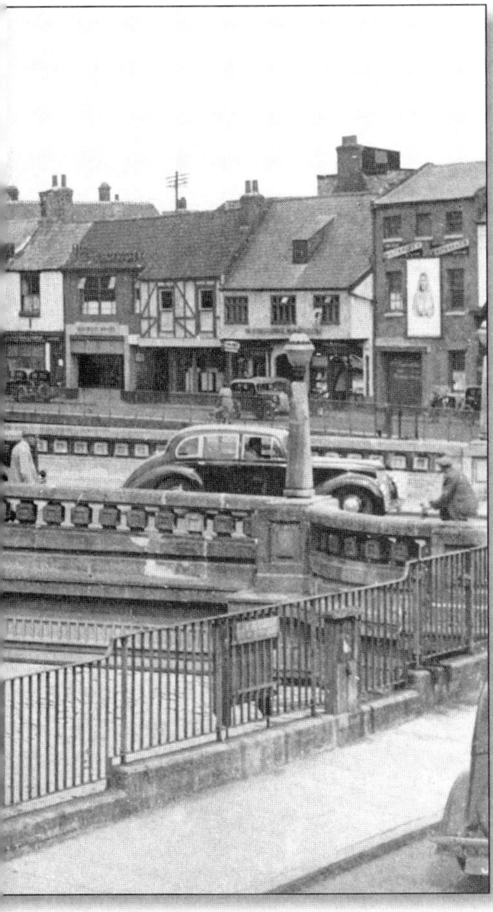

Left:
THE BRIDGE c1955 W115037

To the left, at the junction of Cornhill and the Old Market, can be seen the Midland Bank which was built in 1921. Across the road, the row of small shops, which included Forum Cleaners & Dyers, J D Gillett & Son (seed growers) and the Covent Garden Stores, have been removed and replaced by a garden area - dedicated to the late W H Carlisle, a prominent local surgeon. In the background can be seen the premises of 'Mush' Friend which dominates Nene Quay.

Below Left:
NENE QUAY c1965 W115079

The quay was once an unloading point for ships, carrying cargoes of wines and spirits to the town.

Below:
THE RIVER NENE 1923 73574

On the right, a coaster can be seen berthed at R & W Paul's granary. Also visible: the harbour line of the M & G N Railway that linked the harbour to the goods yard off Leverington Road, and the line to Sutton Bridge.

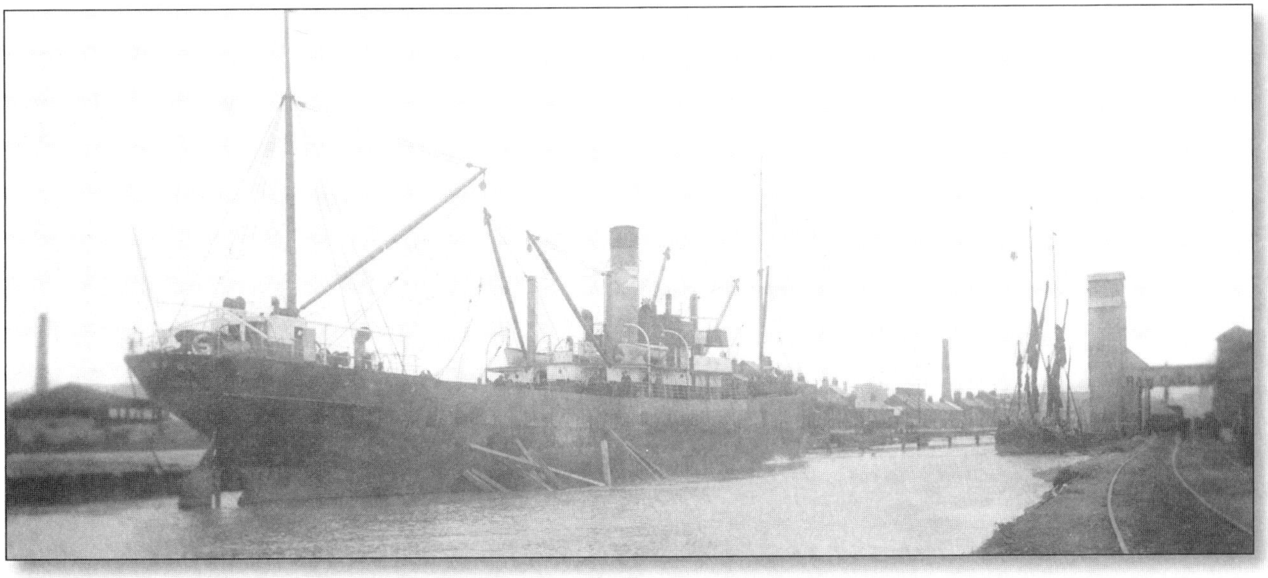

THE BRINKS

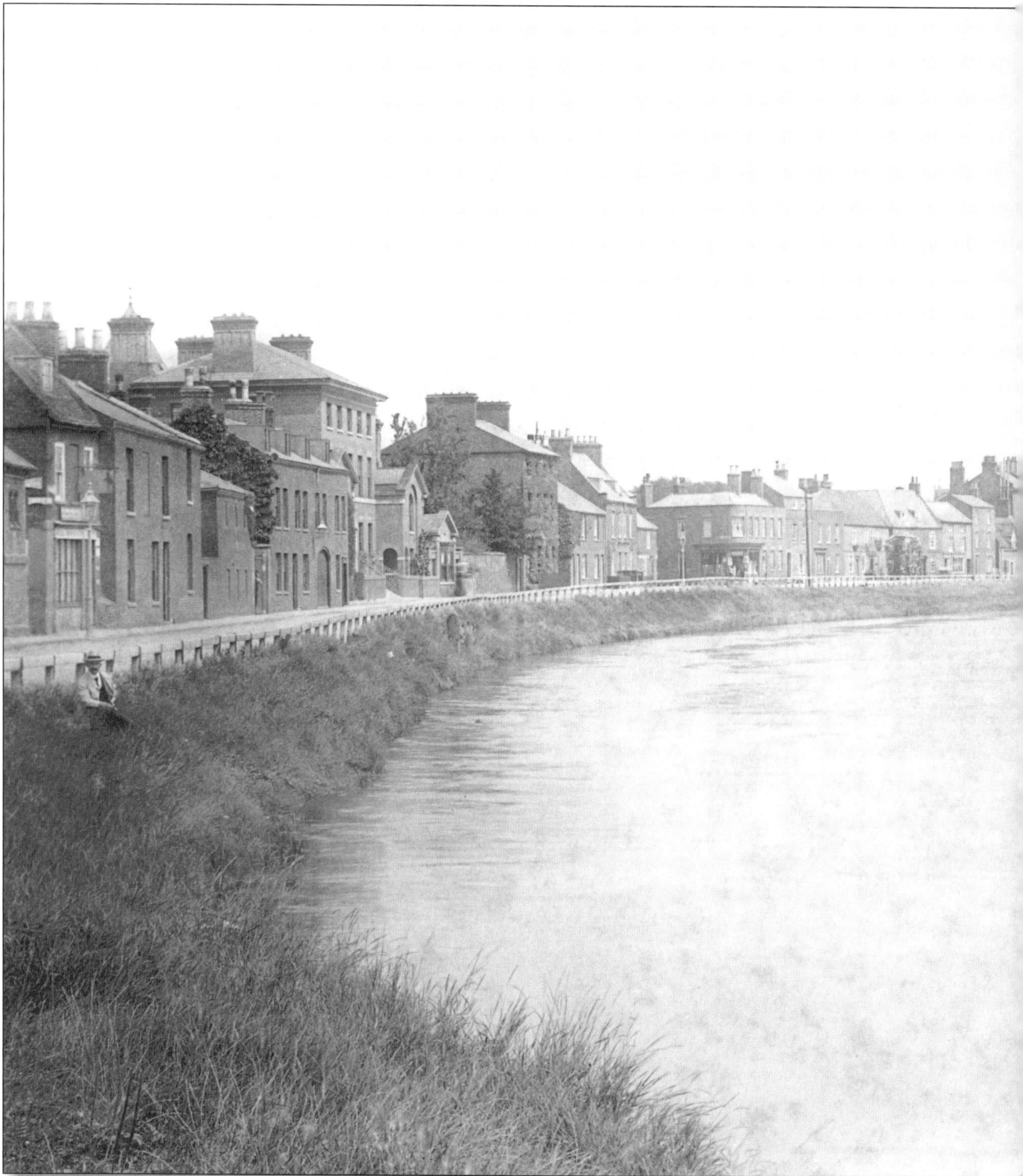

THE BRINKS

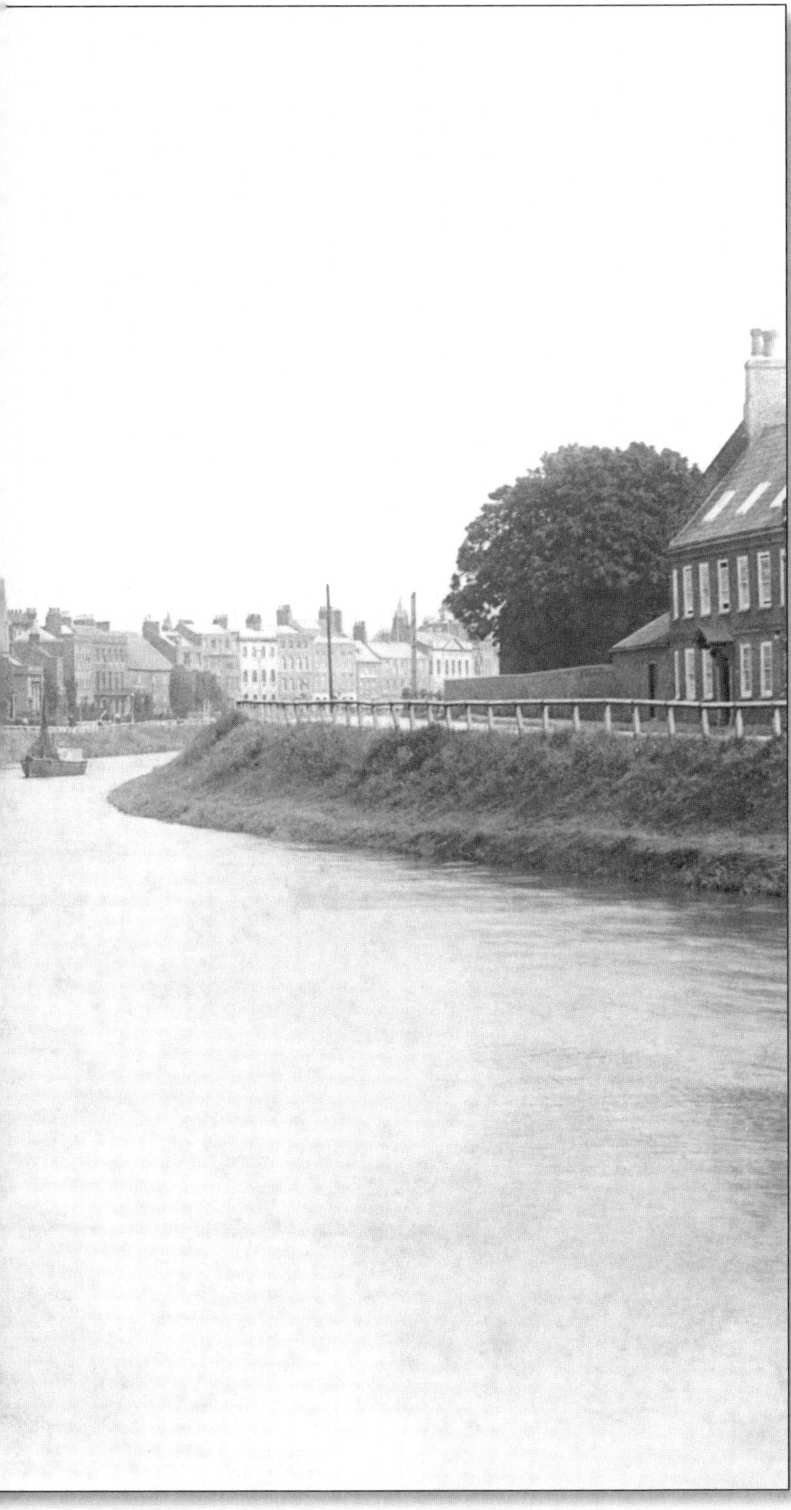

When approaching Wisbech from Peterborough, either by road or river, the traveller passes through the industrial outskirts and is then greeted by the wonderful prospect of the River Nene flanked by the North and South Brinks. The Italianate Harecroft House dominates the surrounding houses, situated on the North Brink between Barton Road and Chapel Road. Designed by Algernon Peckover in the mid-19th century, the house became the home of the Girls' High School, founded in 1904, which subsequently merged with the Grammar School in late 1970 to form a co-educational establishment.

Extract from 'Hills and the Sea' by Hilaire Belloc 1906

'As I sat there in the White Hart, waiting for steak and onions, I read in a book descriptive of the place that a whale had come to Wisbeach once, and I considered that a whale coming up to Wisbeach on a tide would certainly stay there; not indeed for the delights of the town (of which I say nothing), but because there would be no room to turn round; and a whale cannot swim backwards.'

North Brink 1901 47585

THE BRINKS

Below: North Brink 1923 73572

Below Centre: North Brink c1950 W115004

Bottom: The River Nene c1955 W115014

Bottom Right:
The River Nene and North Brink c1965 W115098

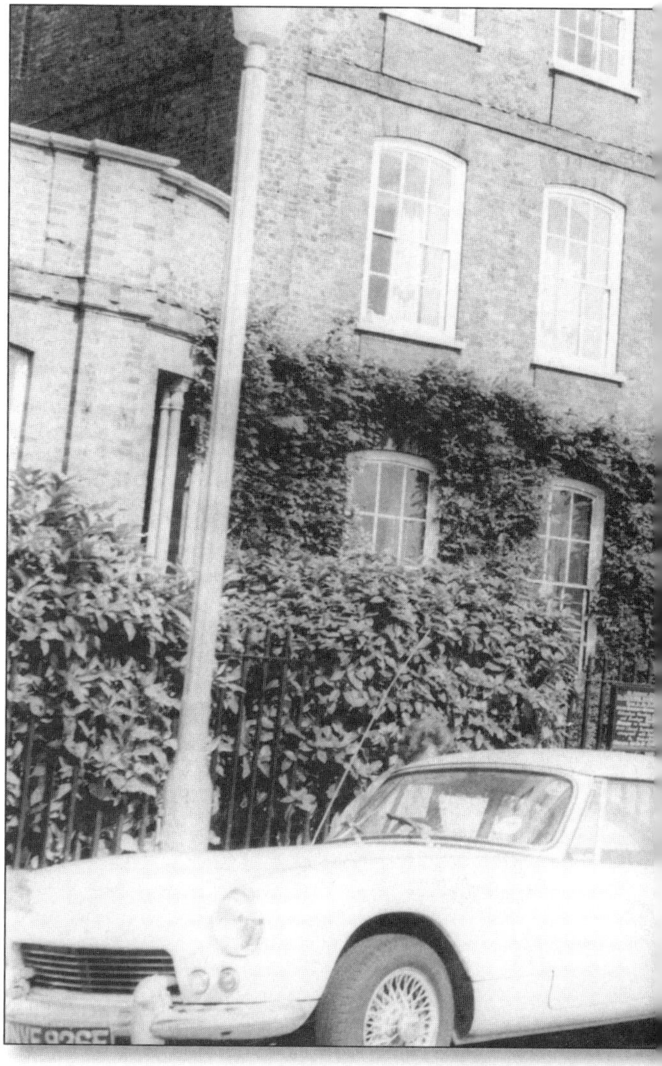

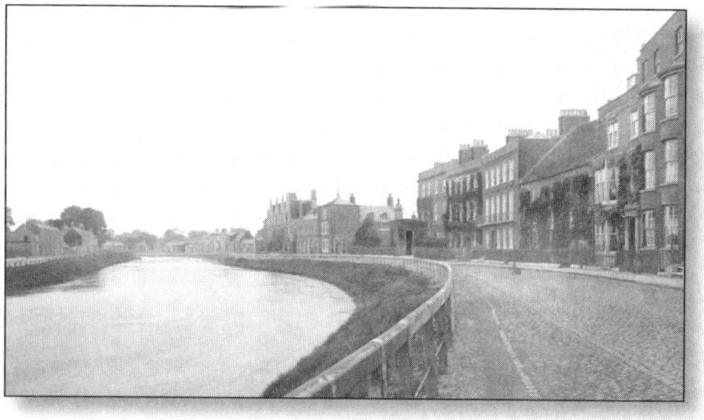

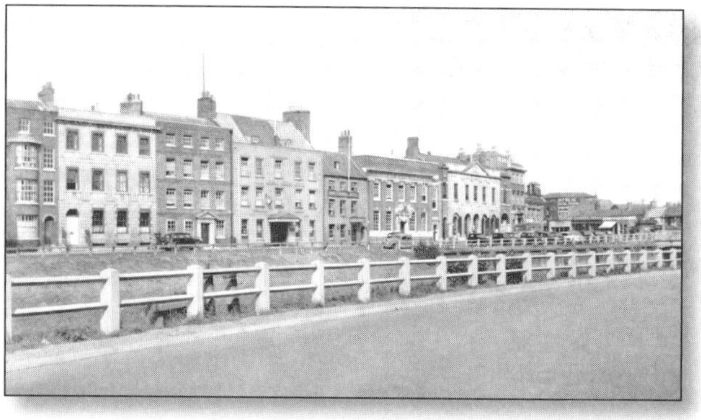

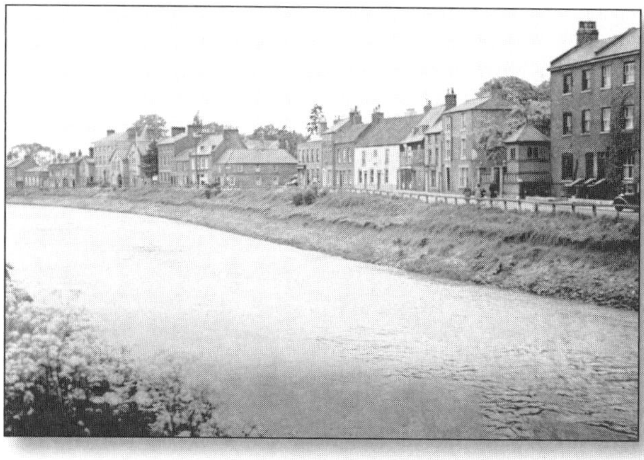

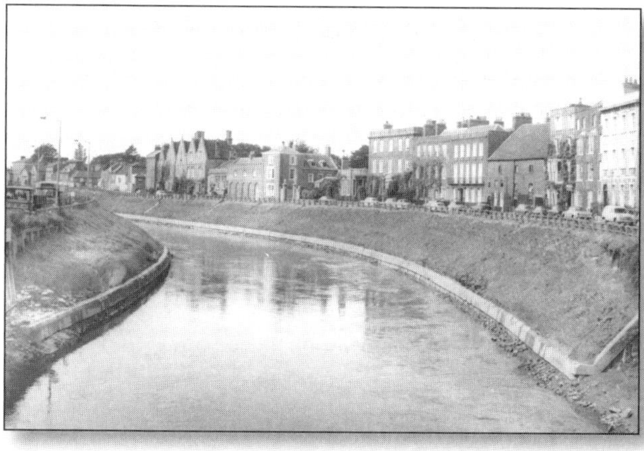

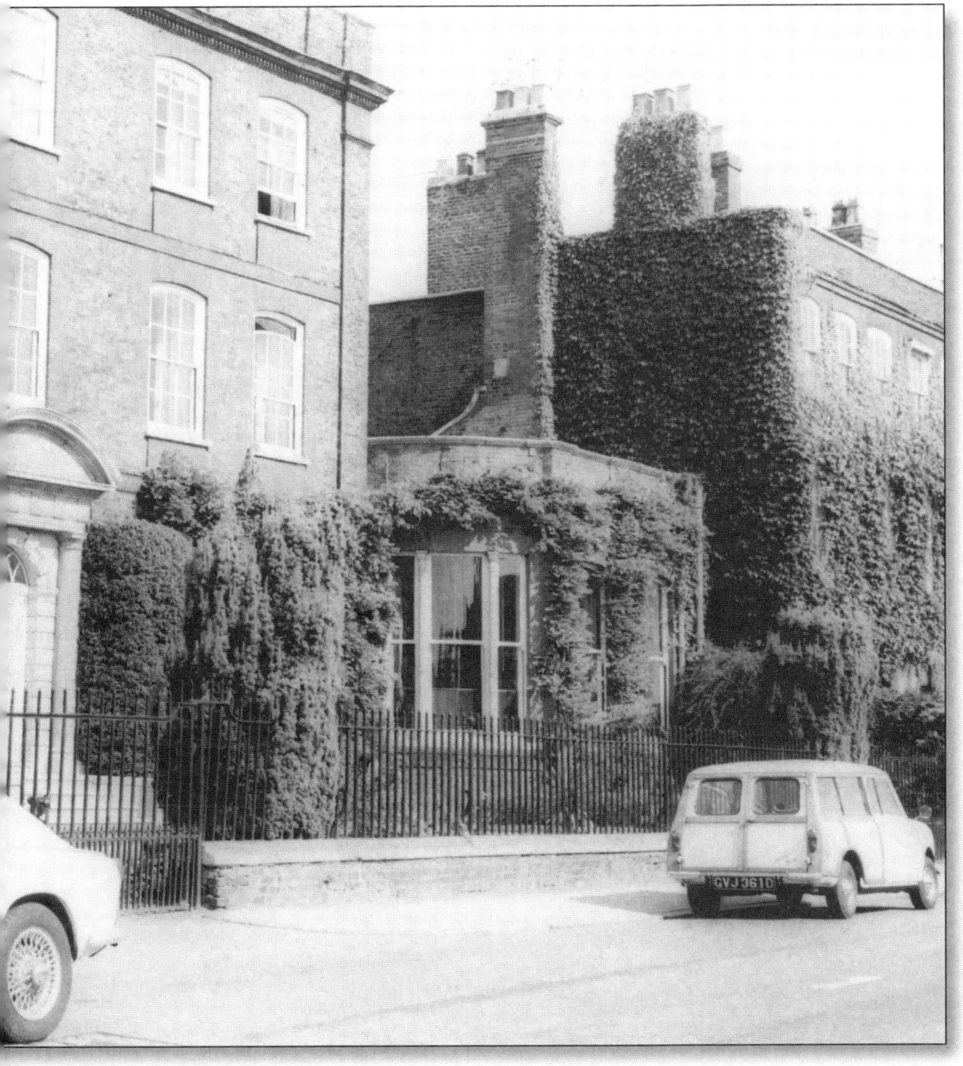

Left:
PECKOVER HOUSE c1965
W115101

Jonathan Peckover bought the house in 1794 and it was here that the family carried on its banking business in the west wing of the house. With the removal of the business to the new branch in the Old Market in 1878, the old banking room was demolished, and the present library (seen on the right) with matching wing were added to the plans of Edward Boardman of Norwich.

From the Chapel Road junction, the Red Lion is flanked by other lesser Georgian and Victorian properties, and these gradually give way to the more substantial houses of North Brink (see W115098) that are the core of what the architectural historian Nicholas Pevsner described as 'one of the most perfect Georgian streets in England'. However, Algernon Peckover's Jacobean-style terrace does seem at odds with its neighbours.

Set back from the rest of the houses, Peckover House is the centrepiece of the North Brink. Built in 1722 this fine Georgian property became the home to several generations of the Peckover family, who were Quaker bankers. The family had a marked influence on the town during the 19th and early-20th centuries, supporting such institutions as the Working Men's Institute, Wisbech Museum and Literary Society, and the town's cottage hospital. The family carried on their banking business in the specially-constructed wing of the house, before a new branch of Gurney & Co - of which the Peckovers were partners - was opened in the Old Market in 1878. The house was left to the National Trust after the death of the Hon. Alexandrina Peckover, last surviving daughter of Alexander, Lord Peckover. Formerly known as Bank House, the property was renamed Peckover House.

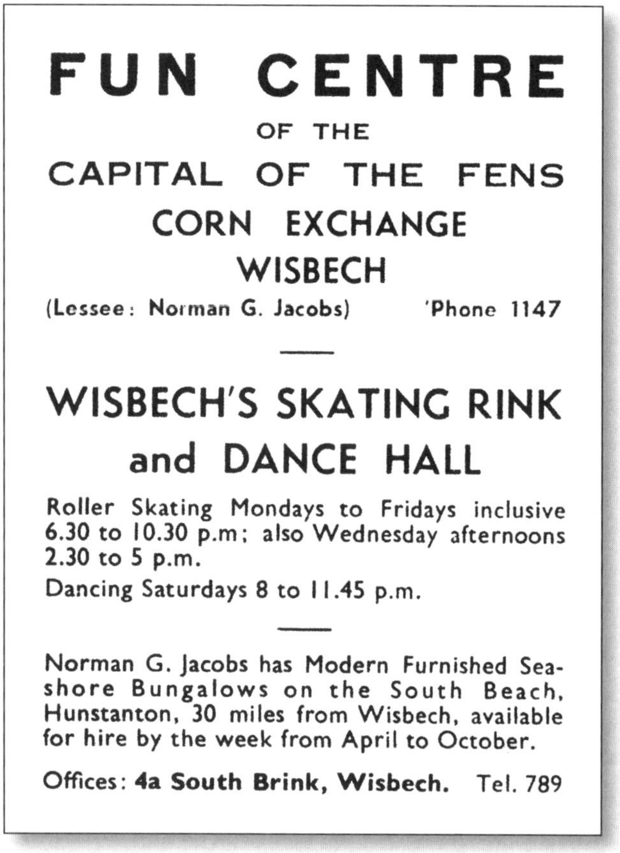

ADVERT FOR ROLLER-SKATING AT THE CORN EXCHANGE c1950

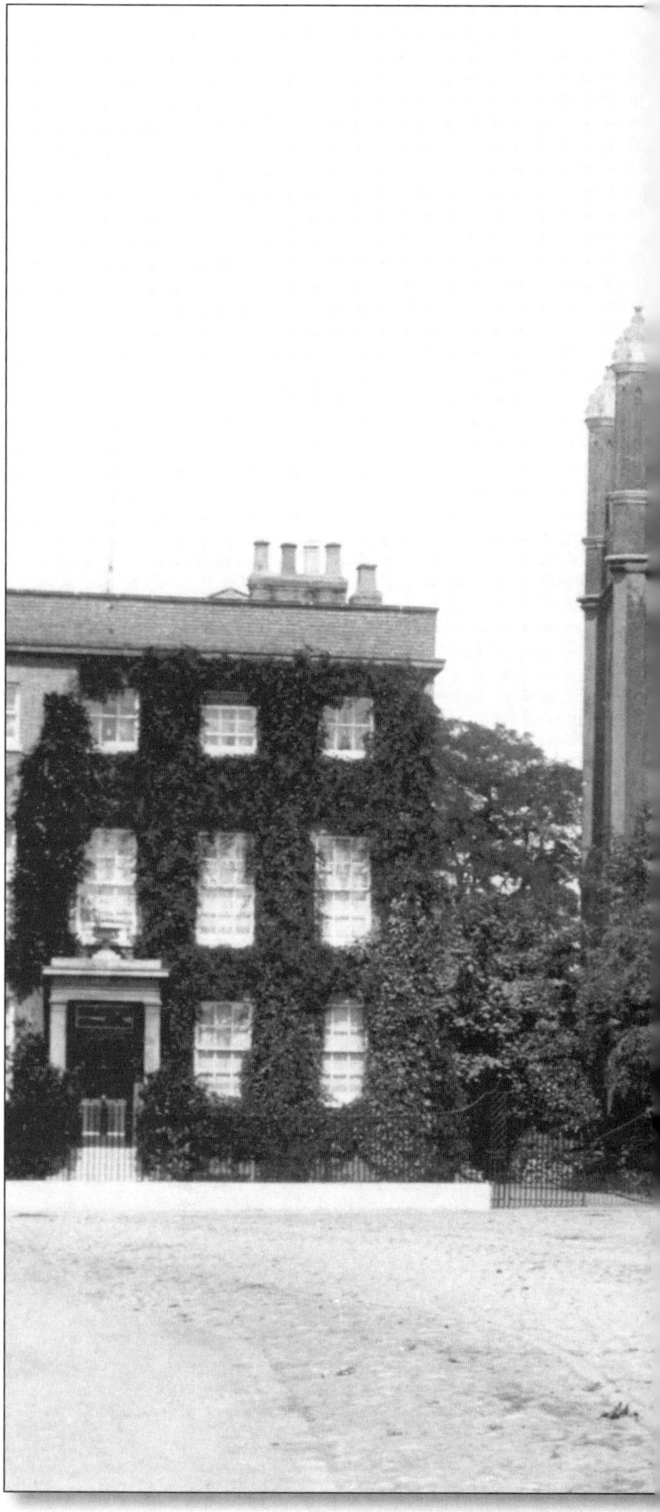

Right: THE OCTAGON CHURCH 1901 47591

To the left of the chapel is 'Glan Dyfi' house: formerly a school for young ladies and now known as Astral House, a branch of the RAF Association. In the foreground is the drinking fountain, 'for man, horses, dogs and sheep', dedicated to George Duppa Collins and his wife. It has since been moved to Lynn Road.

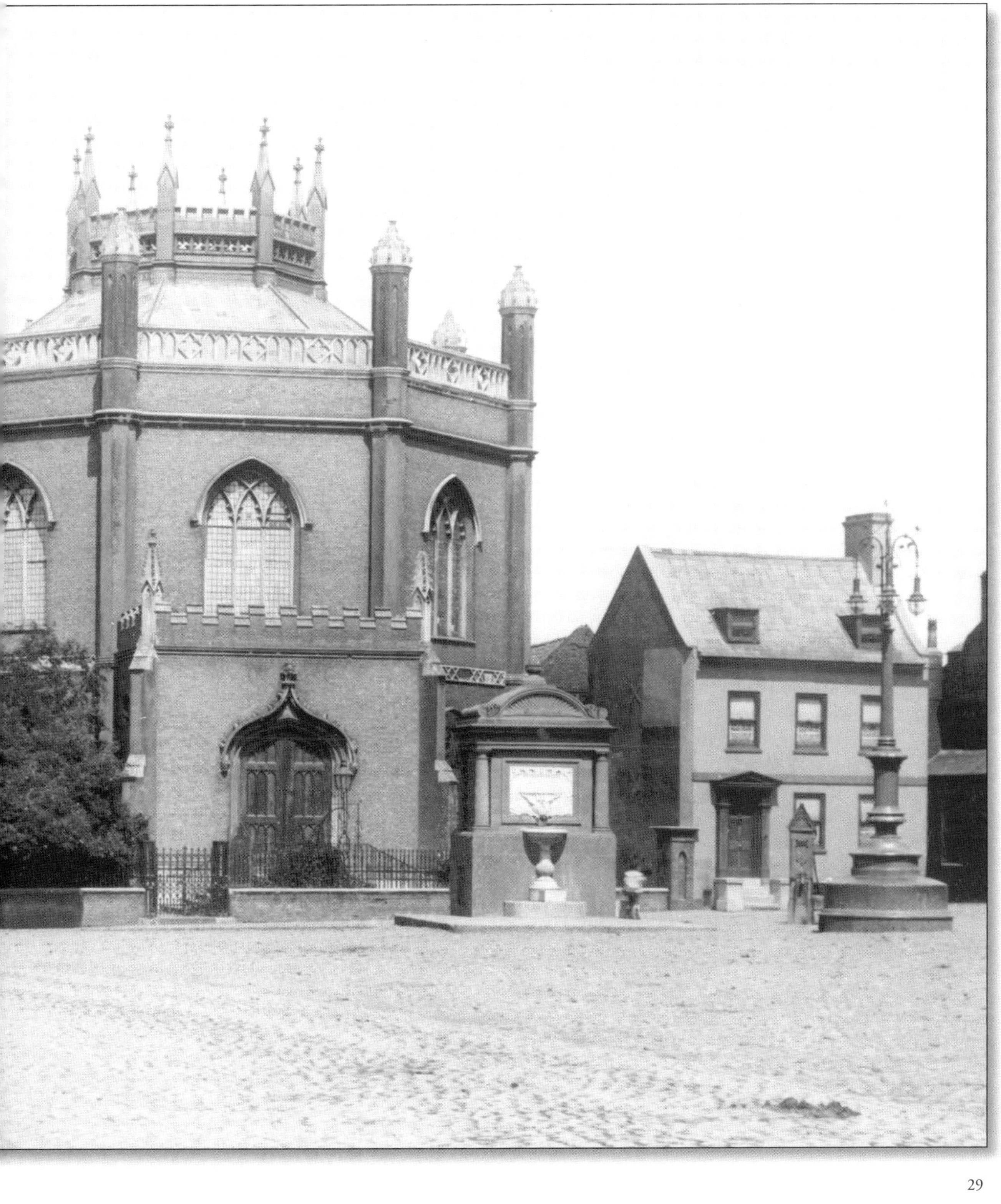

THE BRINKS

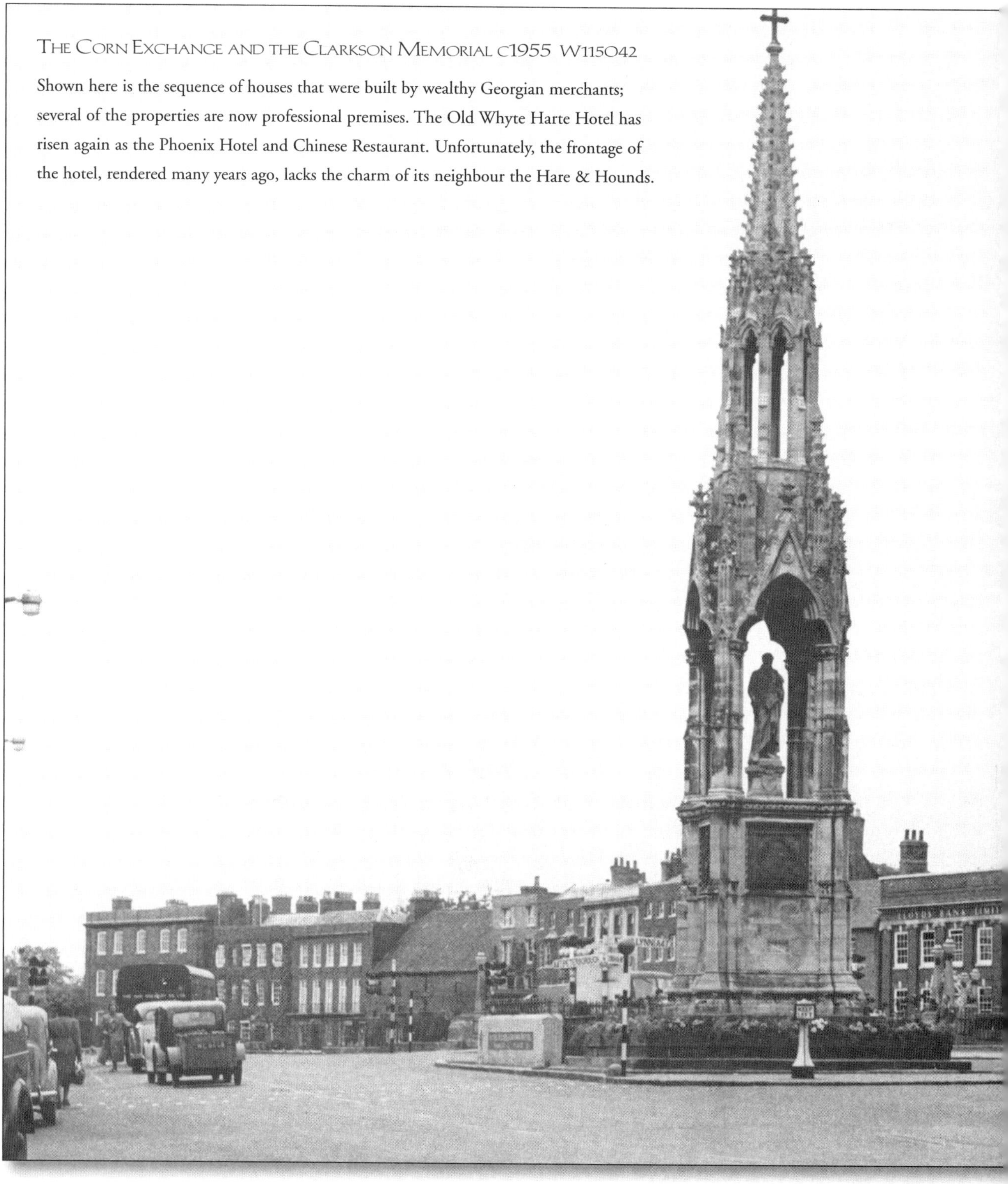

THE CORN EXCHANGE AND THE CLARKSON MEMORIAL c1955 W115042

Shown here is the sequence of houses that were built by wealthy Georgian merchants; several of the properties are now professional premises. The Old Whyte Harte Hotel has risen again as the Phoenix Hotel and Chinese Restaurant. Unfortunately, the frontage of the hotel, rendered many years ago, lacks the charm of its neighbour the Hare & Hounds.

THE BRINKS

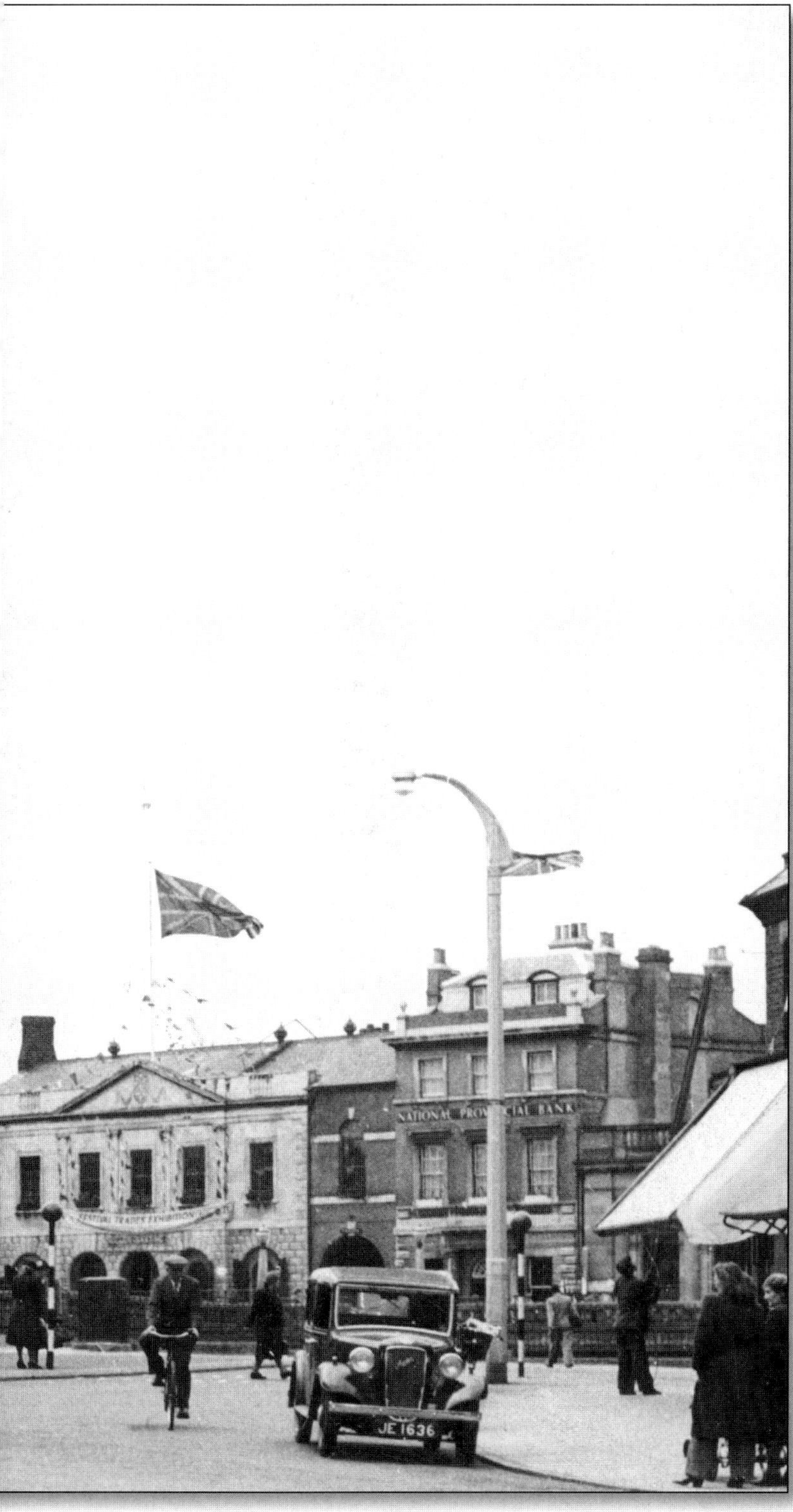

From the Old Whyte Hart, and the Hare and Hounds, we move towards the financial centre of the town. Lloyds Bank, with its wonderful doorway, was built in 1928. The bank was originally a branch of Lacon, Youell and Kemp, of Yarmouth, and opened in 1894; eight years later, the business transferred to the Capital and Counties Bank before being absorbed by Lloyds in 1919. A more recent change has seen the bank become a branch of the giant concern Lloyds TSB.

The Town Hall was originally known as the Exchange Hall (built by Joseph Medworth in 1811); the present stone façade was added in 1856. A year later, the Corn Exchange, to the rear, was opened; thus providing a home for Wisbech's busy corn market. With the closing of the Exchange, the building has been put to many uses. From the Corn Exchange, with its novel double use as Town Council Chamber and a place of entertainment, one proceeds to Cornhill and the Old Market where the rest of the town's banks have their main branches.

When moving into the Old Market today the visitor is unaware of the great loss that befell the town when the Chapel of Ease (commonly known as the Octagon Church) was demolished in 1952. Formed by Act of Parliament in 1826, the church was built by a local man, Mr Swansborough. In 1846 the lantern, which had been modelled on the one at Ely Cathedral, was in such a poor state that it had to be removed. A branch of Lloyds TSB now occupies the site of the chapel.

In contrast to the North Brink, the South Brink is slightly overlooked. Yet, it too has houses of note such as the White Lion Hotel, which was re-fronted and enlarged in 1883/4 at a cost of around £950 by Rands & Son. Further along is the birthplace of Octavia Hill (see W115076, page 32), and then the former Sessions House, the Old Grammar School and the charming Edes' Terrace.

THE BRINKS

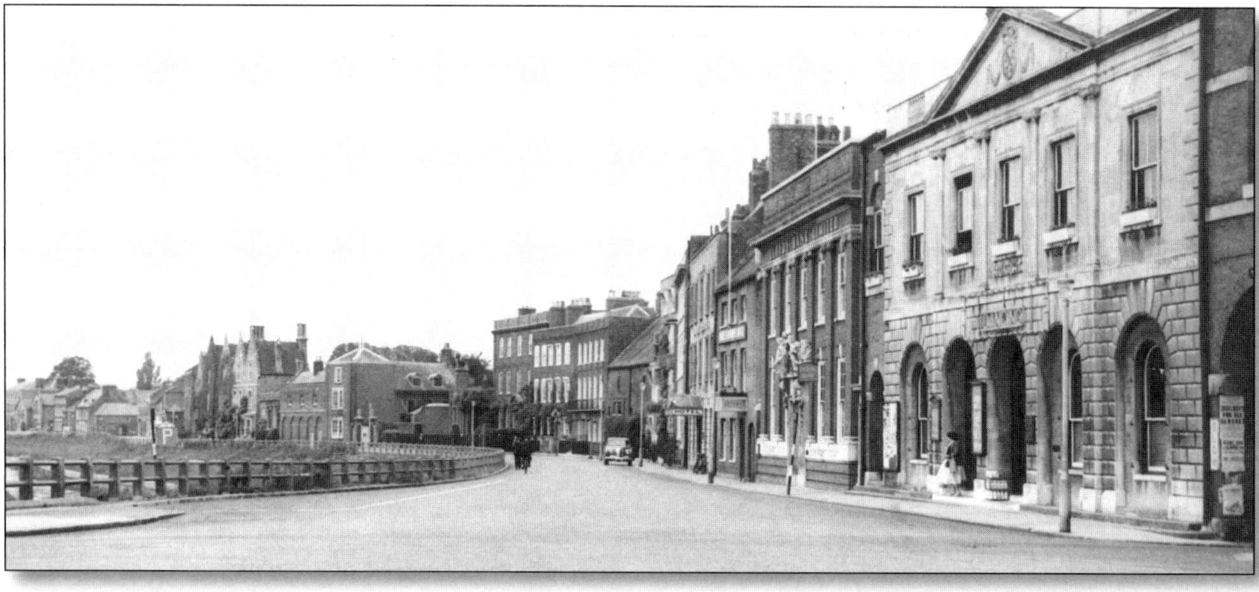

CORNHILL AND THE TOWN HALL c1955 W115064

The upper front storey of the Corn Exchange houses the Town Council's chamber and offices. Corn markets were held to the rear and other of its uses have included: a drill hall for the Volunteers, dancing (as in the advert on page 28), exhibitions, roller-skating and bingo (in more recent years). It is proposed to convert the building into a cinema, which should keep the councillors amused!

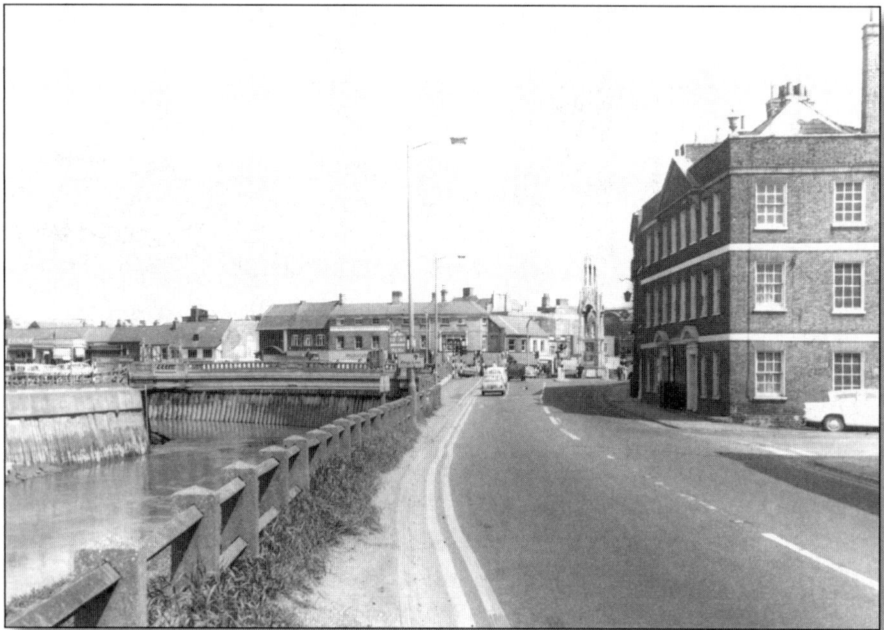

THE SOUTH BRINK c1965 W115076

On the right of the photograph is 7/8 South Brink where Wisbech's most famous daughter, Octavia Hill (1838-1912), was born. Miss Hill was a tireless housing and social reformer and was a co-founder of the National Trust. It is ironic that this fine house should be frequently disregarded in favour of the Trust's own Wisbech property, Peckover House. The house has been divided into two, and the smaller part (where the Ford Anglia is) is now a museum dedicated to Octavia's life and work.

THE TOWN BRIDGE AND BRIDGE STREET

On entering the approaches to Wisbech town centre, one is greeted by the Clarkson Memorial, which dominates Bridge Street - the roadway that historically led from the bridge to the entrance of Wisbech Castle.

The wide expanse of the street has shrunk over the years with the alteration of the road layout, to accommodate the increased amount of motor traffic. Long gone are the days when a large part of the two annual fun fairs would occupy a significant part of this area. Nowadays, all that can be fitted in is Rocky Thompson's rock stall, on the island that surrounds the base of the memorial.

Bridge Street remains a vibrant part of Wisbech. The main Post Office, built in 1887, is a focal point around which services such as estate agencies, legal practices and insurance firms have moved over the years. Another institution worth mentioning is the Tourist Information Centre that now occupies the former PO sorting offices - vacated when the concern transferred to premises on the outskirts of town.

Moving from Bridge Street one enters the High Street, which in turn leads into the Market Place. Nowadays the High Street is a sad sight with many empty and boarded-up shops; it is to be hoped that the anticipated regeneration scheme comes to fruition, to produce a more attractive prospect for locals and visitors.

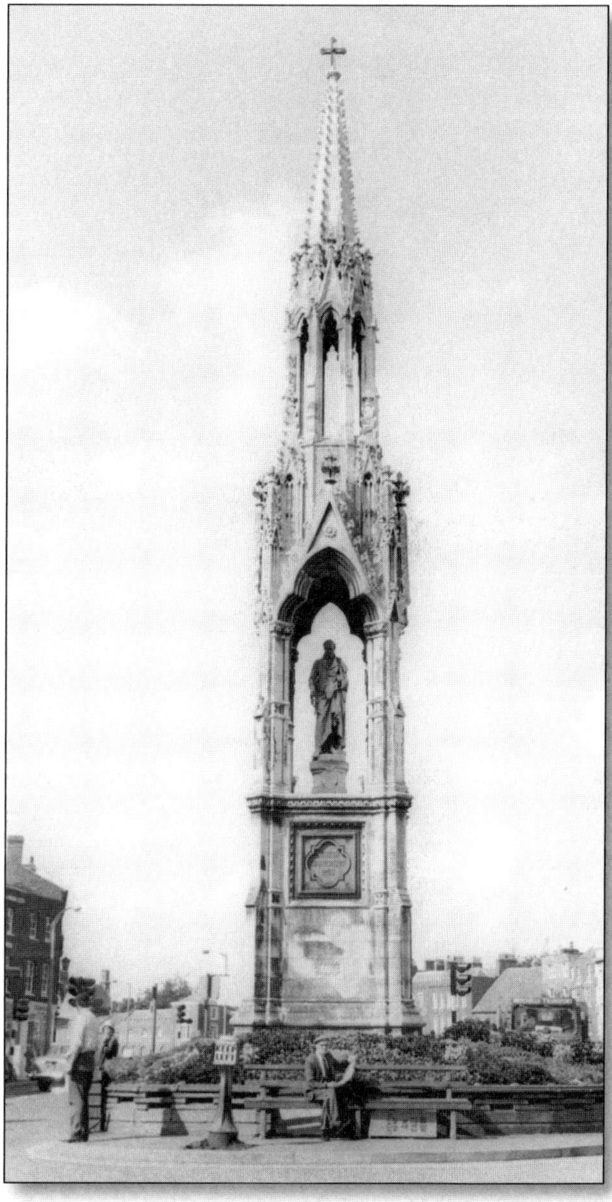

THE CLARKSON MEMORIAL C1965 W115096

Dedicated to Wisbech's most famous son, Thomas Clarkson (1760-1846): one of the key figures in the movement for the abolition of the slave trade in the 18th and 19th centuries. Designed by Sir George Gilbert Scott, who died before it was completed, the memorial cost just over £2,000 and was unveiled by the Speaker of the House of Commons, the Rt Hon Sir Bouverie Brand, MP.

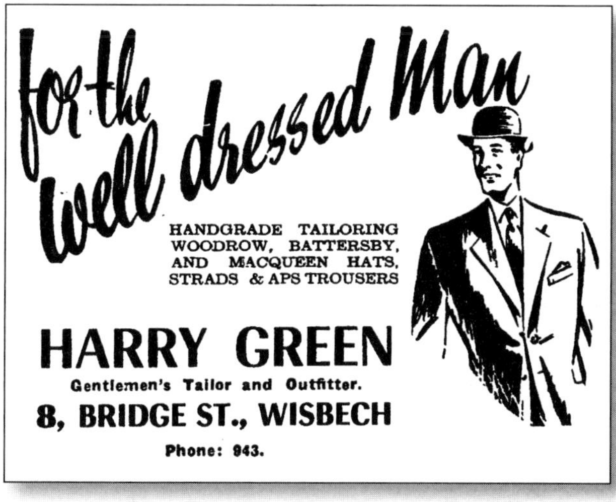

ADVERT FOR HARRY GREEN, GENTLEMAN'S TAILOR 1953

THE TOWN BRIDGE AND BRIDGE STREET

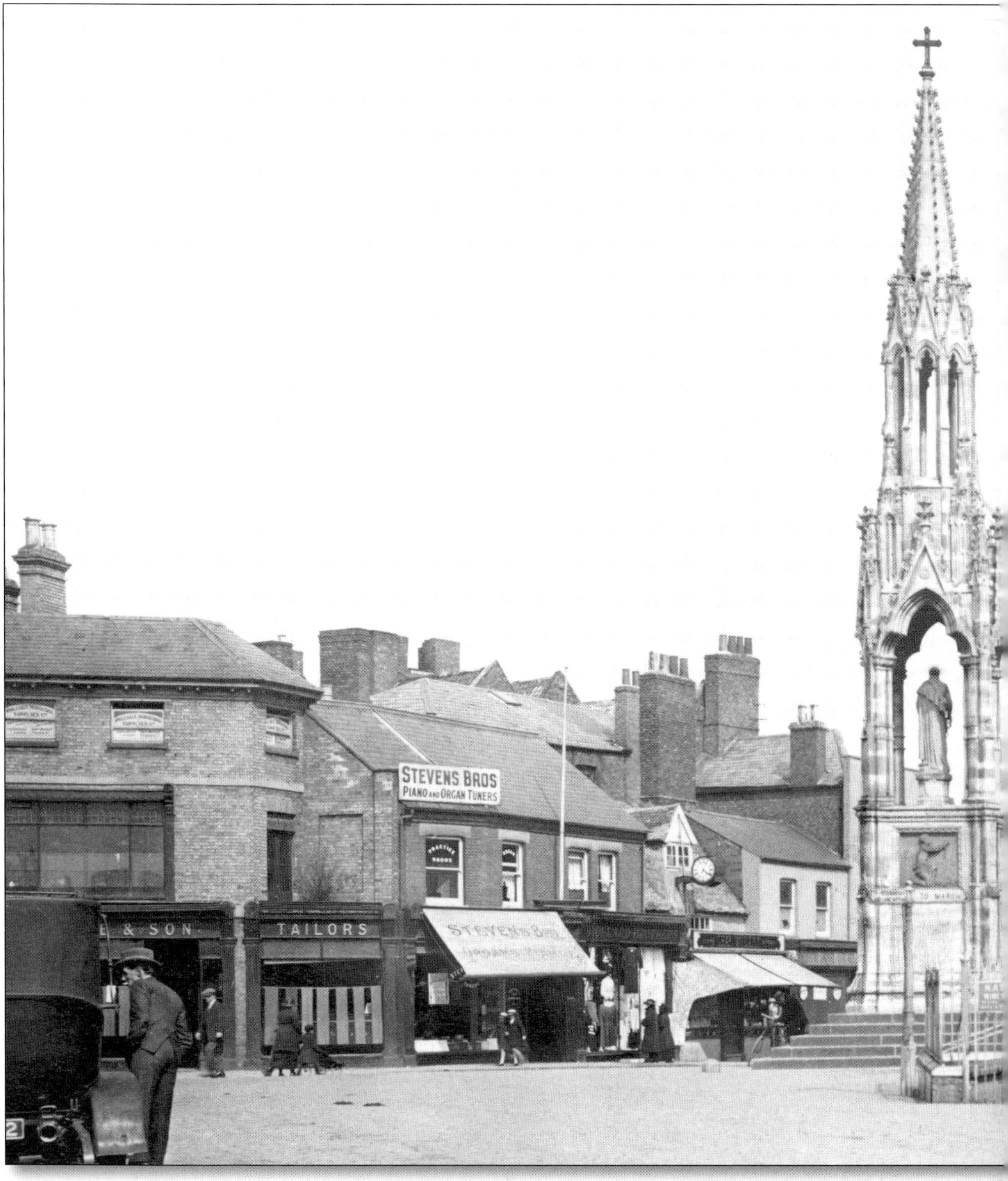

The Clarkson Memorial 1923 *73569*

Since this view was taken considerable changes have occurred. The tailor's shop to the left was shortly taken over by Fells, Cycle & Wireless dealers (see W115023 on page 38-39), who also had premises in Norfolk Street, and until recently was Belfast's linen store. The next two shops, Stevens Bros (suppliers of pianos and organs) and the drapers, Pollard Brothers, are now one building - occupied by estate agents. One point of stability is Evison's clothing store which has traded here for over hundred years.

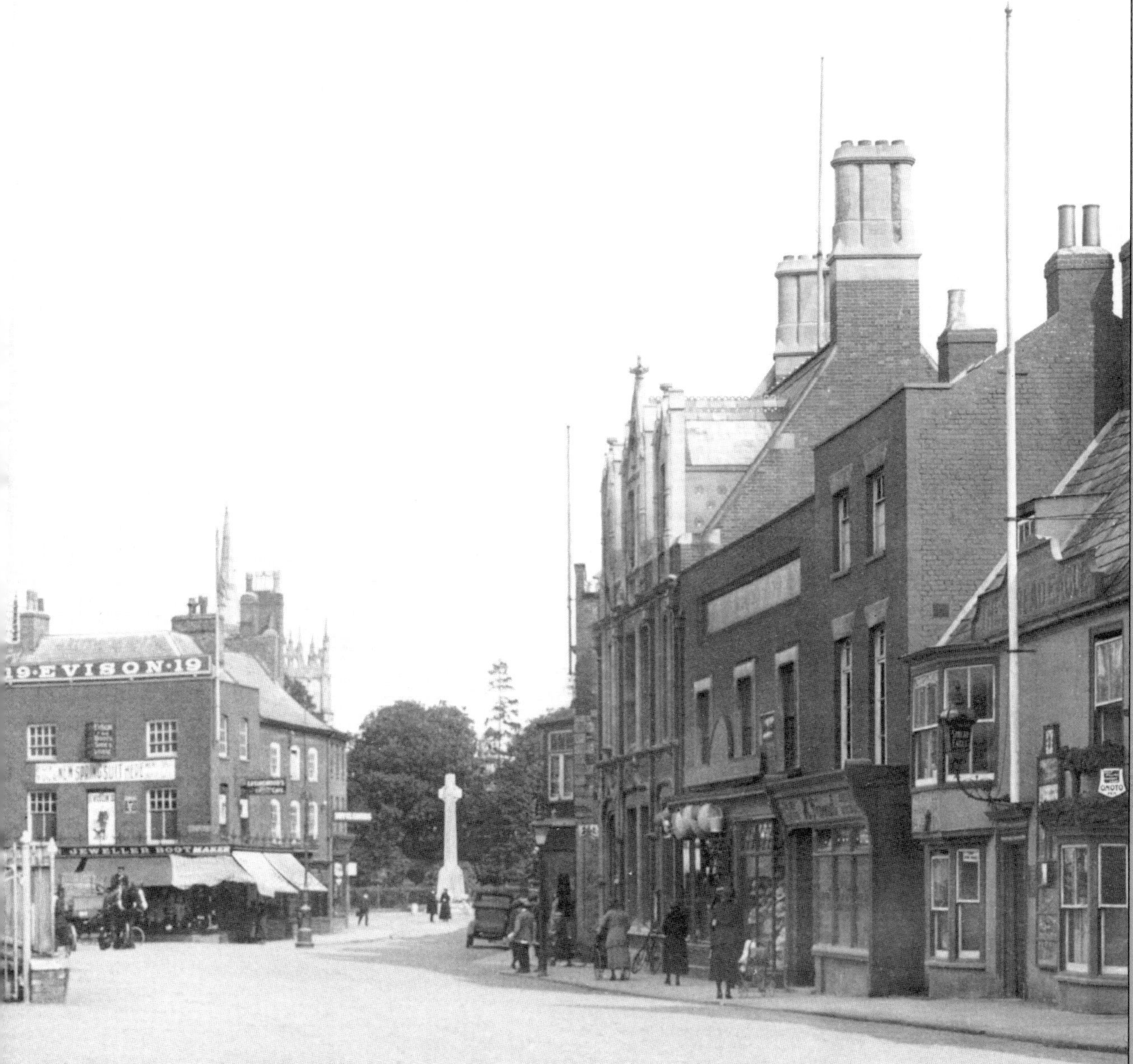

THE TOWN BRIDGE AND BRIDGE STREET

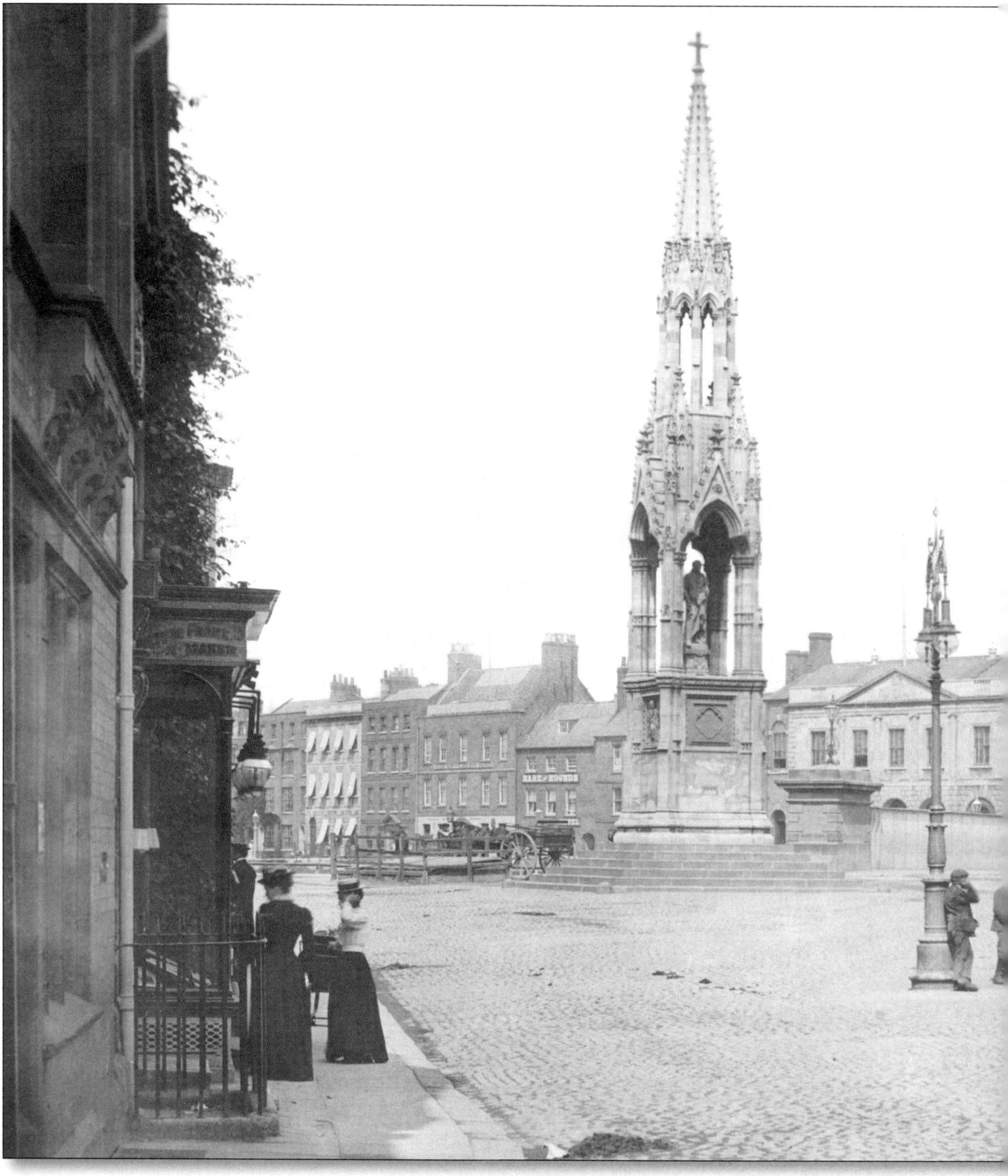

THE TOWN BRIDGE AND BRIDGE STREET

Whilst the High Street is a shadow of its former self, the Rose & Crown Hotel, located at the junction with the Market Place, is enjoying somewhat of a renaissance, with its current owners investing heavily in restoring the hotel to its former prominence in the town and locality. The provision of good accommodation for visitors and tourists must be seen as a priority, if Wisbech is to tap into the tourism market and give a welcome boost to the local economy.

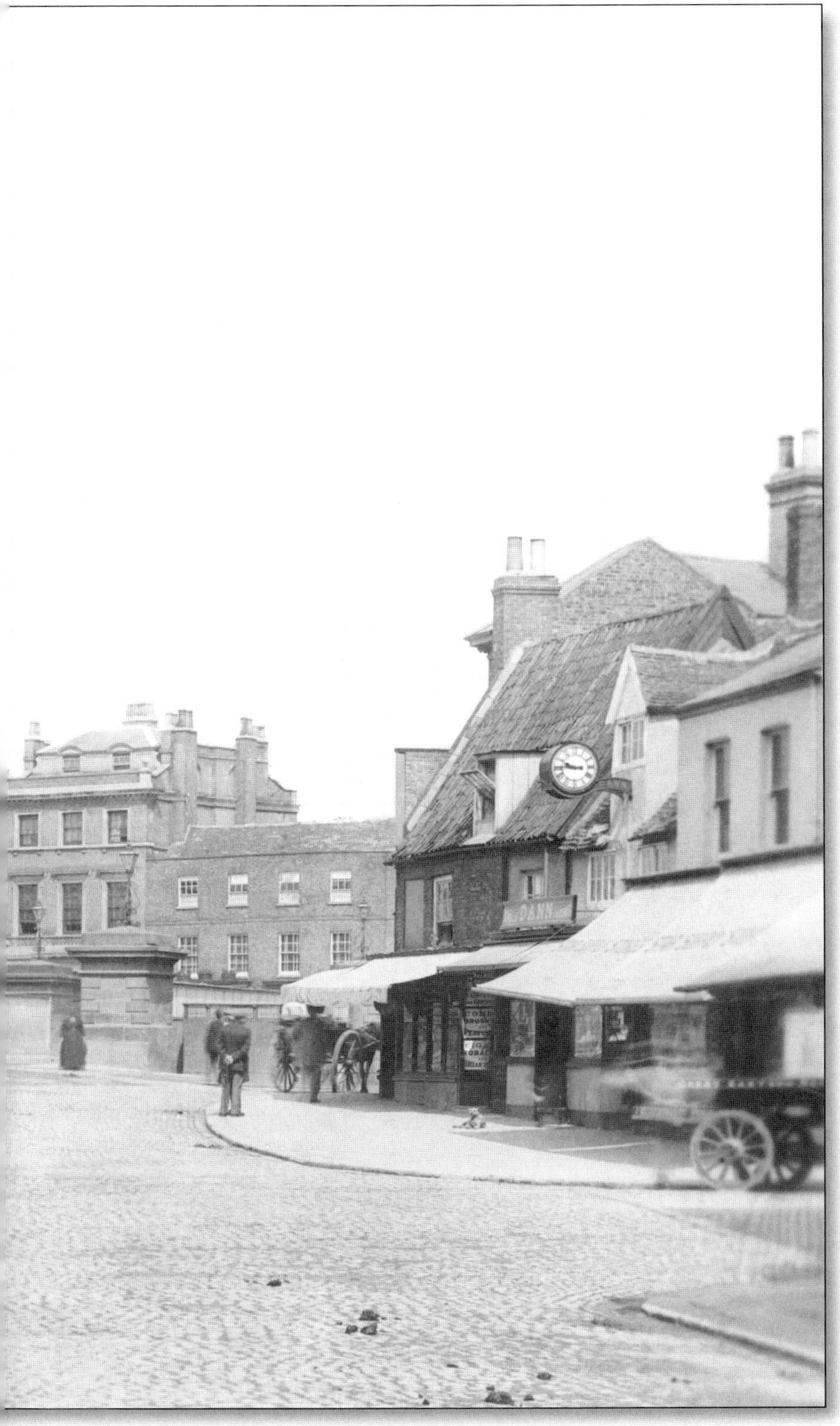

THE CLARKSON MEMORIAL
1901 47583

The ladies on the left are perusing the windows of the Borough Studio, the photographic and picture framing business of J L Brown. These premises were subsequently bought by Lilian Ream - the leading photographic studio in the town, until the 1960s. Across the road can be seen one of Wisbech's familiar landmarks, the 'illuminated clock' on the clockmaker's shop, of Mr Dann. The Corporation paid Dann to light the clock during the hours of darkness. Fortunately the clock was retained when the shop was re-fronted for W R Smith, tobacconist.

THE TOWN BRIDGE AND BRIDGE STREET

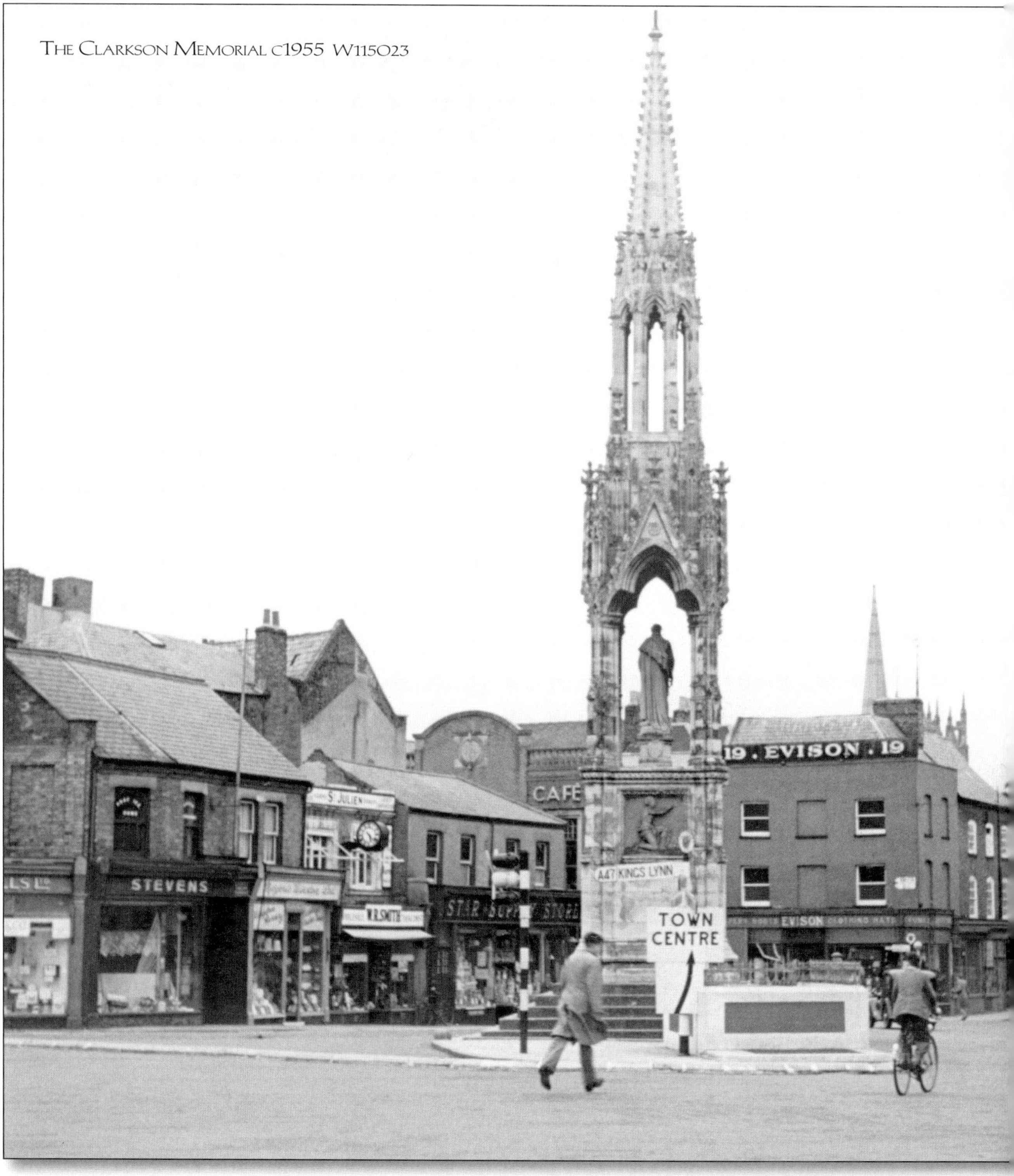

THE CLARKSON MEMORIAL c1955 W115023

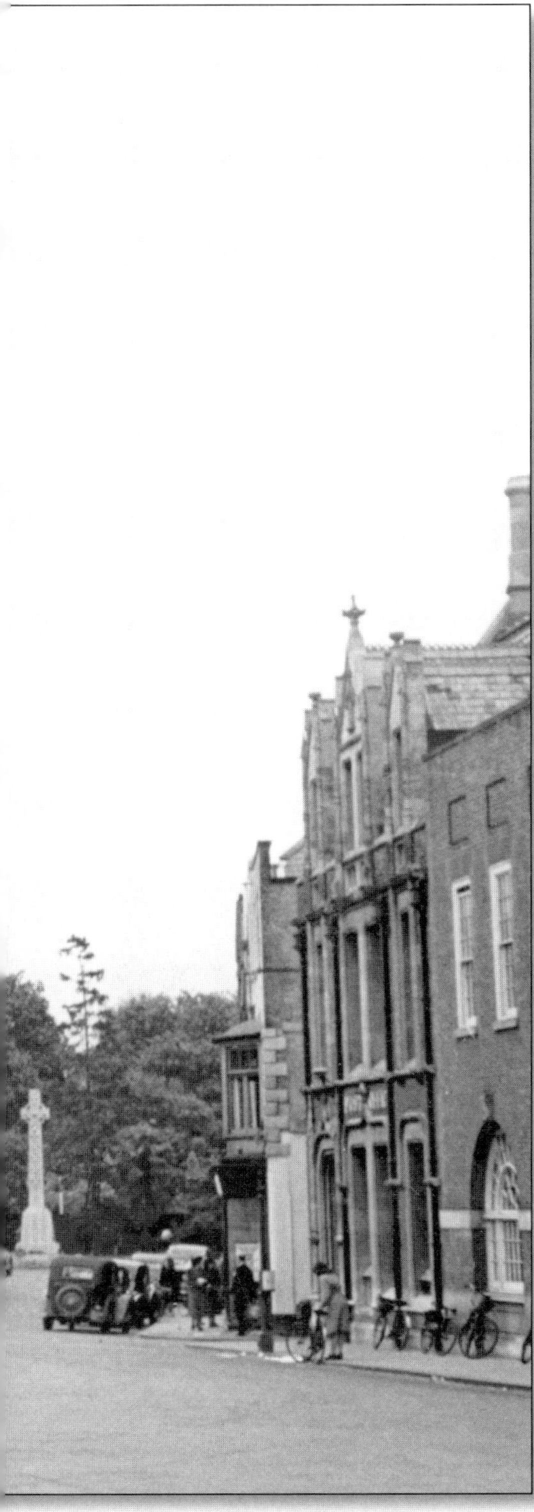

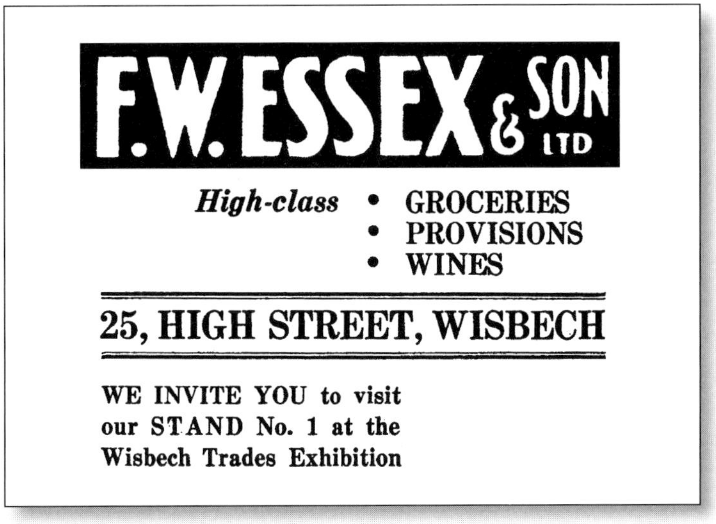

ADVERT FOR F W ESSEX & SON LTD 1953

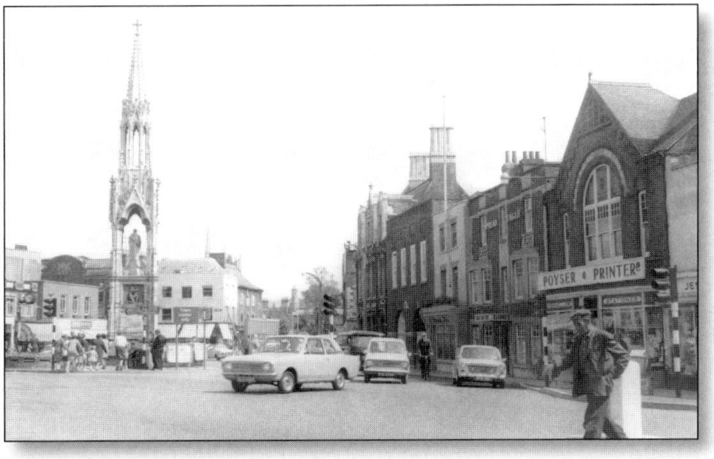

BRIDGE STREET C1965 W115077

The Spread Eagle was re-fronted in 1932 and another storey added; it has recently closed its doors as a public house. Both the stationers, Poysers, and the shop of the noted Wisbech footballer, Jesse Pye, now form part of Robert Goddard's clothing outlet.

THE TOWN BRIDGE AND BRIDGE STREET

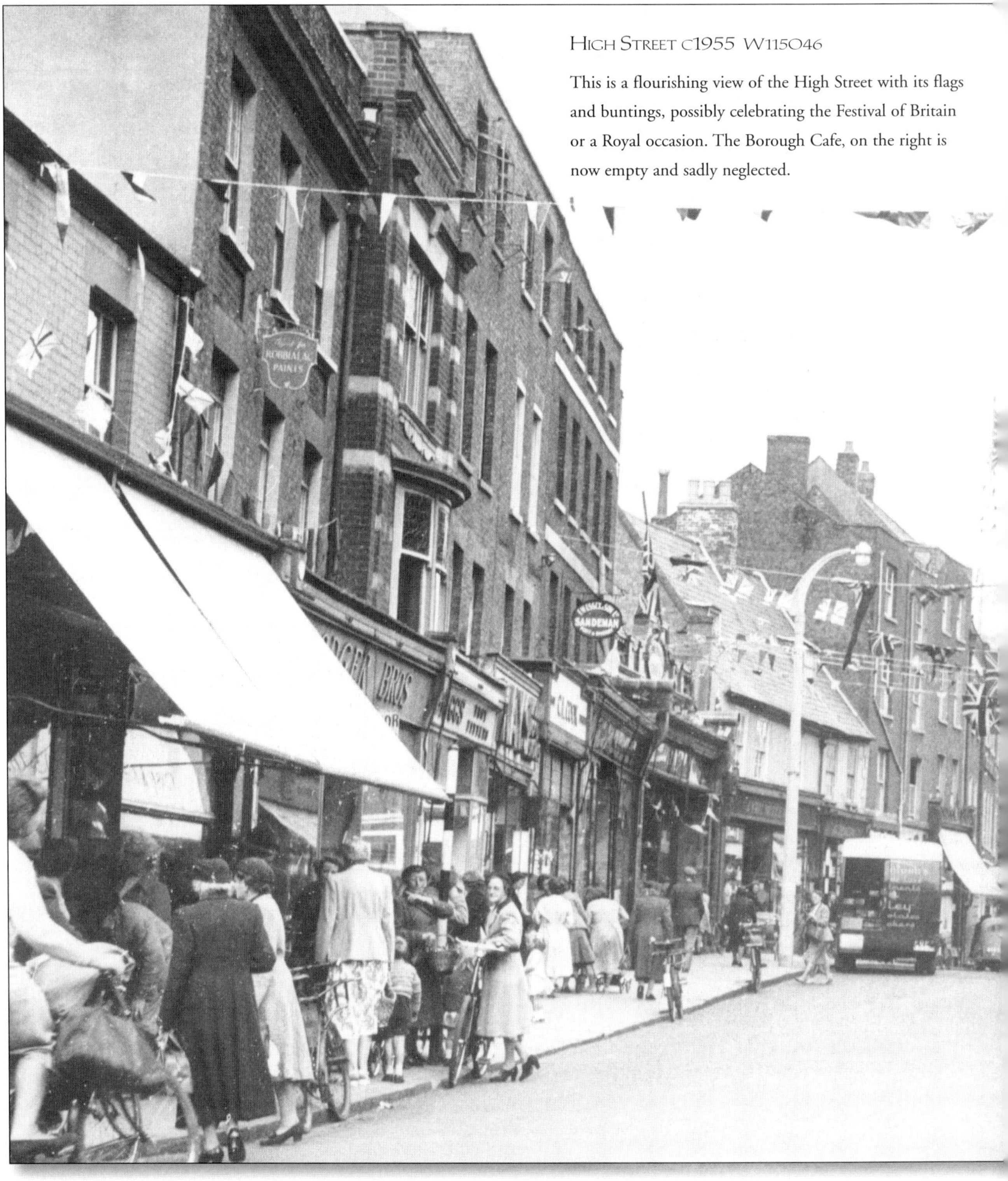

HIGH STREET c1955 W115046

This is a flourishing view of the High Street with its flags and buntings, possibly celebrating the Festival of Britain or a Royal occasion. The Borough Cafe, on the right is now empty and sadly neglected.

THE TOWN BRIDGE AND BRIDGE STREET

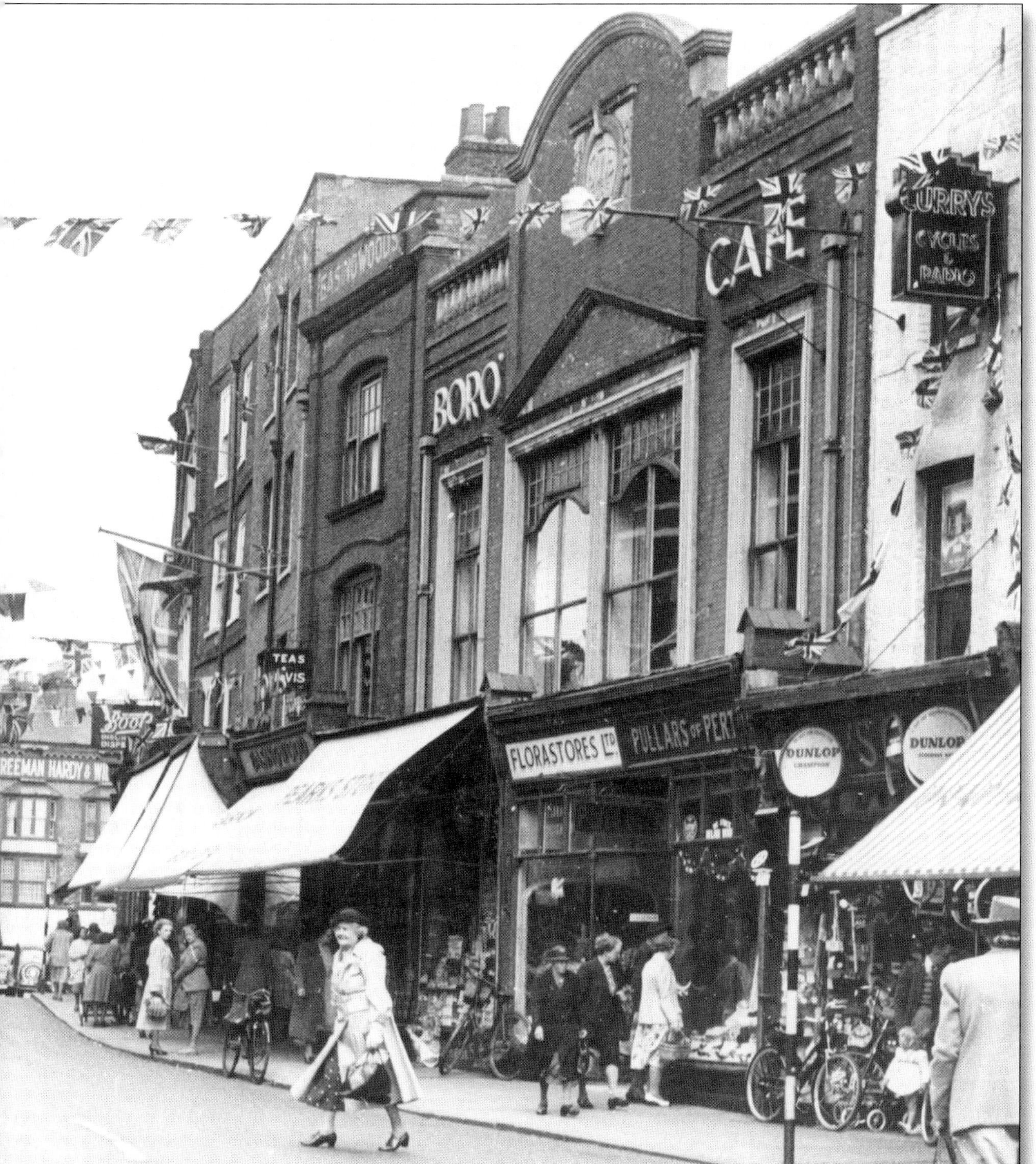

THE TOWN BRIDGE AND BRIDGE STREET

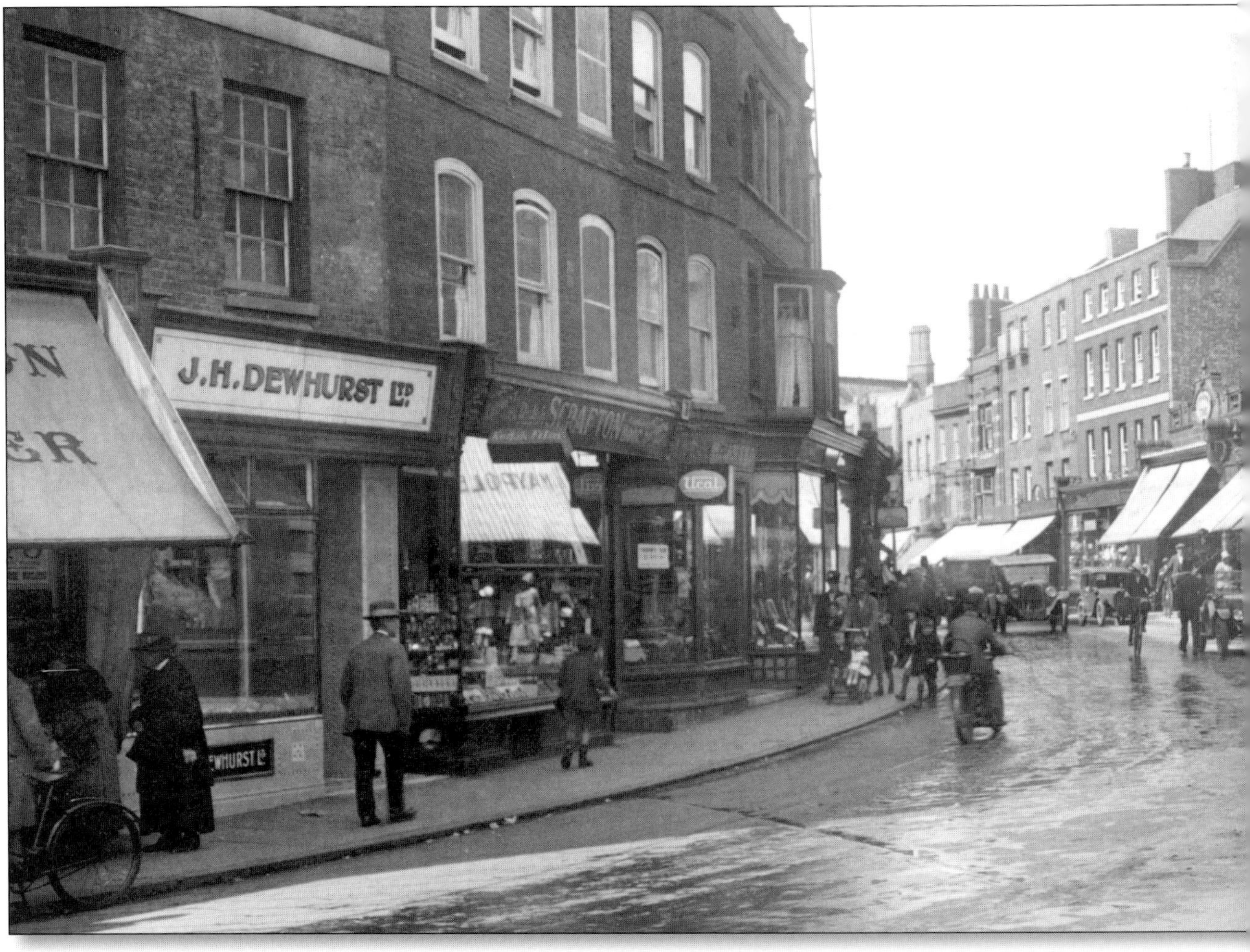

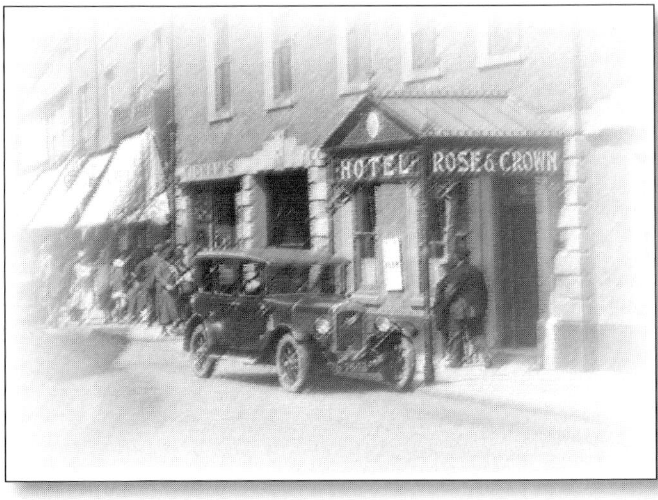

Above: HIGH STREET 1929 81966

Right: DETAIL FROM 81966

Far Right: HIGH STREET c1965 W115099

Comparing these views gives an inkling of the decline that was to befall the street in later years. Because of the relatively small shop sizes the larger retail chains, such as Boots and Burtons, have moved to bigger and better premises in the new Horsefair development - a successful retail location between the Market Place and the bus station.

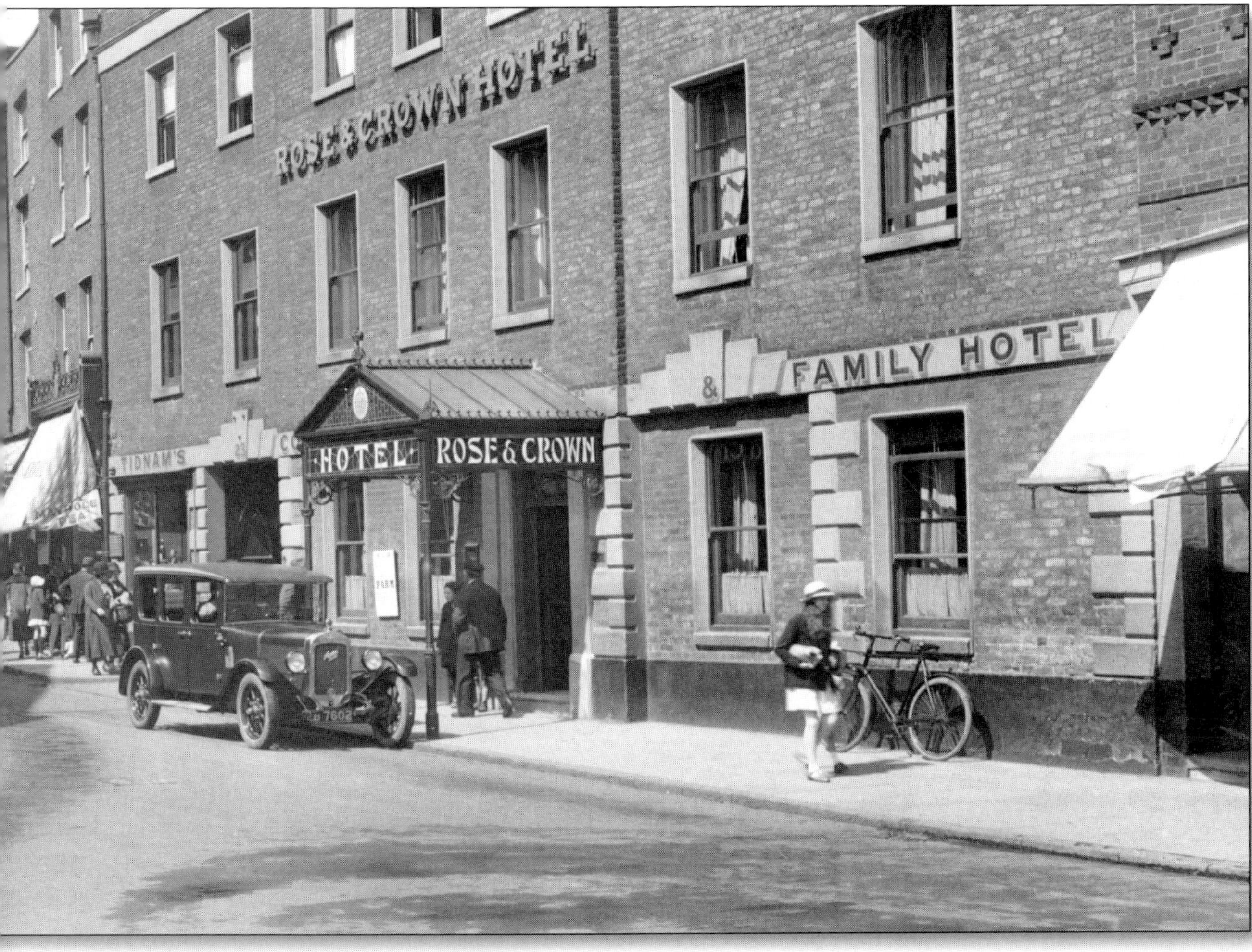
ROSE & CROWN HOTEL
HOTEL
ROSE & CROWN
& FAMILY HOTEL
TIDNAM'S

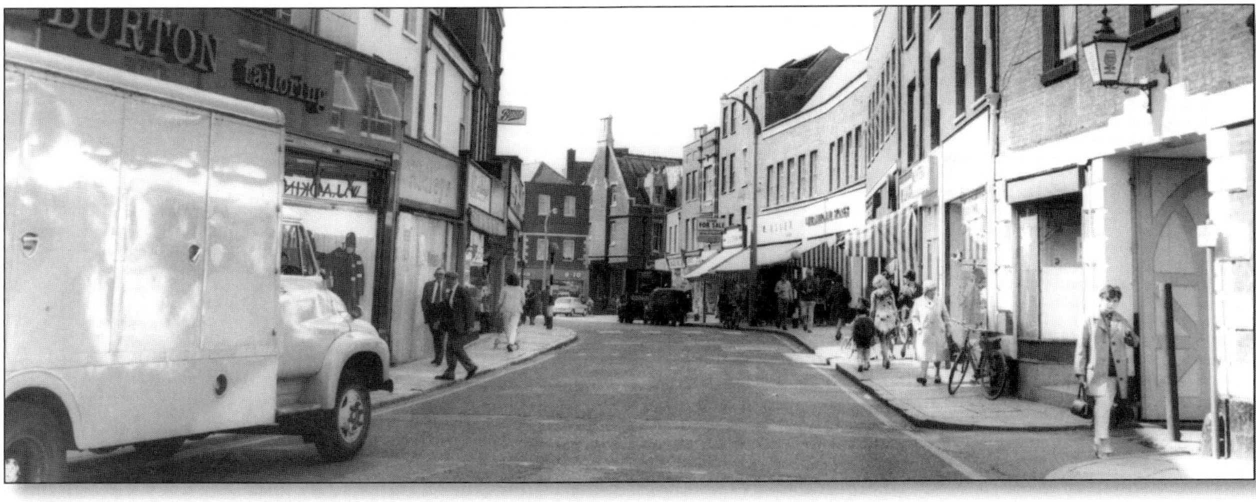
BURTON
tailoring
FOR SALE

CAMBRIDGESHIRE COUNTY MAP

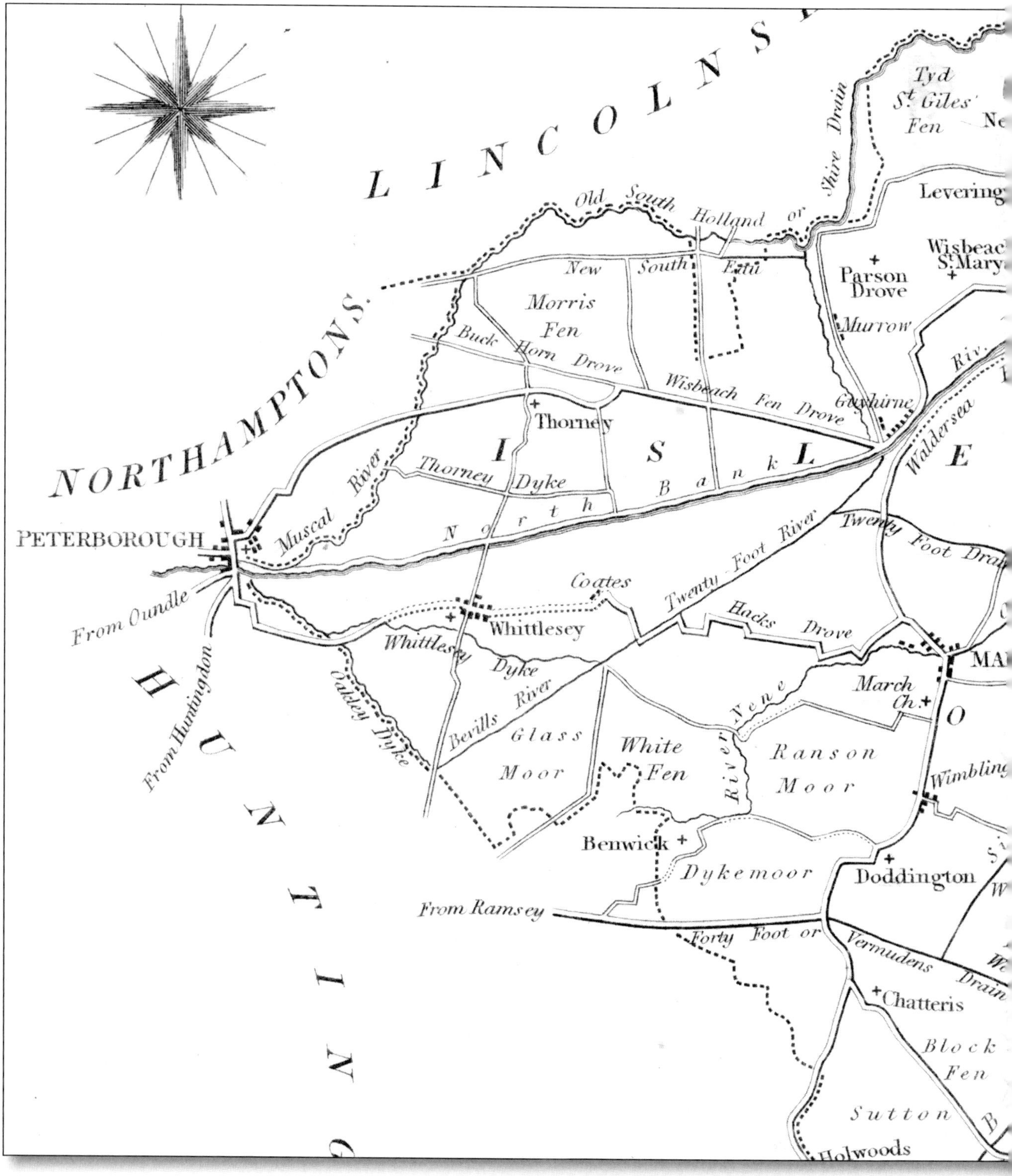

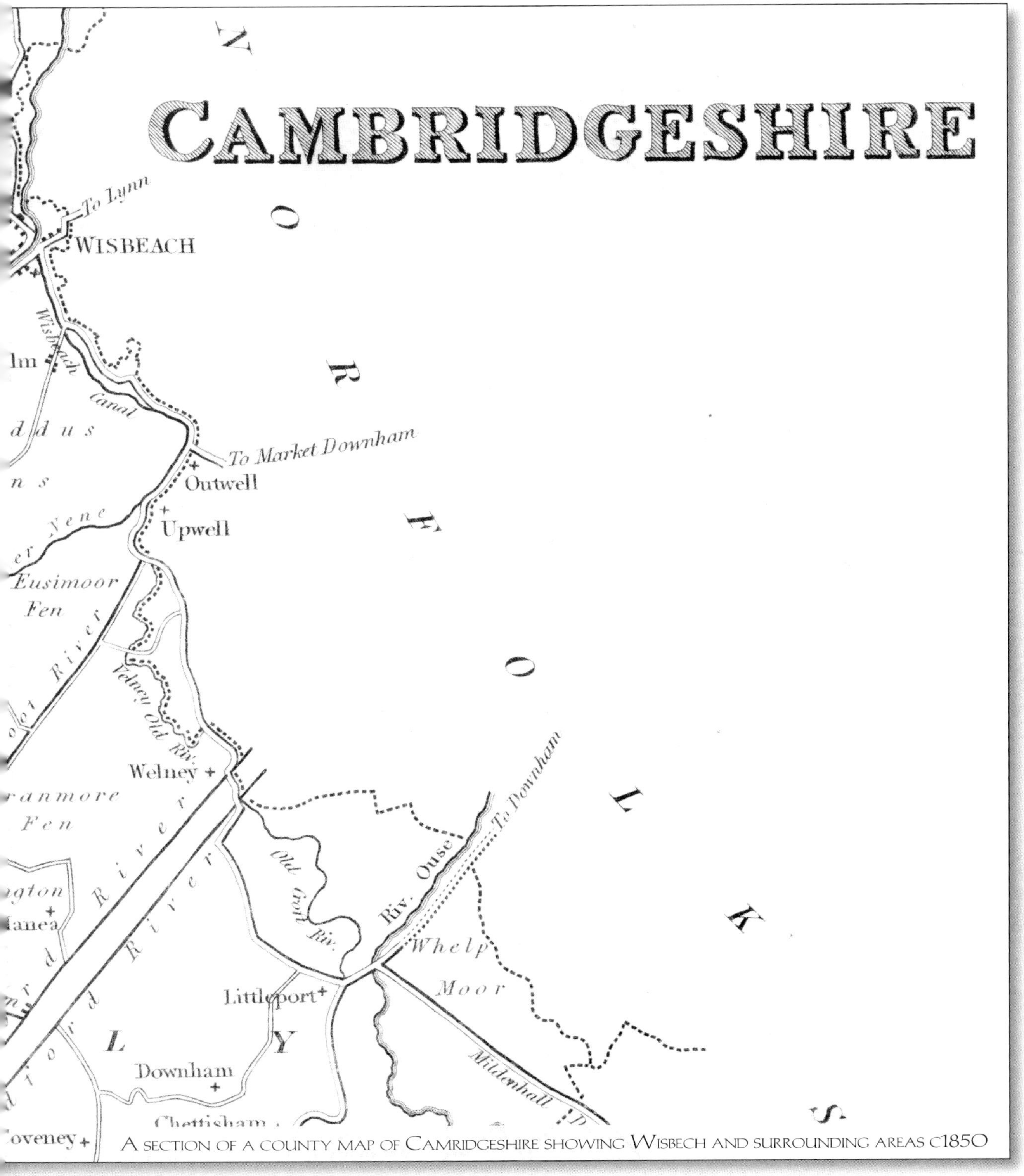

A section of a county map of Camridgeshire showing Wisbech and surrounding areas c1850

MARKET PLACE

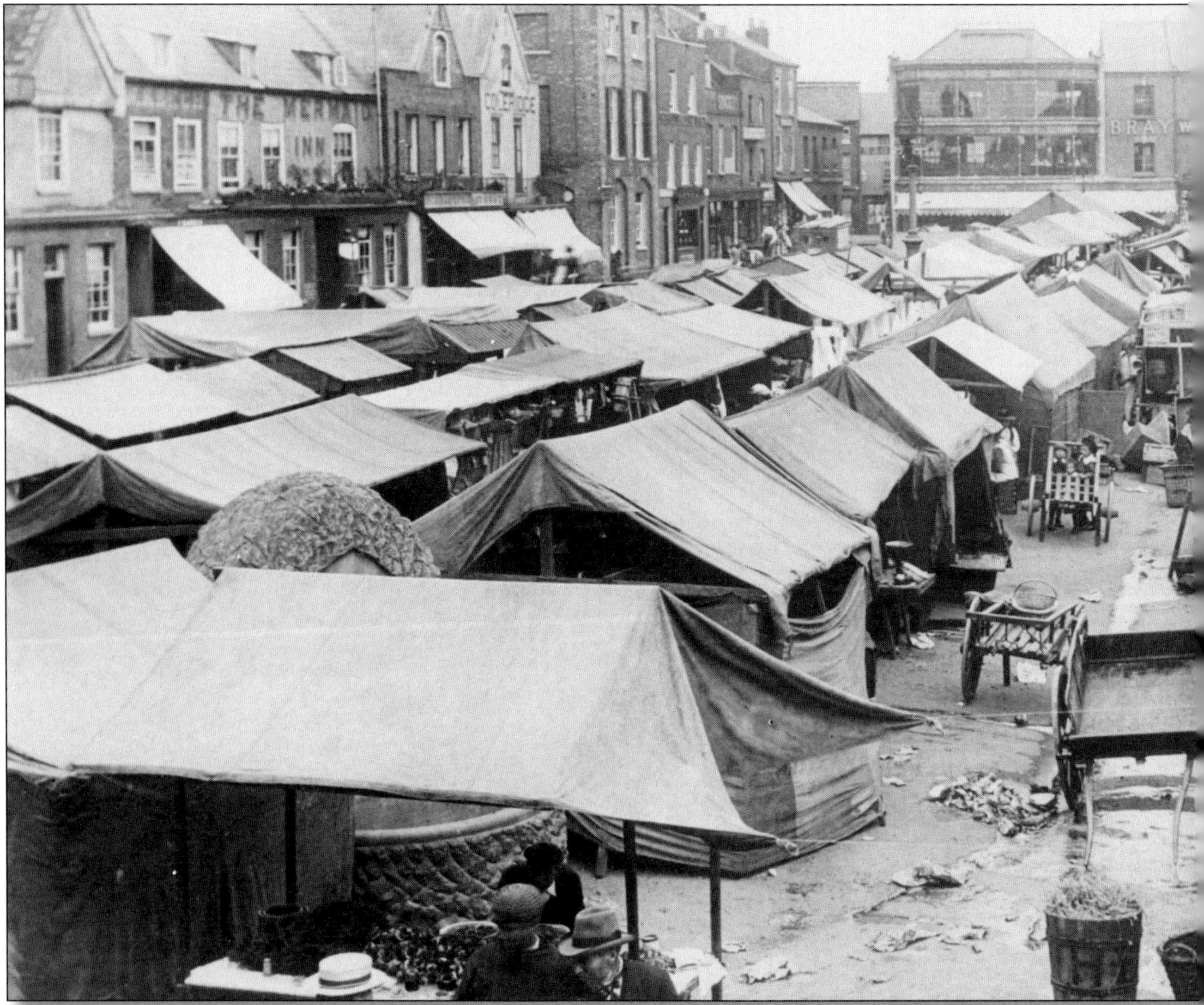

A market had existed on the left bank of the River Nene in Saxon times; as early as 1223, it was known as the 'Old Market'. This market became the centre for farming, fruit and horticulture and, in the past, sheep and cattle. The newer Market Place was formed just outside the walls of the Norman Castle, and dealt with locals' goods as well as those from outside the district. During the mediaeval period, the town was subjected to periods of building, flooding and re-building, as revealed by recent archaeological digs.

Very few early buildings survive in Wisbech, and Market Place is no exception, although it is possible that some remnants may be found behind the later Georgian and Victorian façades. In 1588 the Shire Hall, which had a pillory on top, and the Shambles were built towards the east end of the Market Place, at a cost of £85. The upper storey of the Shambles was used to store flour or corn, and the space underneath was divided into individual butcher's shops. The buildings stood until 1810 when they were removed and the whole area was properly paved for the first time; thus ending the need for planks to cross the muddy surface.

Although extensively rebuilt over the years, including the adding

MARKET PLACE

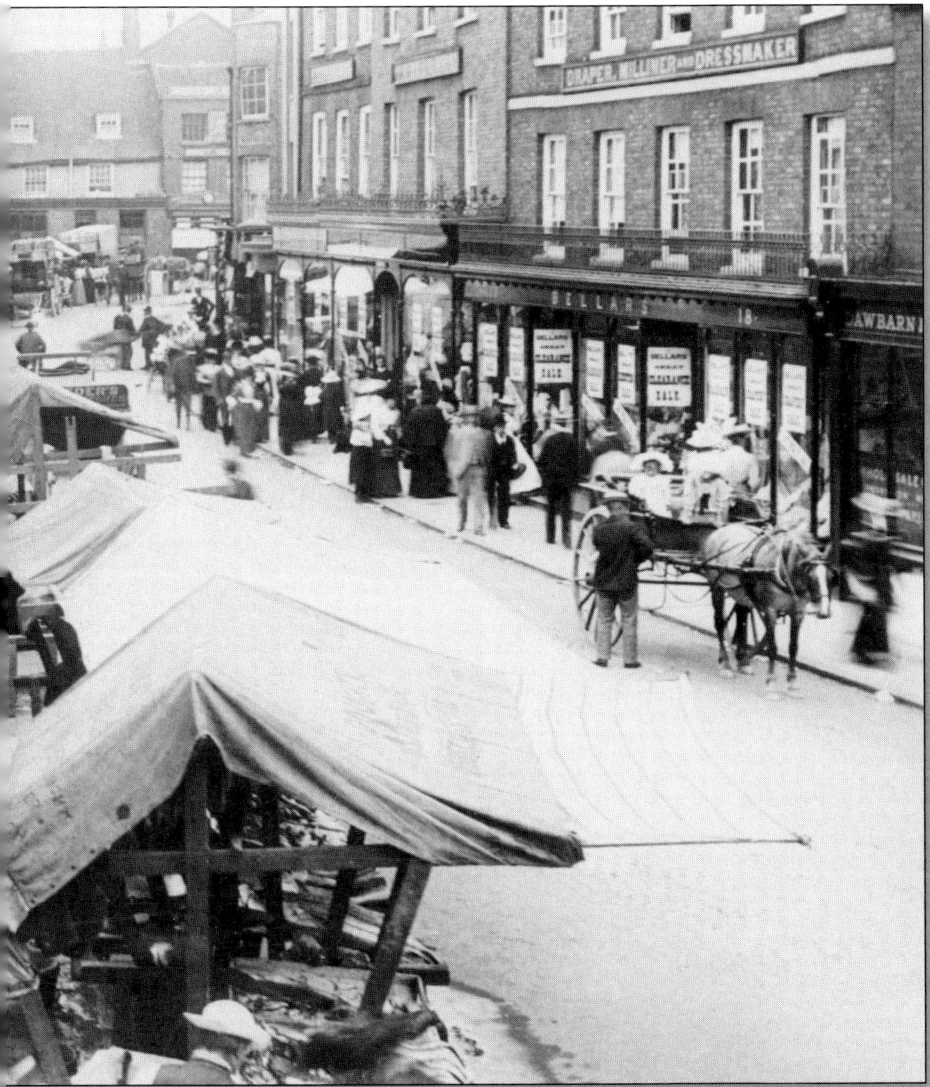

MARKET PLACE 1901 47580

Here is a typical market day in Wisbech, at the beginning of the 20th century. In the distance can be seen Racey's Arcade Stalls. The Arcade was located just off the Market Place in Blackfriar's Road, where the Empire Cinema is now. Many retailers with shops elsewhere in the town would also have a stall on market day. At the east end of the Market Place is Bray's showroom, for the household furniture that was manufactured in their works in Agenoria Street near the canal.

of the present imposing frontage, the Rose & Crown Hotel still possesses an interesting mixture of different architectural periods, as witnessed by its Tudor vaults and the courtyard, which dates back to 1601. The Swan stood on the site in 1435 and 40 years later the inn had become the Pheasant & Horn. The hotel was for many years the foremost coaching house in the district; it was re-fronted in about 1857, when it was purchased by William Tidnam, who developed it into a base for a thriving wine and spirit business. In 1895, Harry Augustus Tidnam succeeded his late father, and further expanded the wine and spirit business. The enterprise made good use of the cellars and passageways that ran under the inn and into the Market Place to store the stock. The Tidnams also acquired the cellars in Bridge Street from Peatlings; these ran under the Clarkson Memorial to the corner of the High Street and still exist today.

Originally, a market was only held on Saturday; later a second one was held on Thursdays. To quench the thirst of the many visitors to the markets, no less than eight public houses stood, at one time or another, on the north side of the square. These were in addition to the aforementioned Rose &

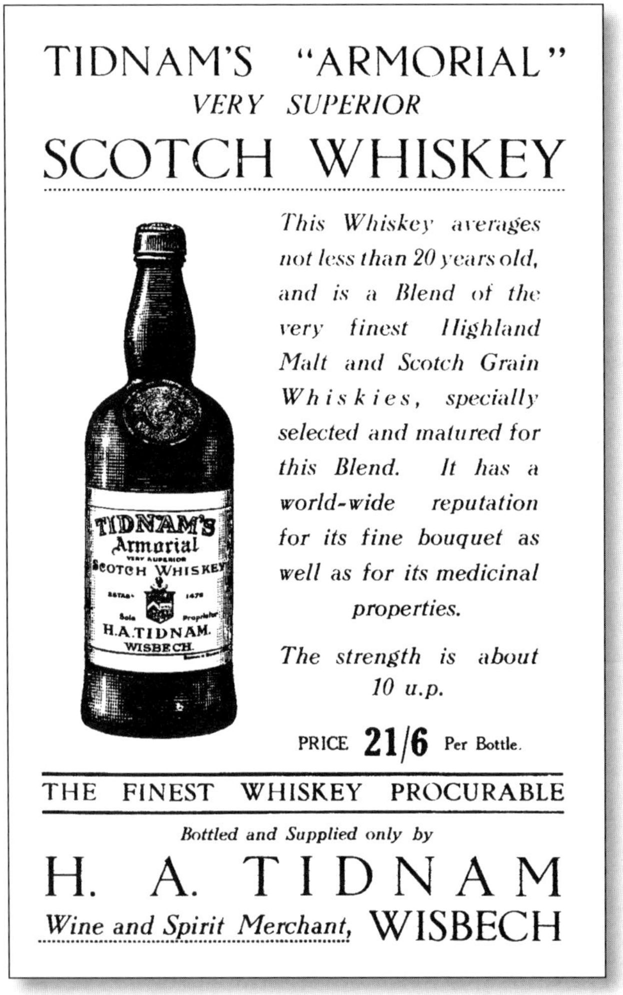

ADVERT FOR TIDNAM'S 'ARMORIAL' WHISKEY 1926

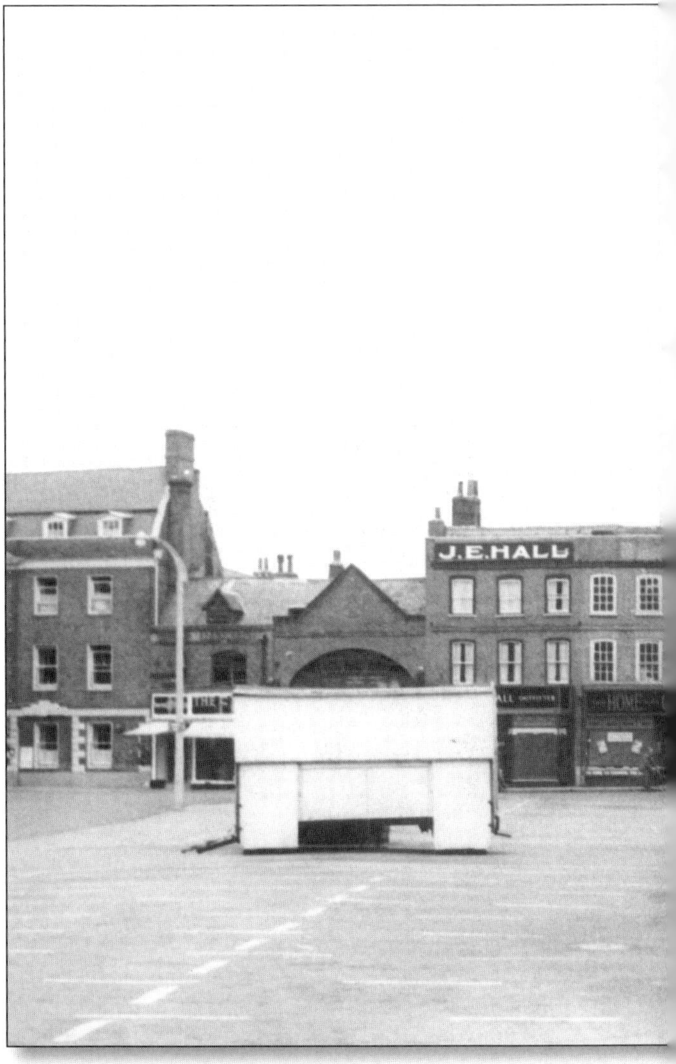

Crown Hotel to the west, and the Globe Inn (now the Market Inn) at the east end.

When the Shambles was demolished in 1810, the Market Place became a suitable area for holding large, public events; a dinner was held there in August 1814 celebrating (prematurely!) the defeat of Napoleon. Just over 20 years later, on 28 June 1838, the Market Place played host to another memorable event: a dinner in honour of Queen Victoria's coronation. This saw 5,000 people regaled, at a cost of £408, with nearly 300 stones of roast beef, 260 stones of potatoes and 542 plum puddings - weighing 7 pounds each. The feast was followed by rustic sports including 'jingling' matches and a tea drinking competition for women of 40 years and above. There was a balloon ascent and the event concluded with a fireworks display. Similar dinners were held for Victoria's two Jubilees and Edward VII's coronation, the latter event being followed by a tea for 3,500 of the town's schoolchildren.

The Market Place has had to redefine itself in recent years, with the removal of the Tesco store to an enlarged superstore on the outskirts, and the rival attractions of the new retail units in the Horsefair development of 1987. This has seen a rise in service businesses such as building societies and travel agents, plus a range of charity shops and specialist traders. However, some long standing

MARKET PLACE

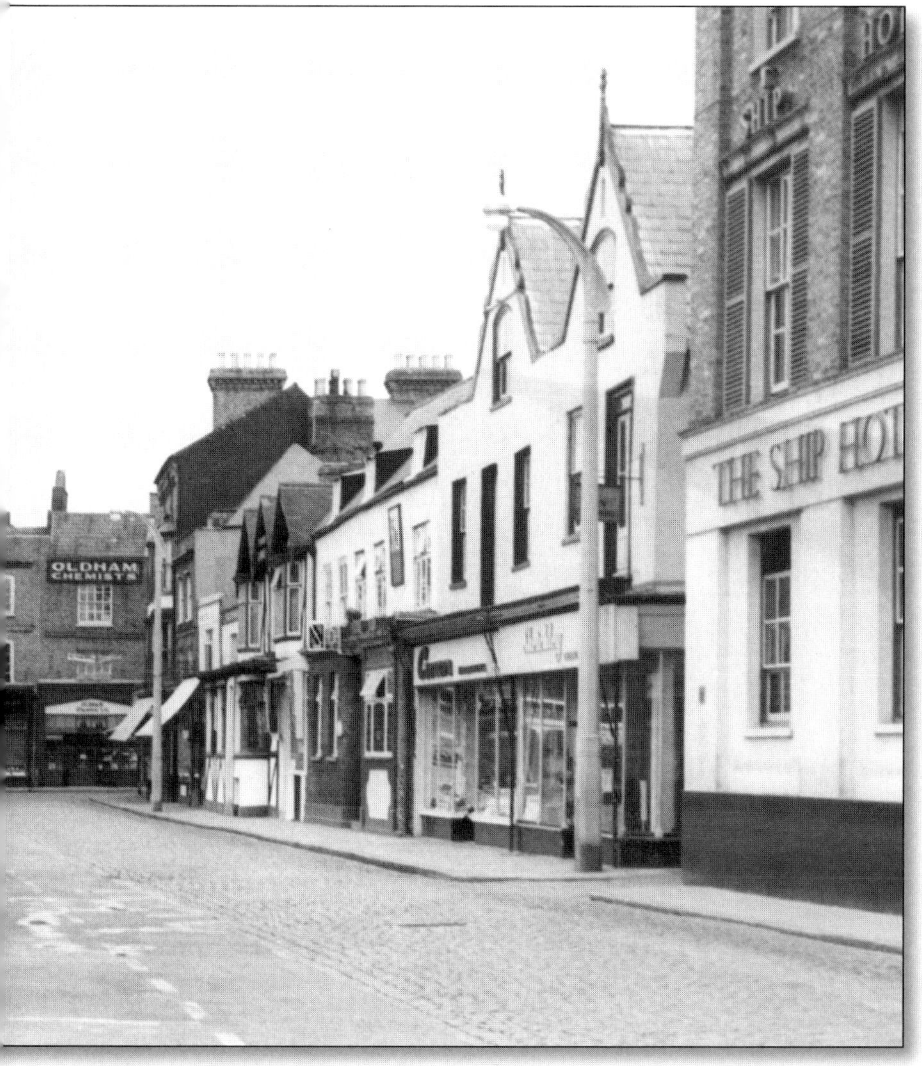

Left:
MARKET PLACE c1955 W115059

The Ship Hotel, on the right of the photograph, was one of the eight inns and taverns that at one time or another stood along this side of the Market Place.

Bottom Left:
THE ROSE & CROWN HOTEL c1955 W115060

The High Street approach to the Market Place is seen here flanked by the Easiephit shoe shop and Woolworth's on one side, and the Rose & Crown Hotel on the other. The Rose & Crown is Wisbech's oldest hostelry and its earliest predecessor, the Swan, is recorded as having been here in 1435.

Below:
THE ROSE & CROWN YARD 1929 81970

Parts of the courtyard date from 1601. When this photograph was taken Harry Tidnam's wine offices, which can be seen on the left, had only recently been established.

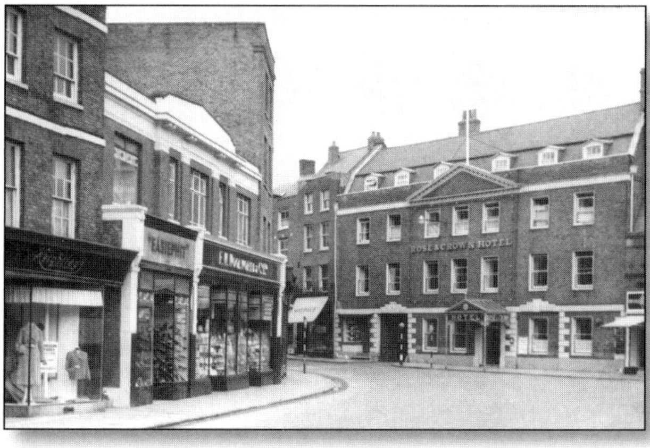

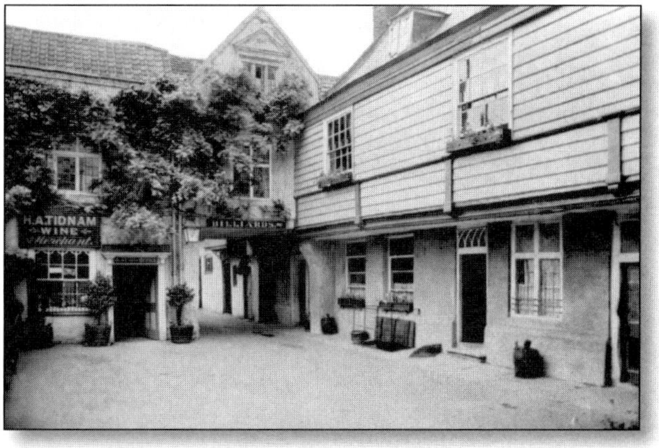

MARKET PLACE

Wisbech shops have flourished here such as G W Frank's butcher's shop and, of course, Woolworth's.

The year 1992 saw the completion of Fenland District Council's enhancement and pedestrianisation of the Market Place; the mix of cobbles and tarmac was replaced, new street furniture installed and several trees planted. The removal of car parking and the resultant open spaces prompted one local wag to describe the Market Place as Fenland's 'Red Square'.

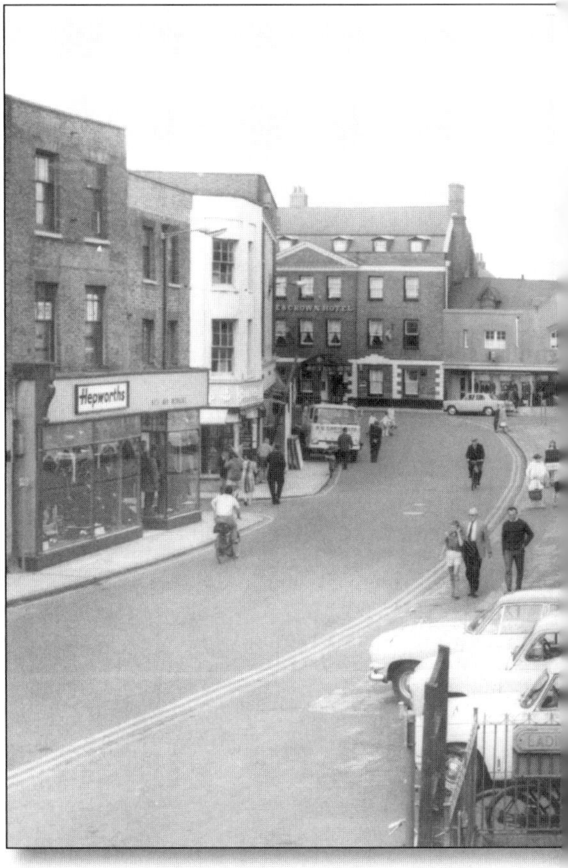

At your Service

Oldham *(Chymists)* Ltd

Managing Director: E. NEWMAN RIGG, M.P.S.
PHARMACIST

Dispensing Chemists
Photographic and Surgical
Toilet Goods

●

Oldham *(Opticians)* Ltd

Managing Director: S. C. DRIVER, F.S.M.C.

Ophthalmic Opticians

●

29 Market Place, Wisbech

ADVERT FOR OLDHAM (CHYMISTS) LTD 1953

The business later removed to the Old Market.

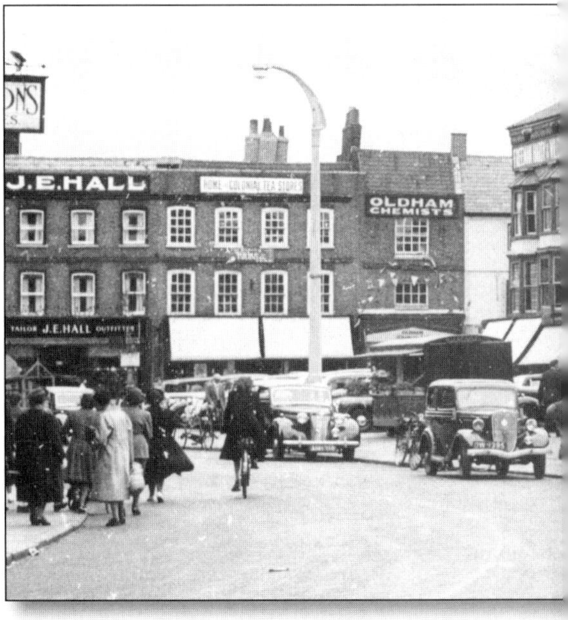

MARKET PLACE

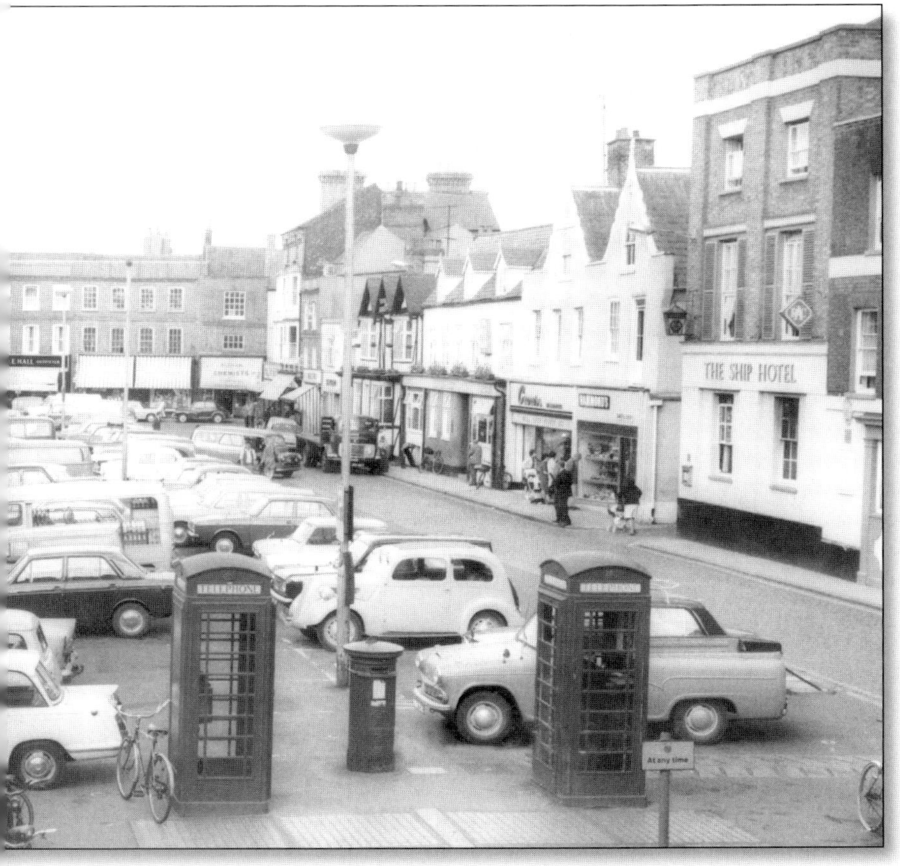

Left:
MARKET PLACE c1965 W115091

We are looking towards the west end of the Market Place. The two tailors and outfitters businesses, John Collier and J E Hall, sit side-by-side, next to the Home & Colonial Tea Store. In the foreground can be seen the underground toilets, which were later filled in.

Below:
MARKET PLACE c1955 W115043

The north side of the Market Place was the drinking heart of Wisbech, whose taste for alcohol saw over one hundred inns, taverns and pubs recorded around the town. In this view the Freeman Hardy & Willis shop stands on the site of the Old Talbot, and two shops along is where the Golden Lion was situated. The 'Tudor' building is the George Inn and next-door is the Mermaid. The lower storey of the Ship Hotel has been opened up to allow greater pedestrian access to the Horsefair, and the Griffin next-door is now a barber's shop.

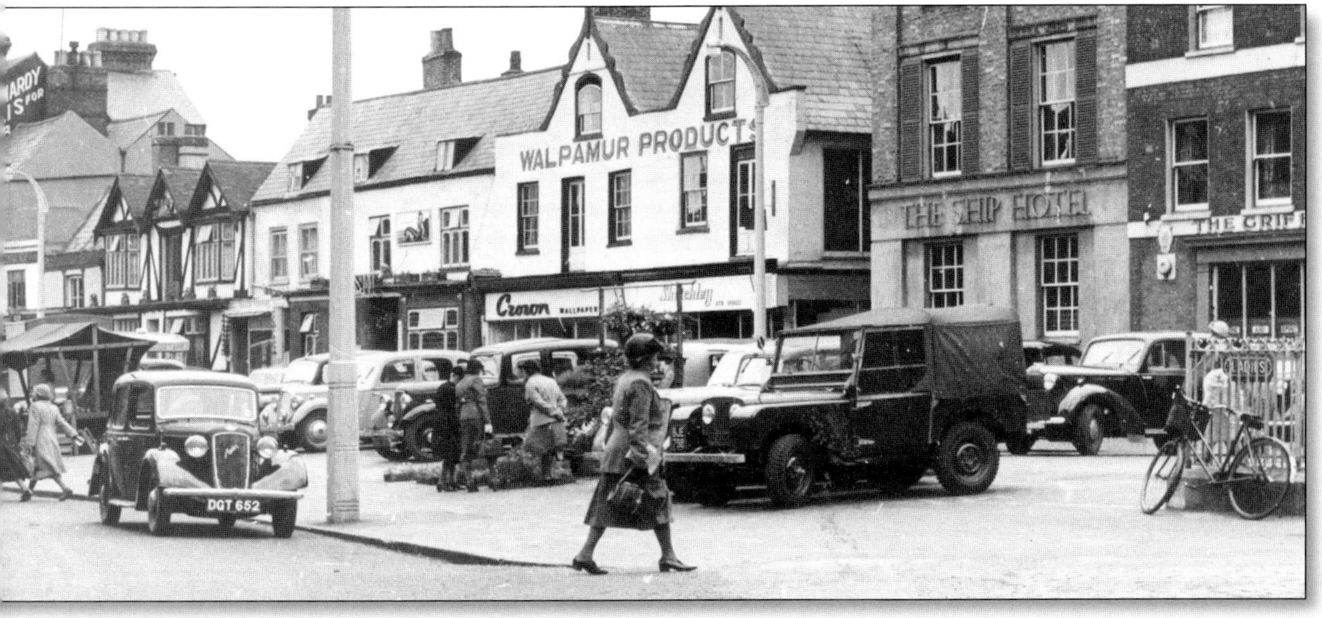

MARKET PLACE

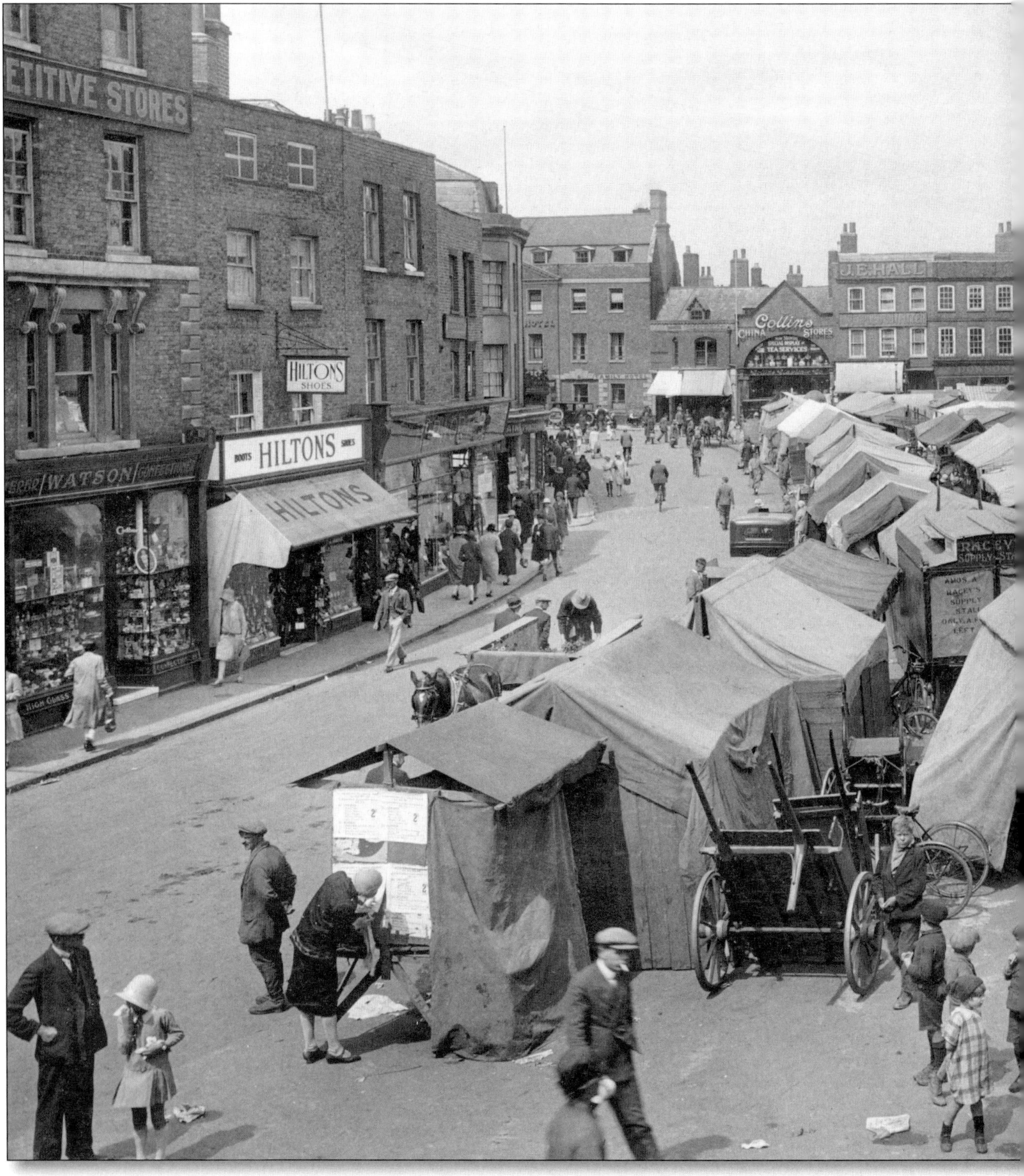

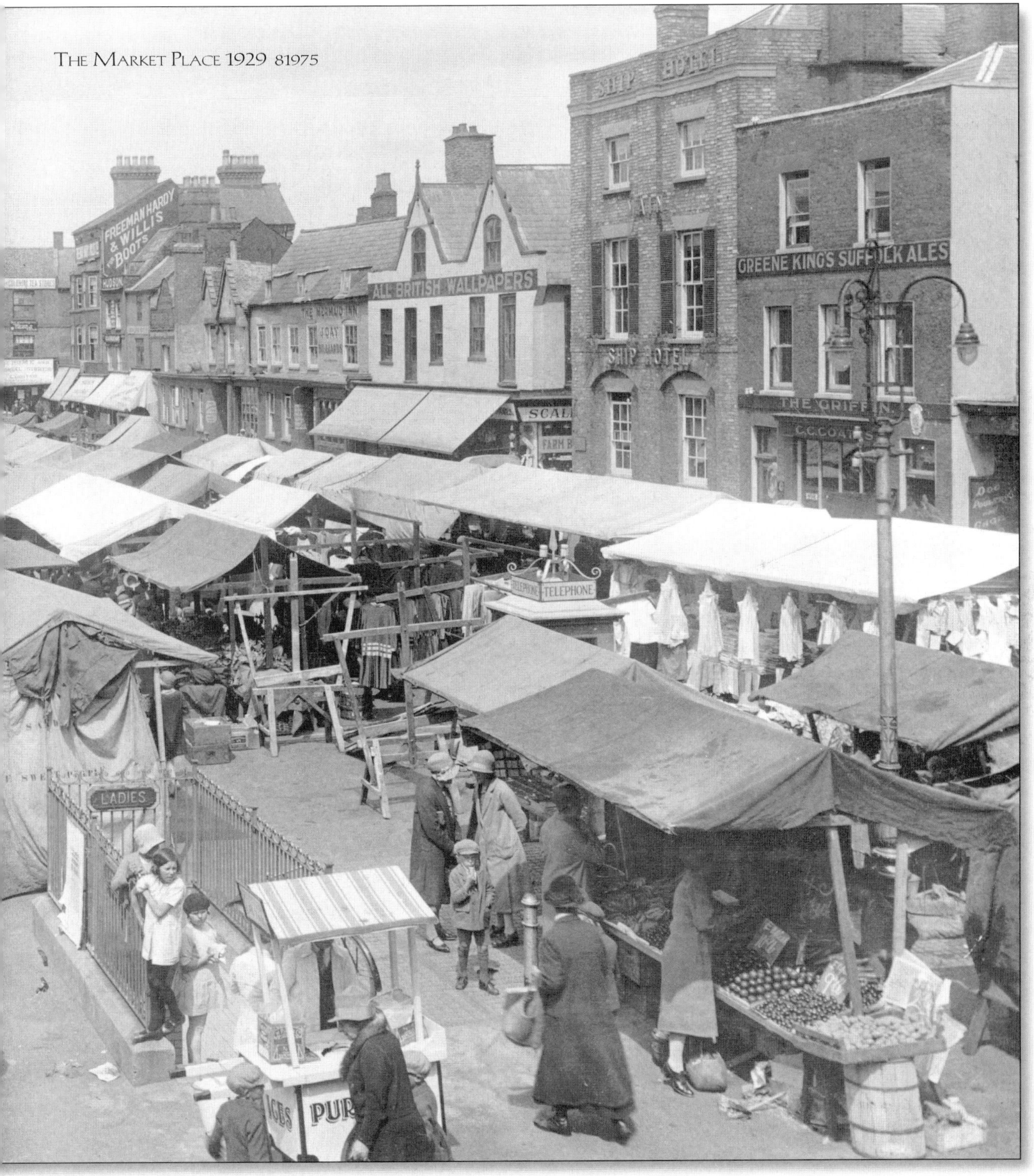

The Market Place 1929 81975

MARKET PLACE

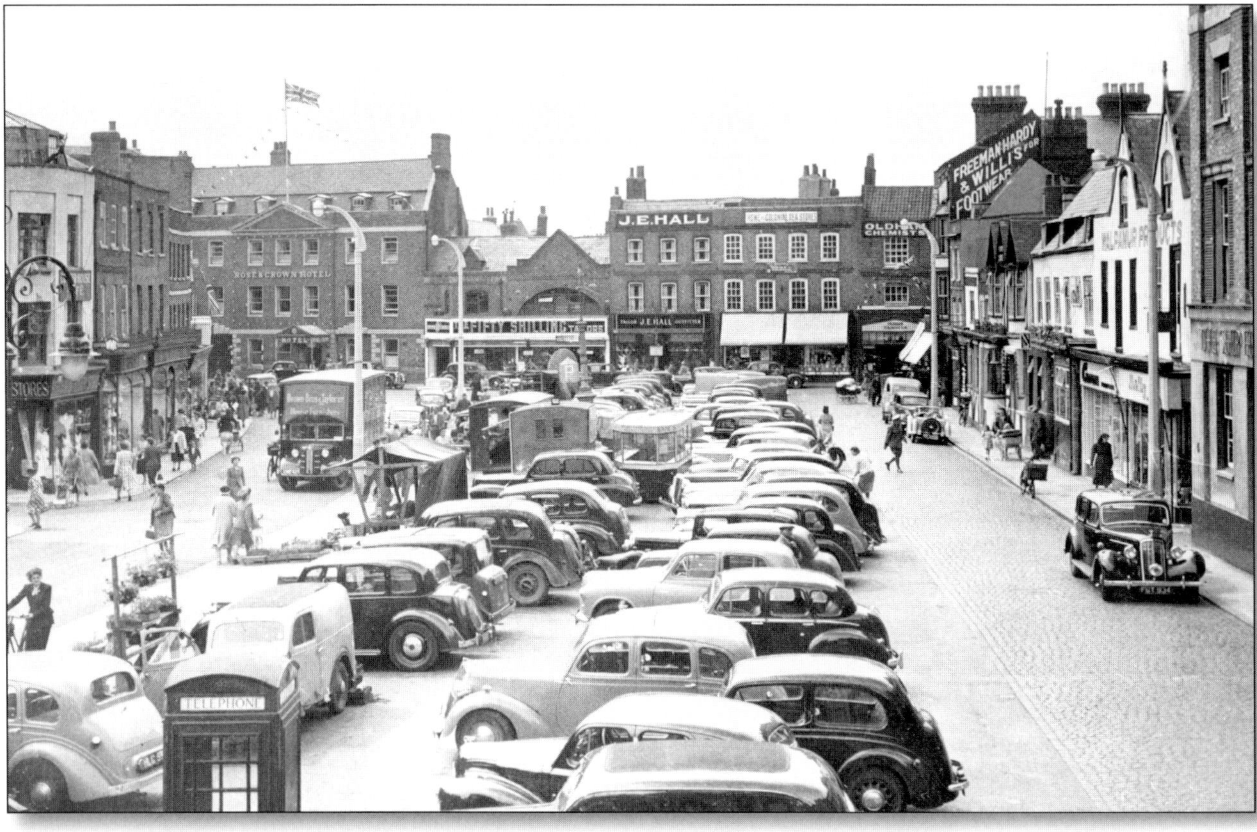

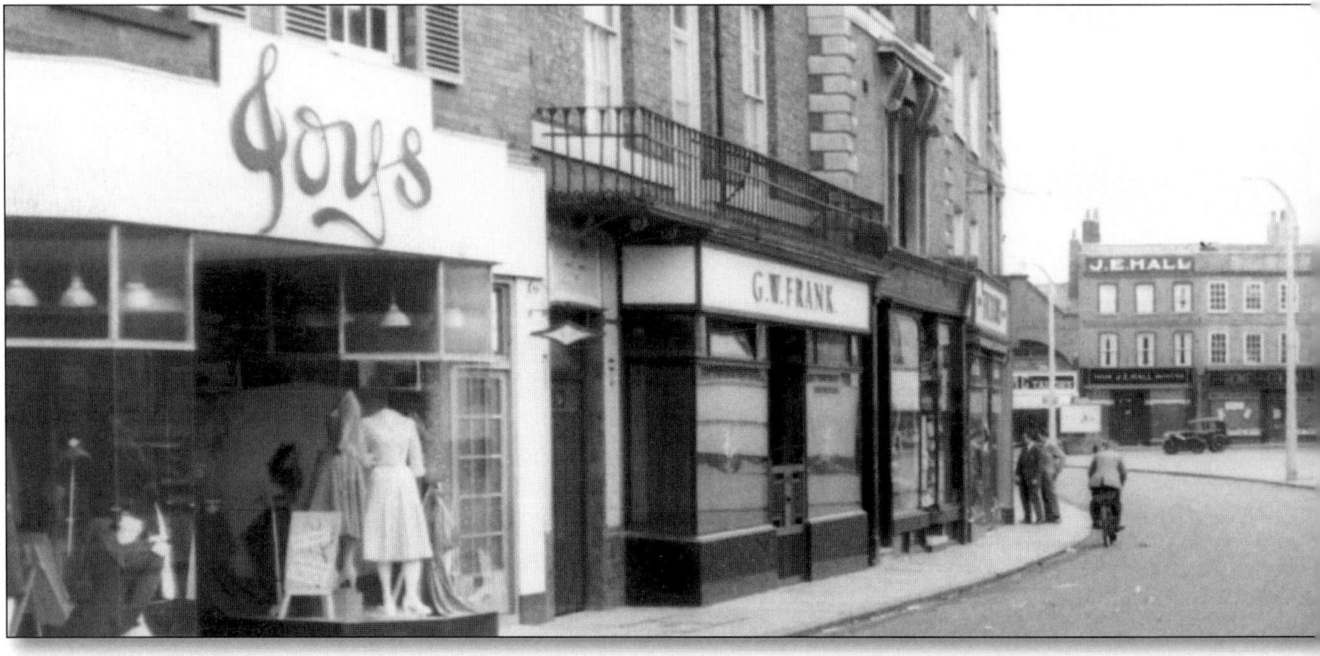

Left: MARKET PLACE c1955 W115044

The appearance of national chain stores was a new threat to the small family business. J E Hall, the People's Outfitter, faced opposition from Hepworth's and was further endangered when Collins China Store moved to Market Street, allowing the Fifty-Shilling Tailor to move next-door (later John Collier).

Below: MARKET PLACE c1955 W115074

G W Frank's butcher's shop possesses perhaps the finest remaining shop frontage in the town, with its original Art Deco design butcher's fittings dating from the 1930s.

Right: DETAIL FROM W115044

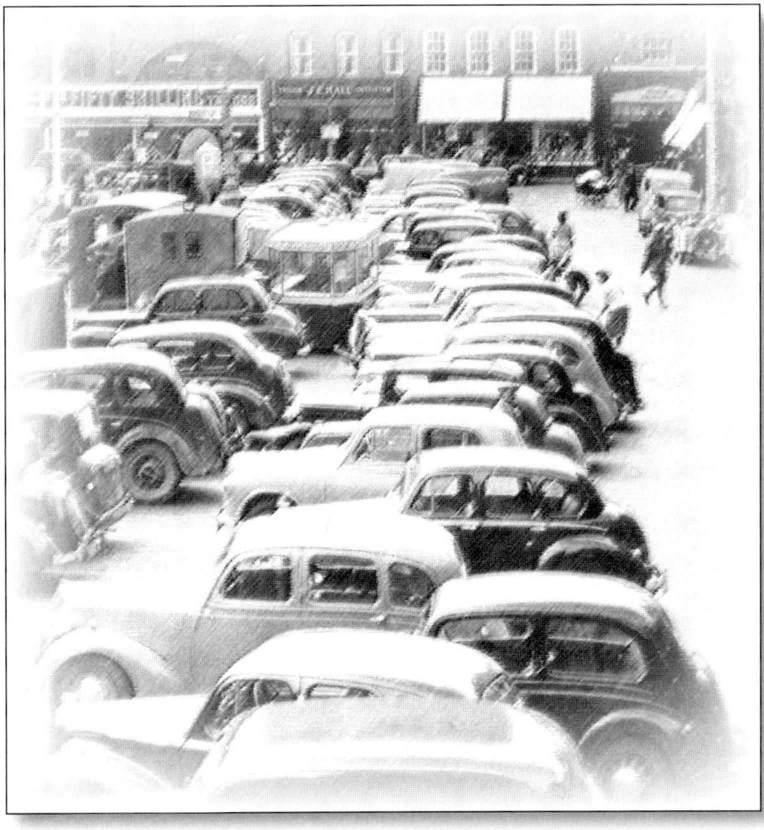

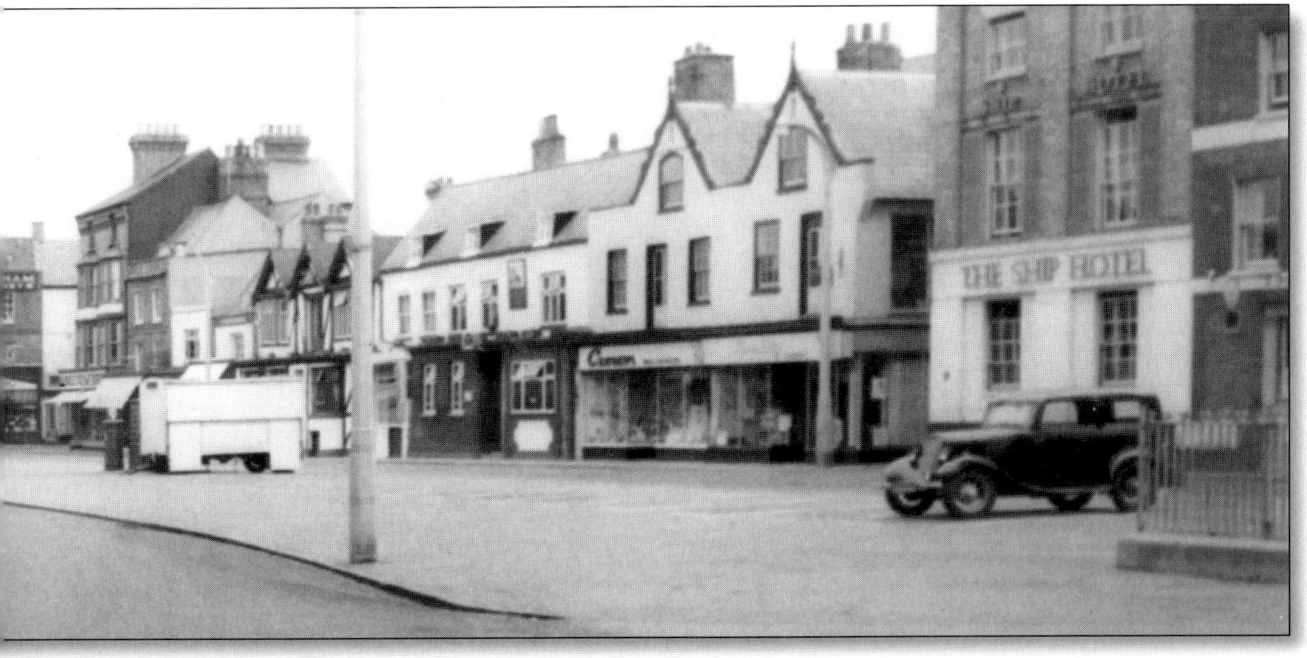

MARKET PLACE

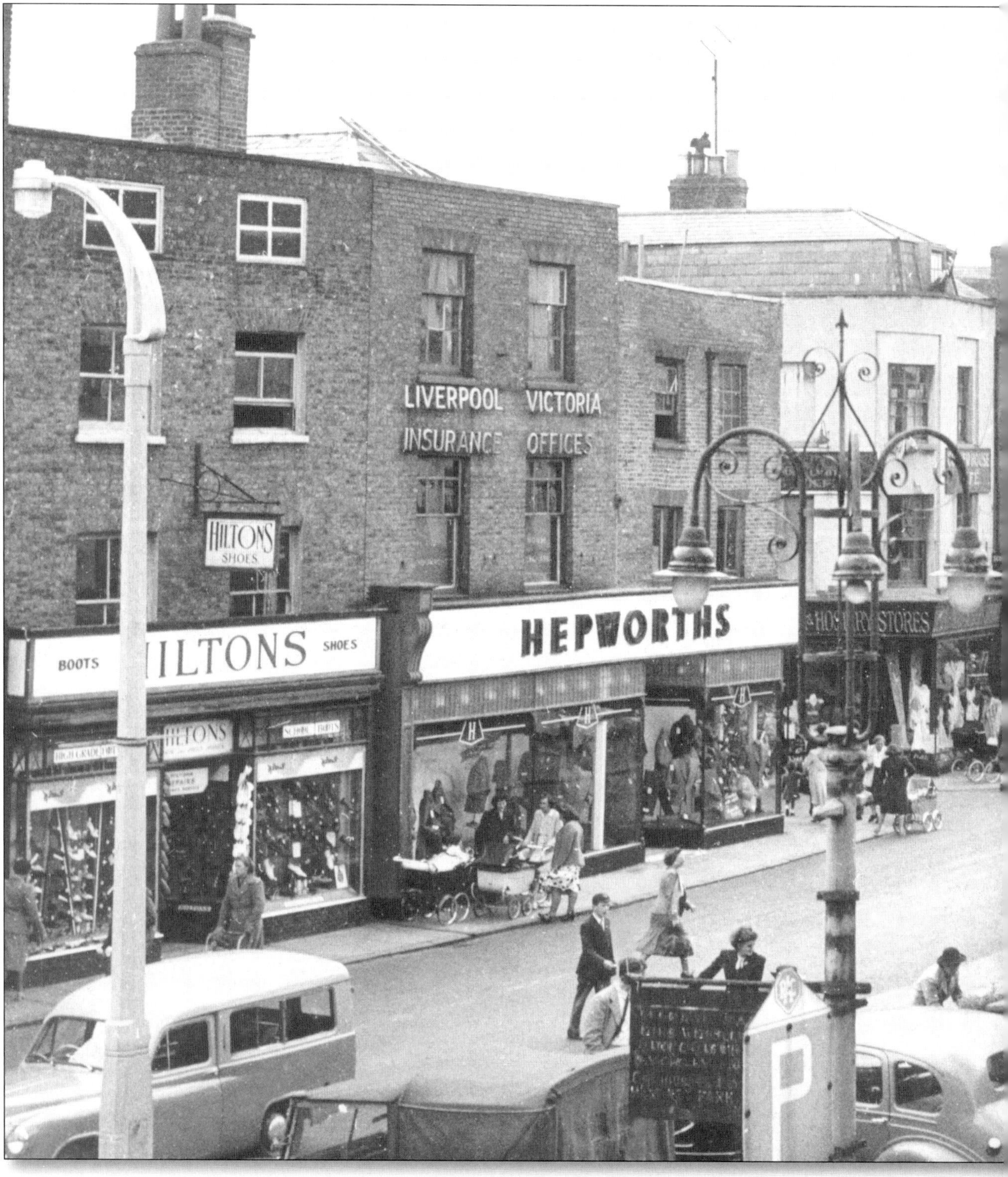

MARKET PLACE C1955 W115045

Before the opening of the Churchill Road in the 1960s the main route from Wisbech to Outwell was through the Market Place onto Church Terrace, then along West Street or Norfolk Street before joining the Elm Road.

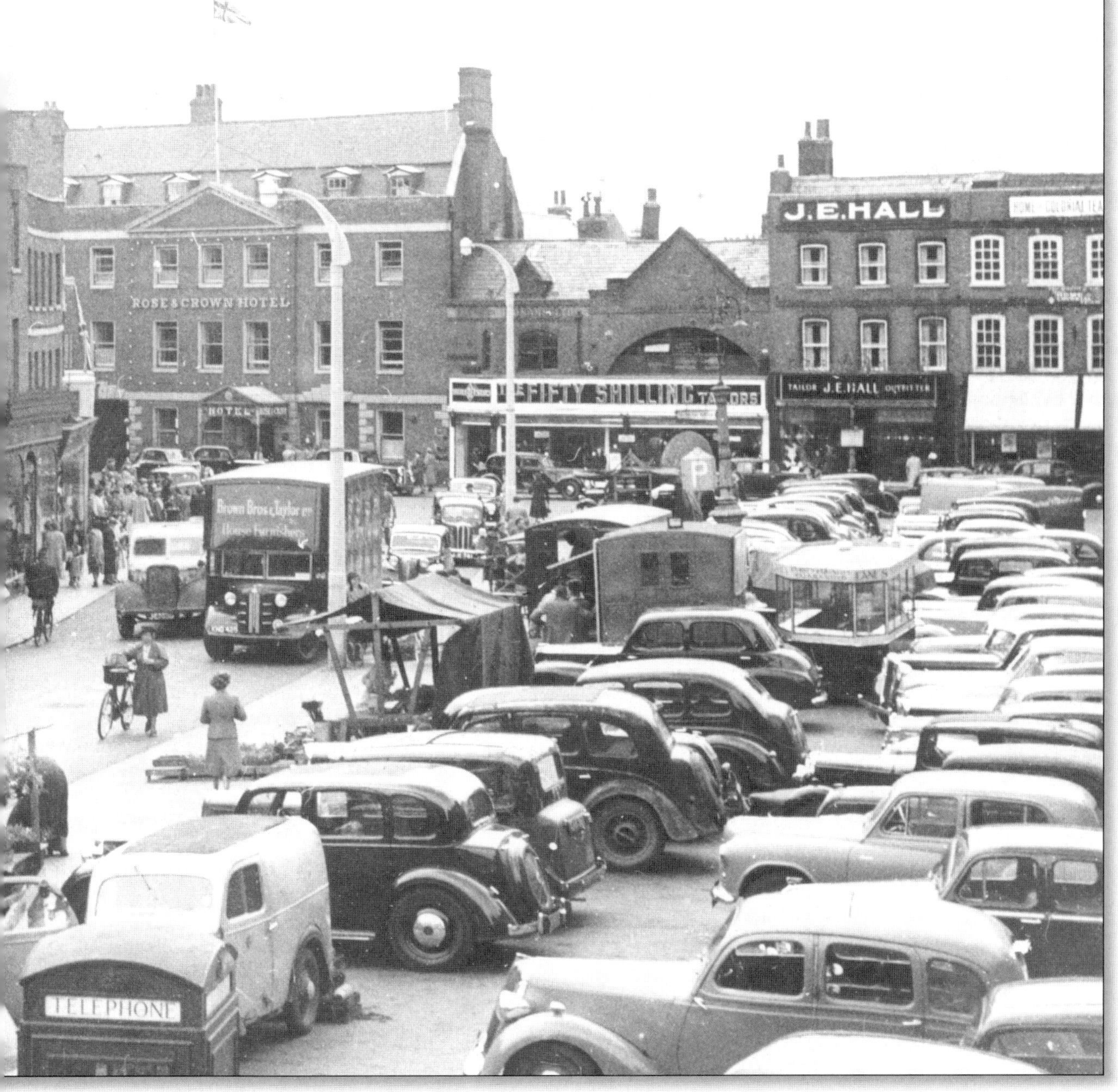

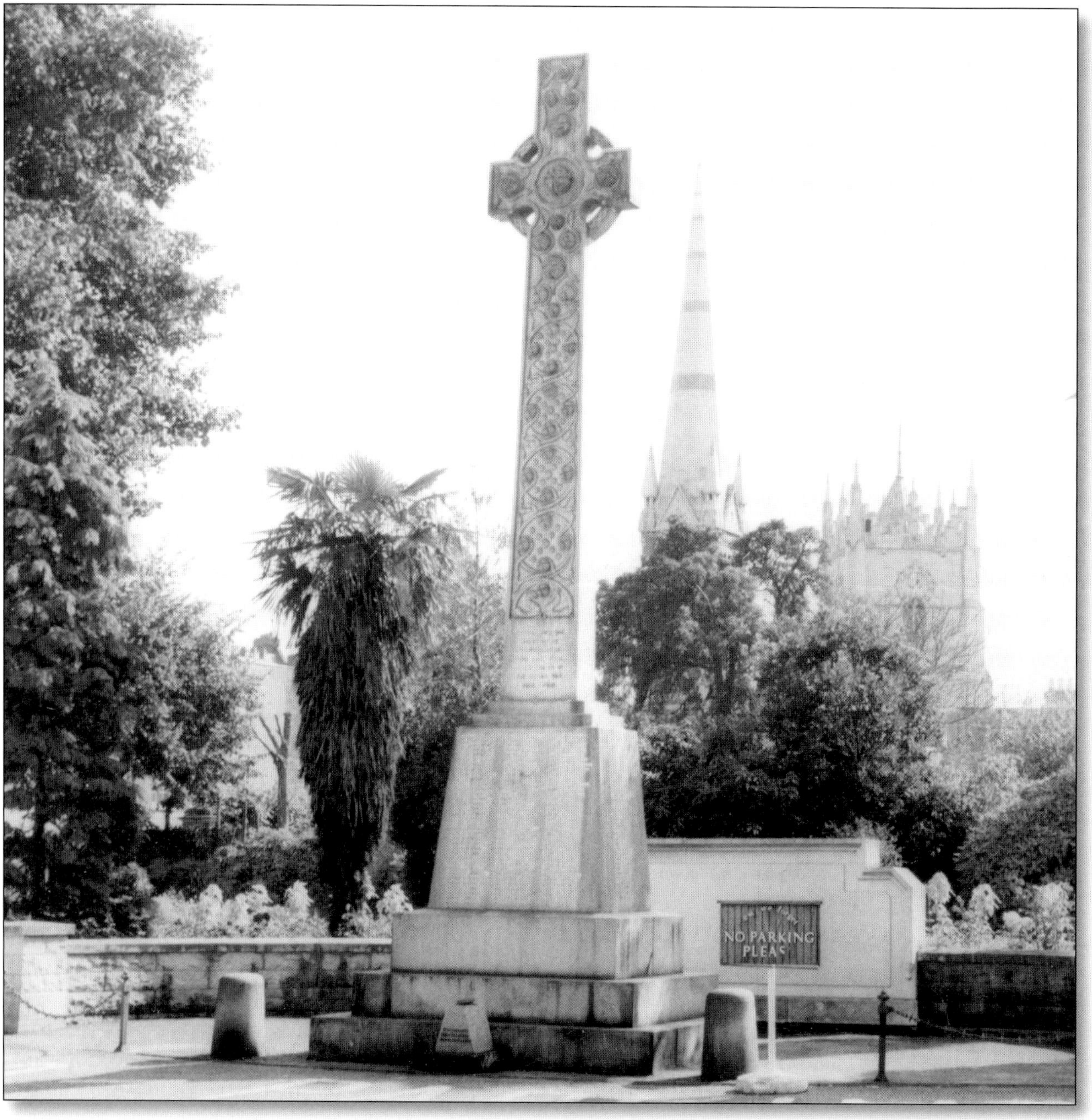

Above: THE MEMORIAL C1965 W115095

Far Right: ELY PLACE BAPTIST CHAPEL C1965 W115081

This rather awkward-looking building was built on the site of a previous chapel. It was opened on 23 March 1873, and cost around £5,000. In the early 1970s the chapel was pulled down and replaced by the present, rather drab, library which opened in 1975.

THE CASTLE, CRESCENT AND CHURCH

The small roadway, Market Street, on the south side of the Market Place leads to one of the most impressive and well-laid-out parts of town: The Crescent. Built on the site of Wisbech Castle, the area has a fine collection of Georgian buildings.

If the commercial significance of the town grew largely from the port, then its administrative importance stems from the Normans' recognition of Wisbech being located at a strategic point, where a castle could guard against incursions into the fenlands from the Wash. After the transfer of the Norman Castle to the See of Ely, it was used both as one of the Bishop's palaces and as a prison. By the 15th century, the stone building had been re-built in brick by Bishop Morton, who caused a channel (which bears his name today) to be cut from Stanground, near Peterborough to Guyhirn; thus significantly improving the drainage and navigation of the Nene at that time.

Castle Square, near York Row, corresponds with the main entrance point to the Castle and is now dominated by the Wisbech War Memorial (see W115095). General Lord Horne unveiled the granite 'runic cross' on 24 June 1921; it lists nearly 300 Wisbech men who died in the First World War. Behind the cross can be seen the plinth erected to commemorate those Wisbechians who were killed during the Second World War. The two palms flanking the memorial stand in the ornamental garden, which was laid out on land given to the Borough by the Hon Alexandrina Peckover, in 1932.

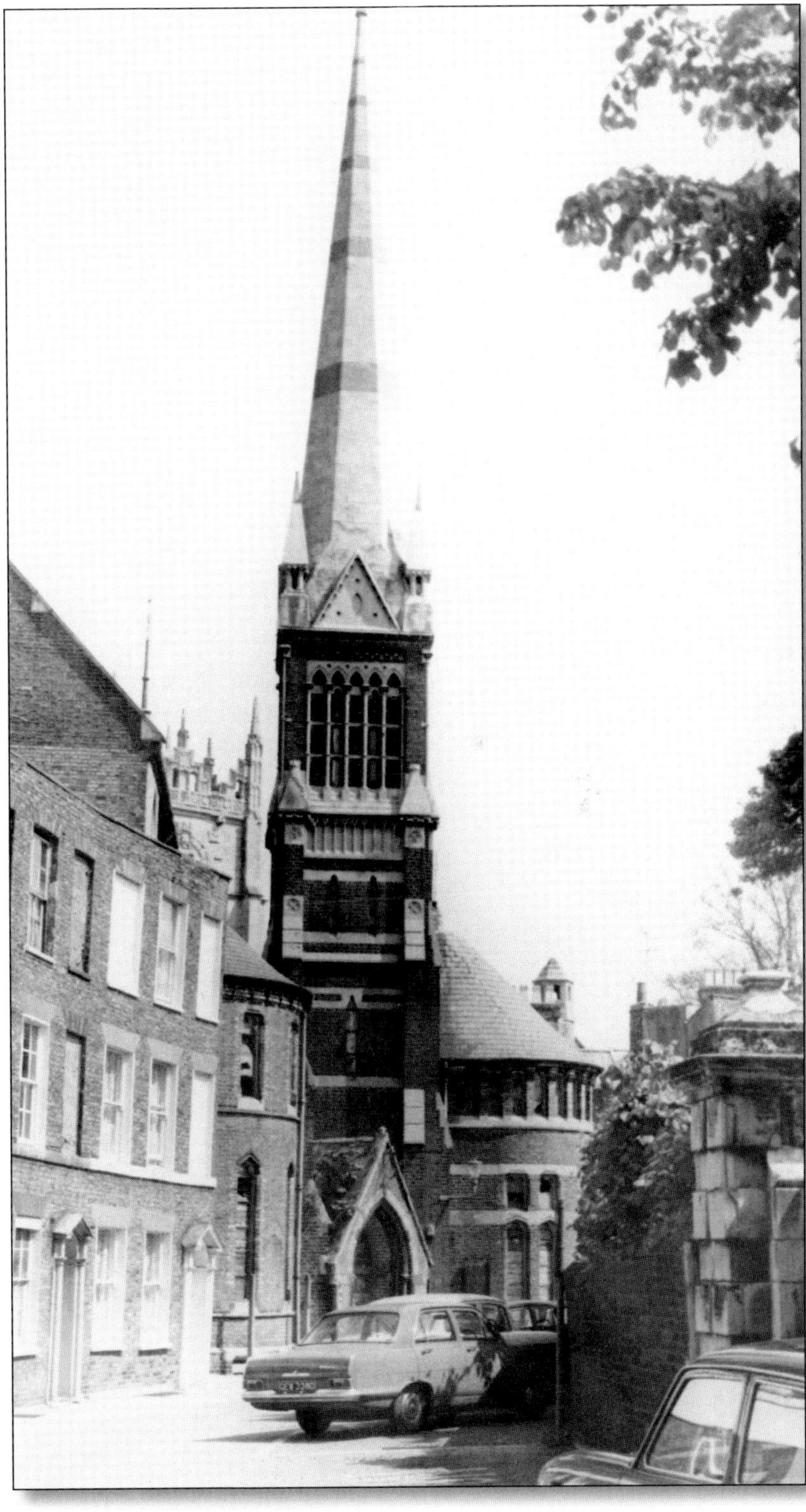

THE CASTLE, CRESCENT AND CHURCH

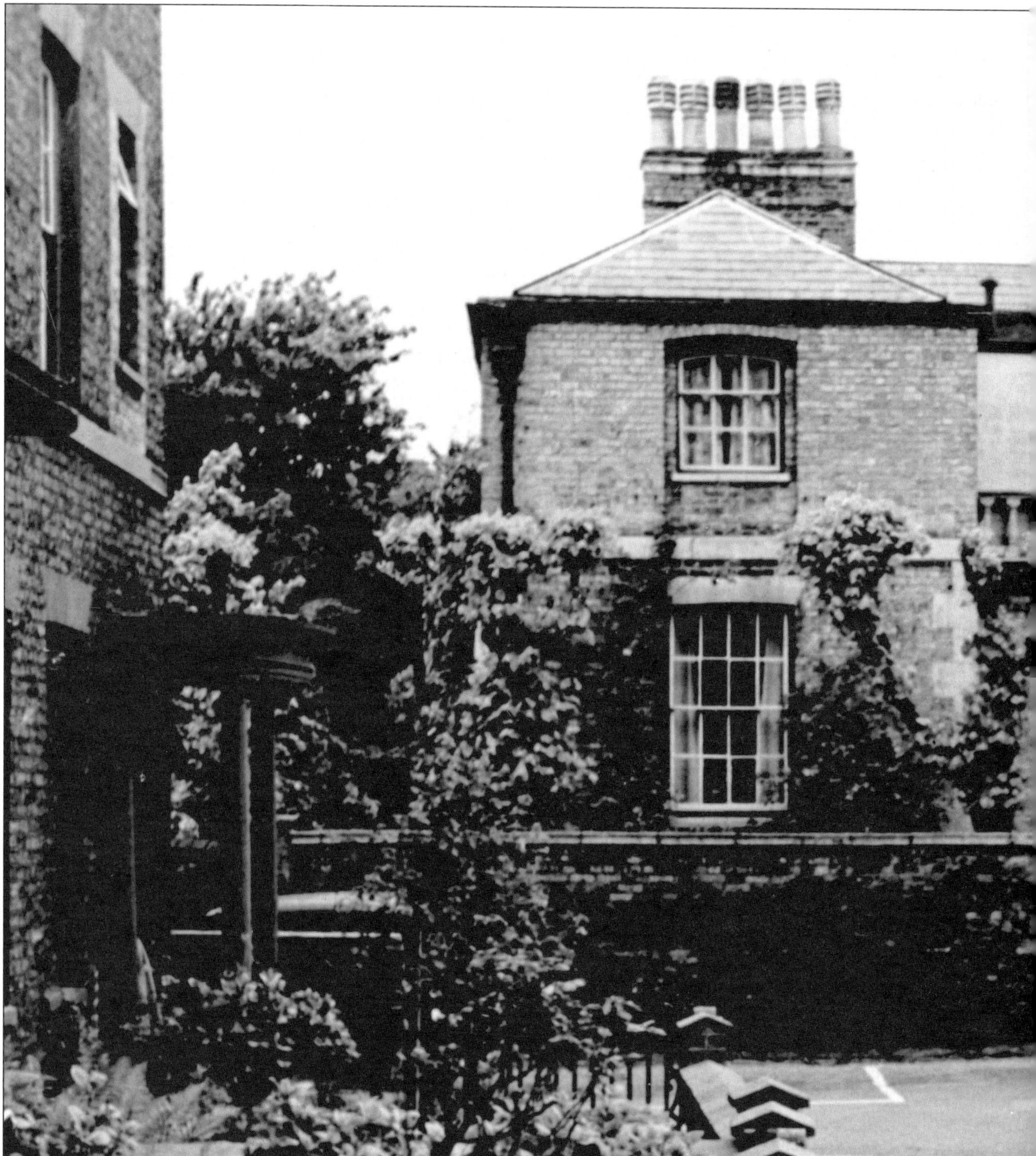

THE CASTLE c1955 W115008

Still referred to as Wisbech Castle, the Regency villa built by Joseph Medworth, about 1816, is the least impressive of the buildings to have born that name.

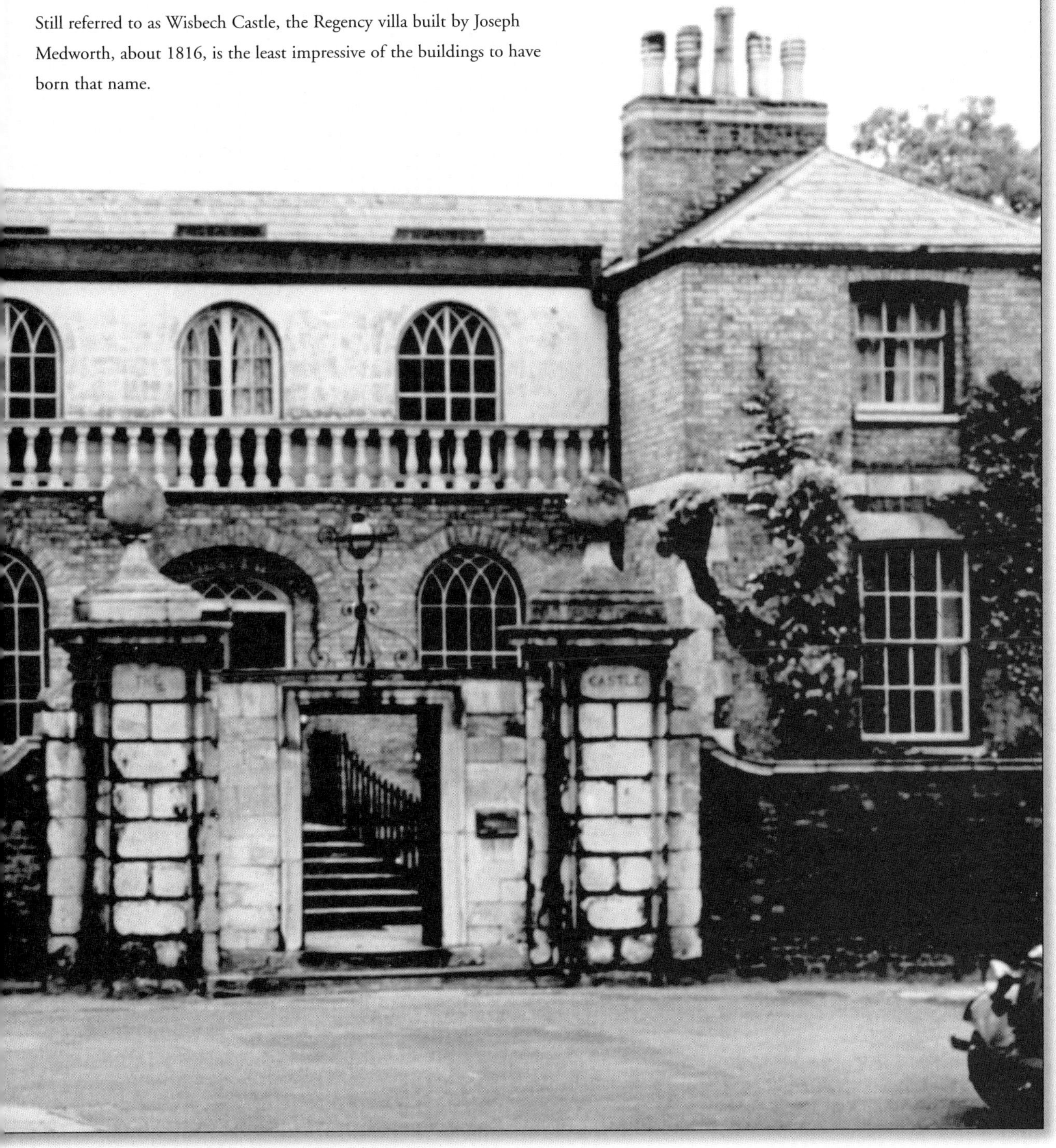

THE CASTLE, CRESCENT AND CHURCH

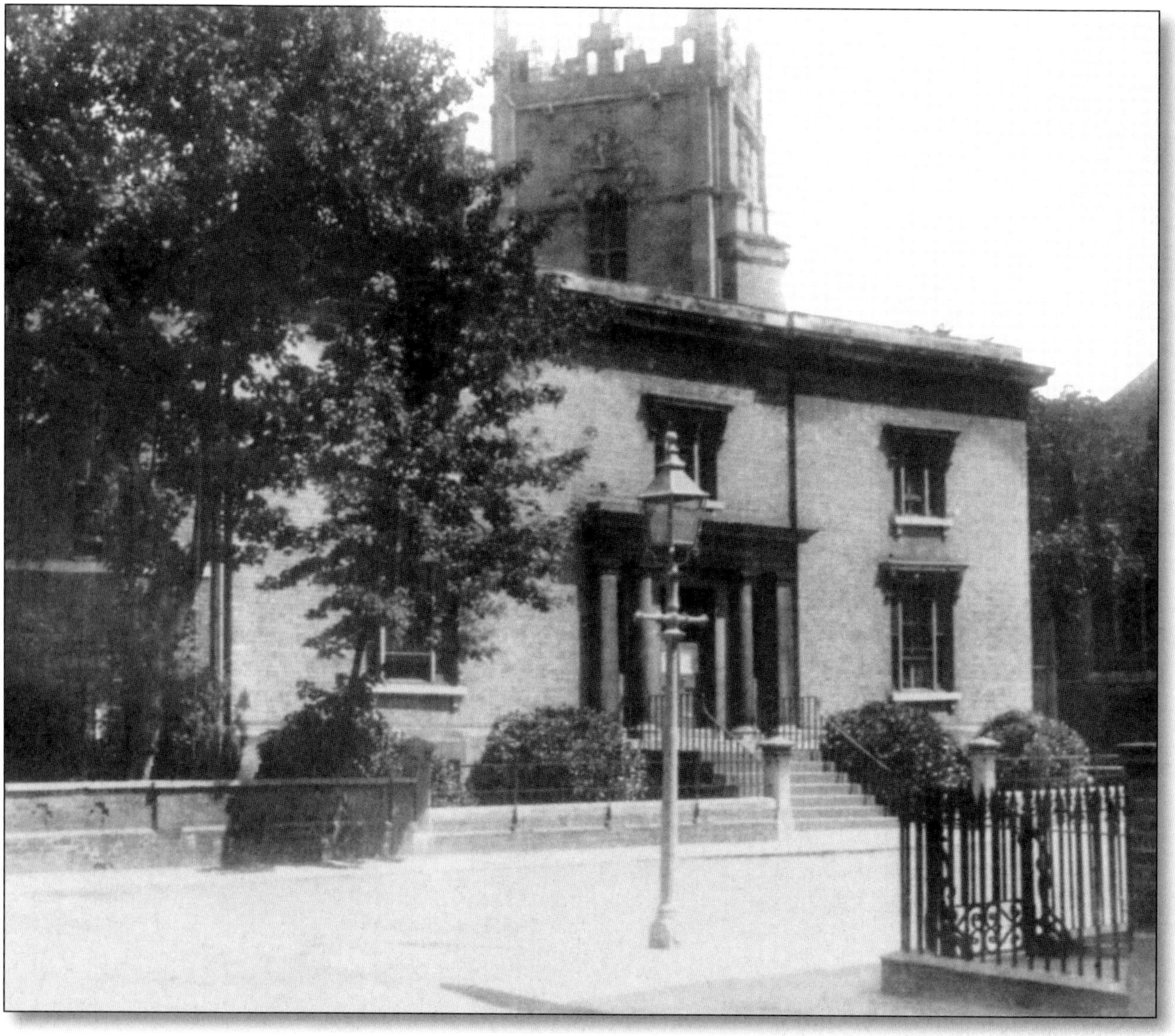

Above: THE MUSEUM 1901 47586

Leading from Museum Square to Deadman's Lane (now Alexandria Road), is Love Lane, which follows the line of the old castle wall. It was in this vicinity that the celebrated author and radical political thinker William Godwin (1756-1836) was born. After leaving Wisbech, Godwin moved to London where he married Mary Wollestonecraft. Their daughter, Mary, married the poet Shelley and was the authoress of 'Frankenstein'.

Opposite: THE PARISH CHURCH, THE INTERIOR 1923 73581

Looking towards the east window which was inserted during the restoration of the church in 1856/7 that was overseen by Sir George Gilbert Scott. To the left can be seen the Norman arches, clearly distinguished from the later perpendicular arches.

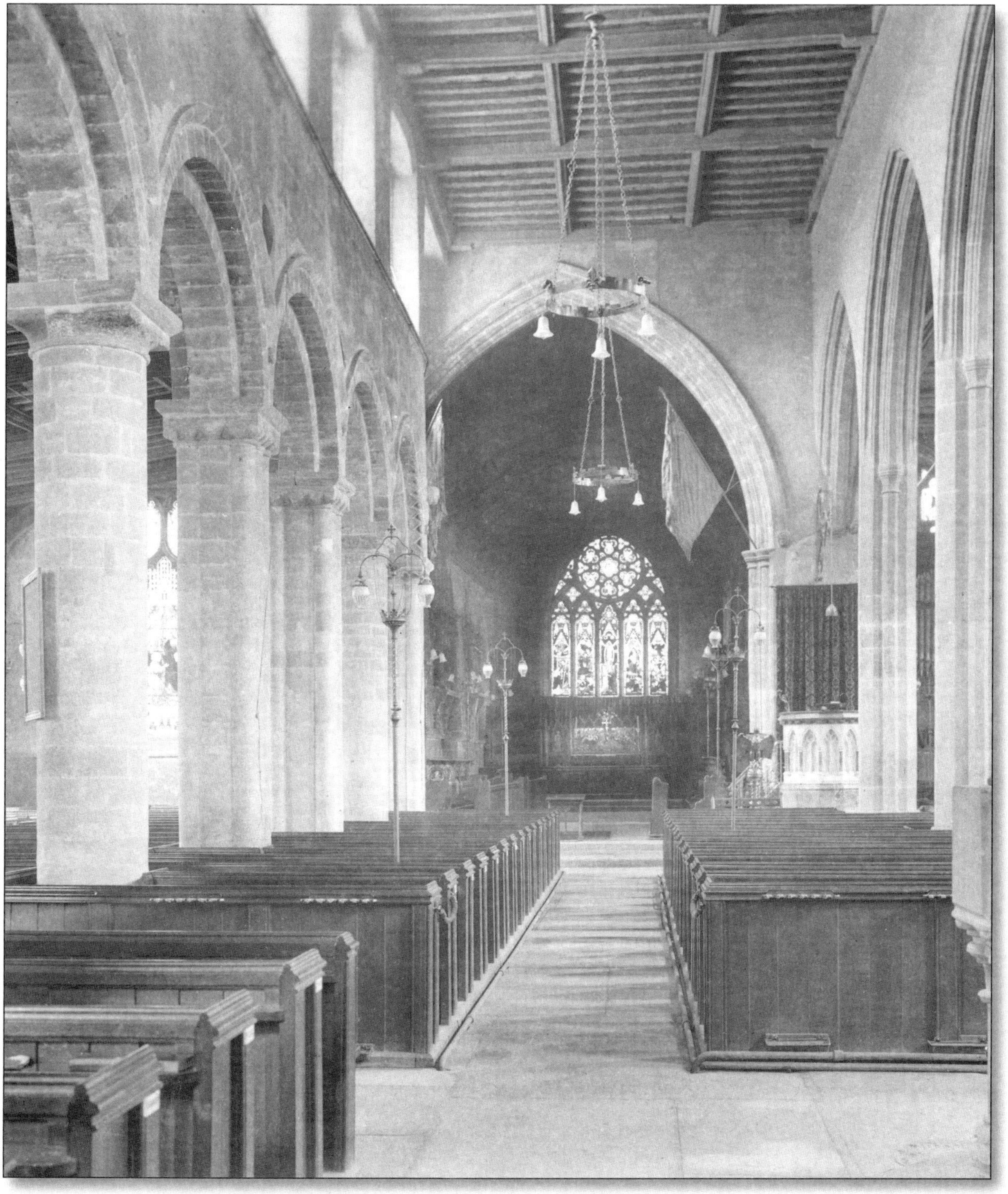

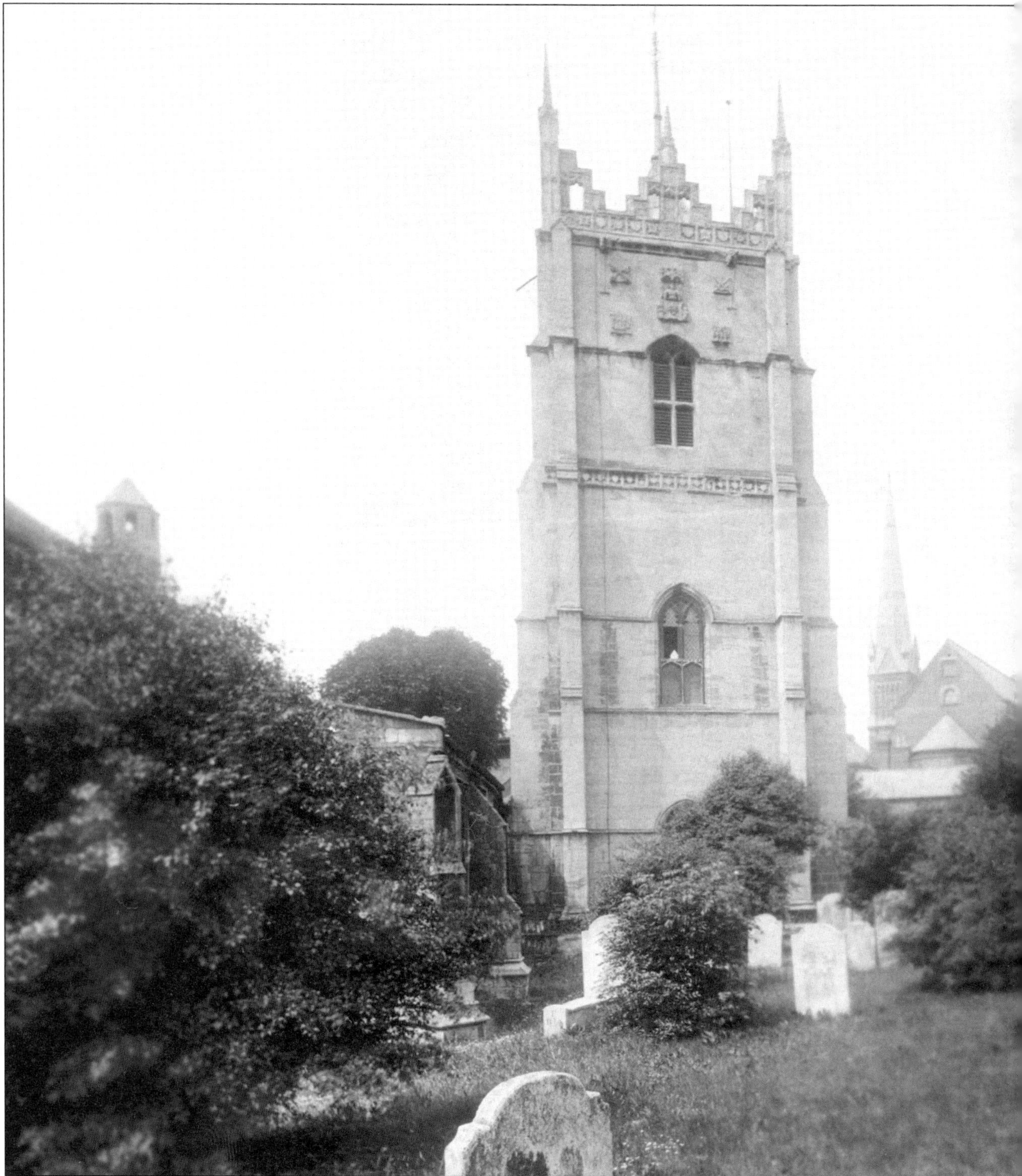

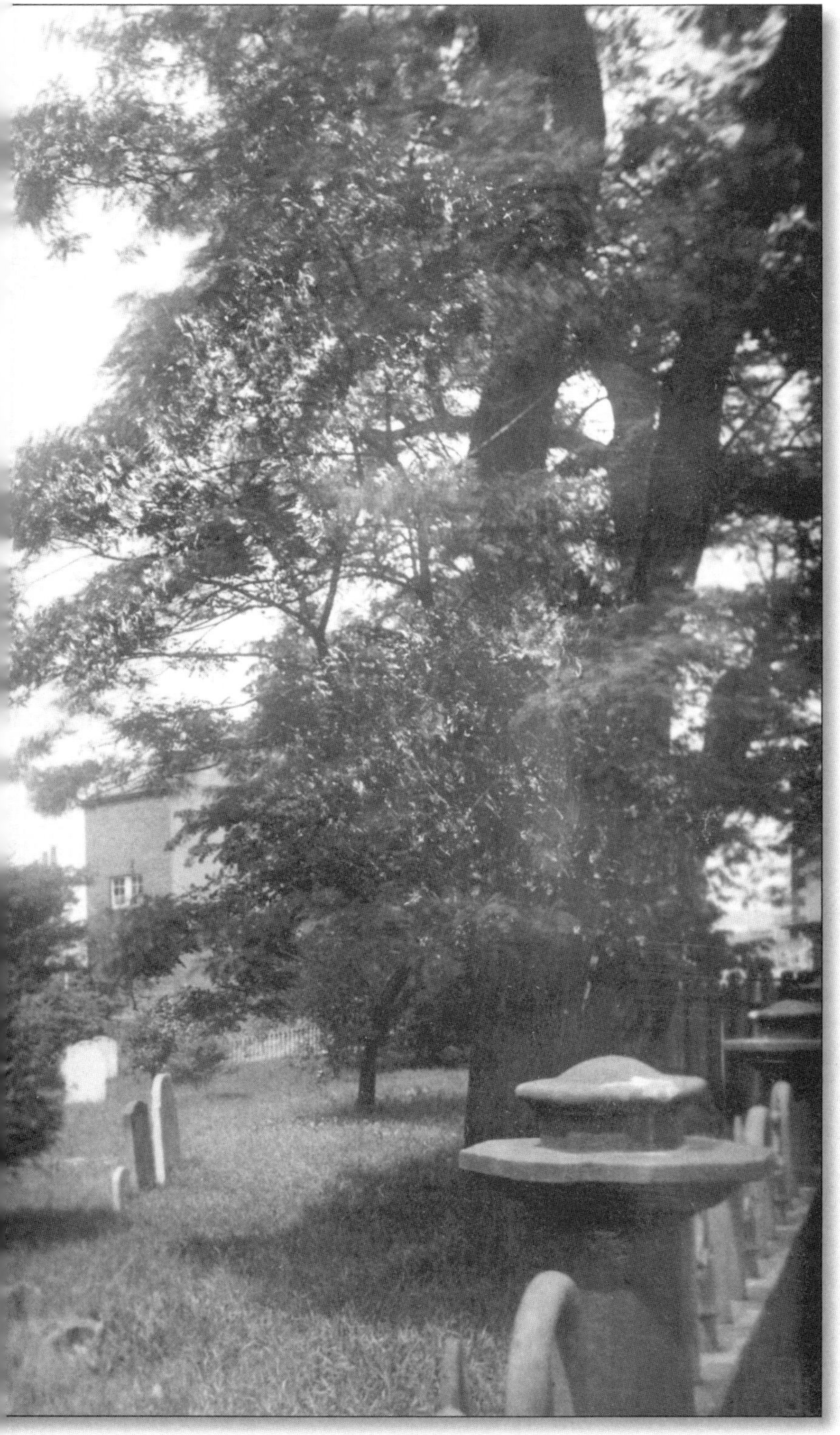

ST PETER'S CHURCH 1929 81984

This view of the church tower clearly shows the tenuous link between it and the main body of the building. Many Fenland churches have detached towers, such as those of Tydd St Giles and St Mary's, West Walton. In the distance can be seen the spire of Ely Place Baptist Chapel.

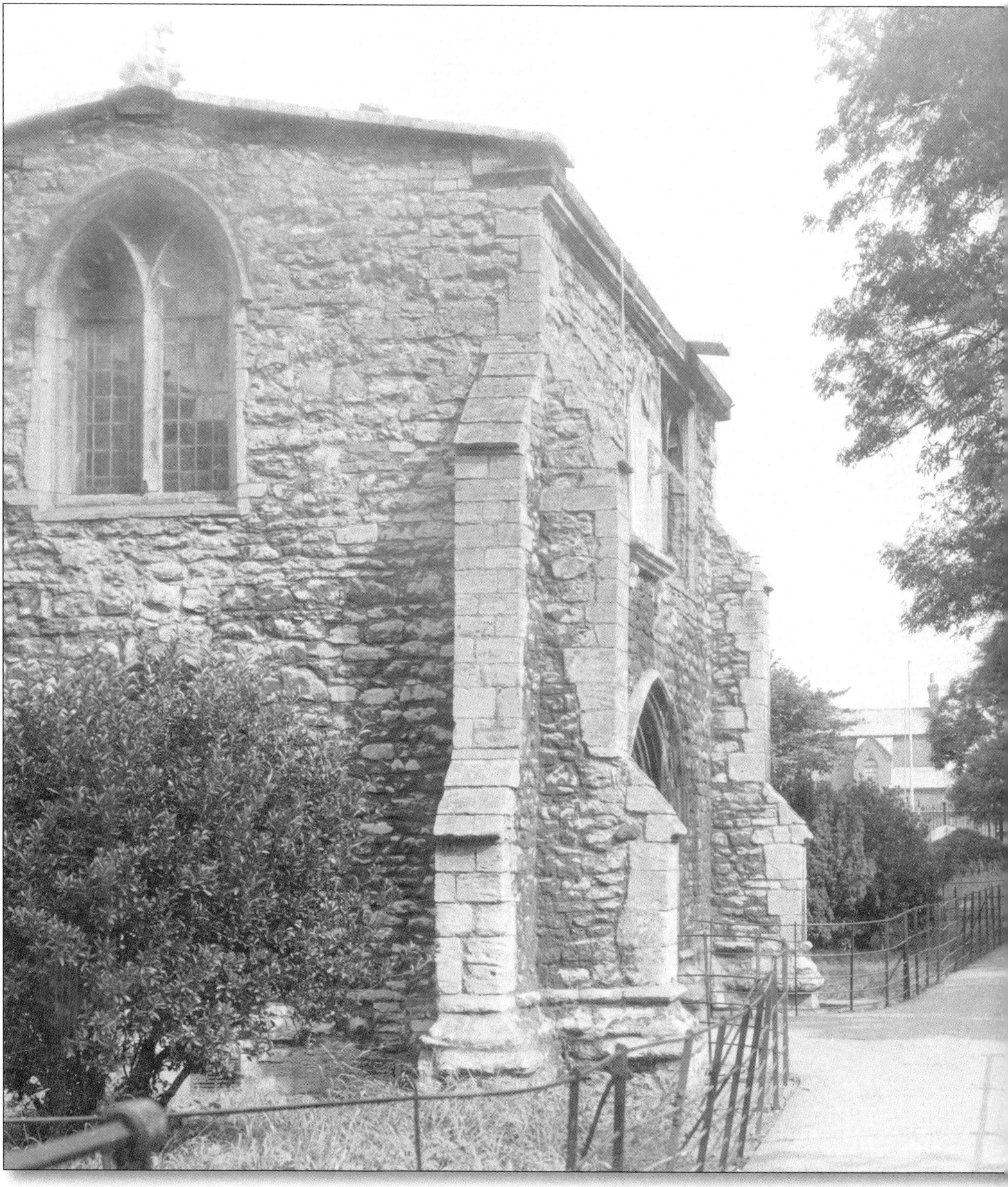

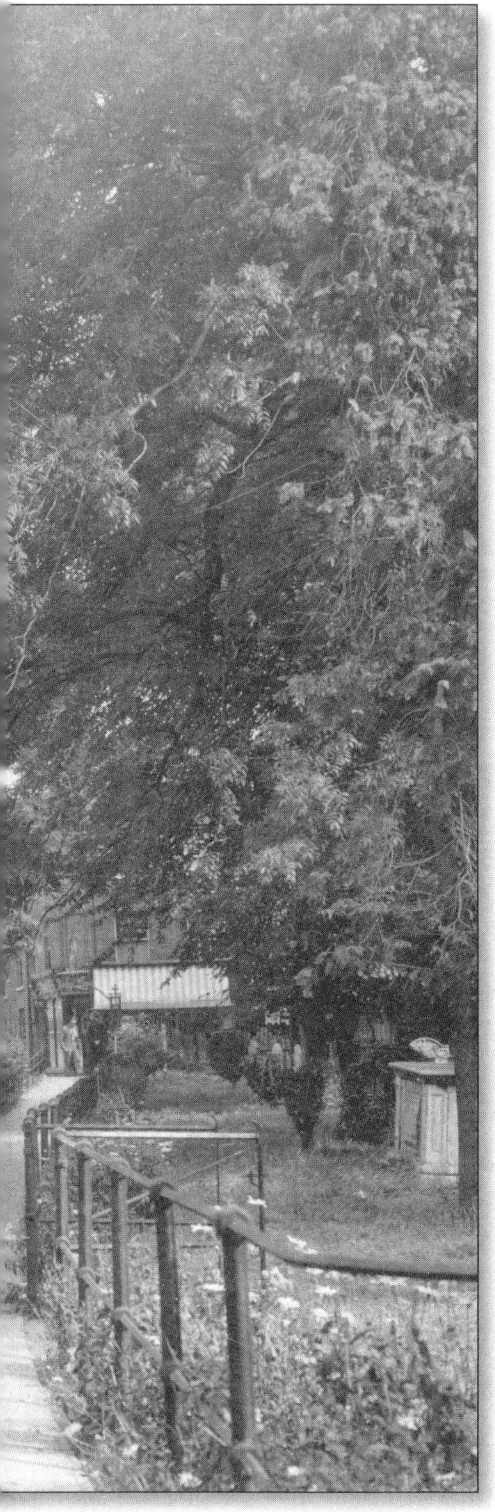

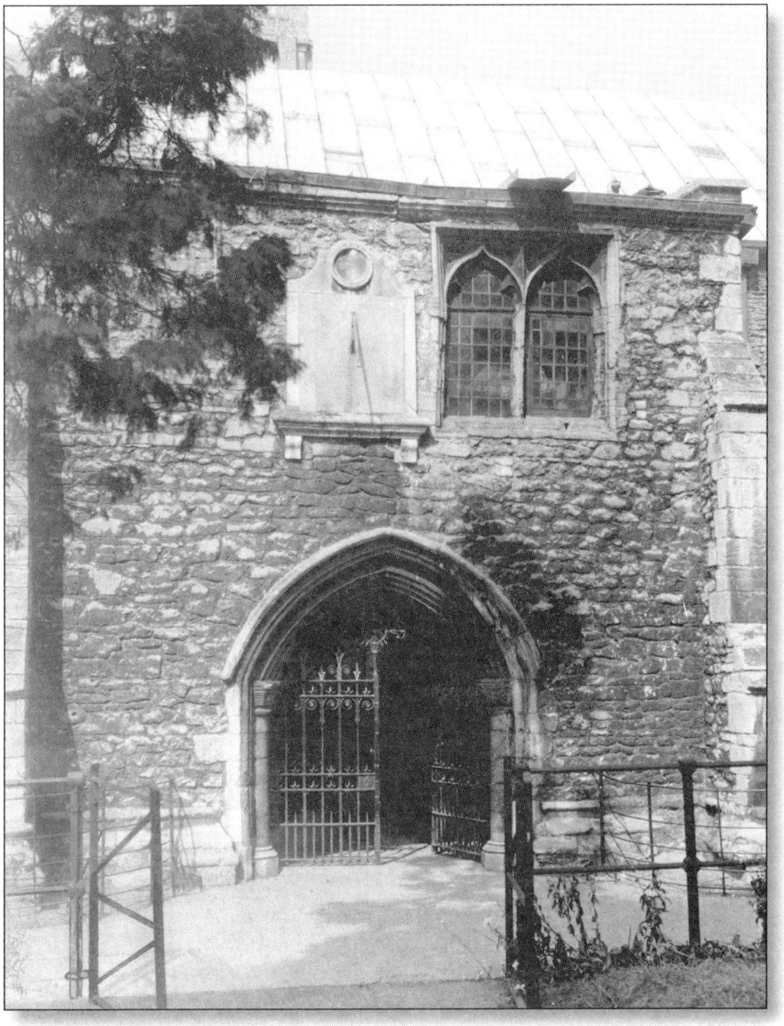

Left:
St Peter's Church Walk c1950 W115007

Looking past the south porch towards Church Terrace.

Above:
St Peter's Church, The South Door c1950 W115001

The room above the south porch has now been converted into the parish office. In early times, it is believed to have been the home of the Grammar School. Later the Town Library, belonging to the Corporation - formed in the 17th and 18th centuries - was housed here. The Corporation removed the library when it was felt that the vicar of the day had begun to think of the library as the property of the church; it was later deposited in Wisbech Museum.

THE CASTLE, CRESCENT AND CHURCH

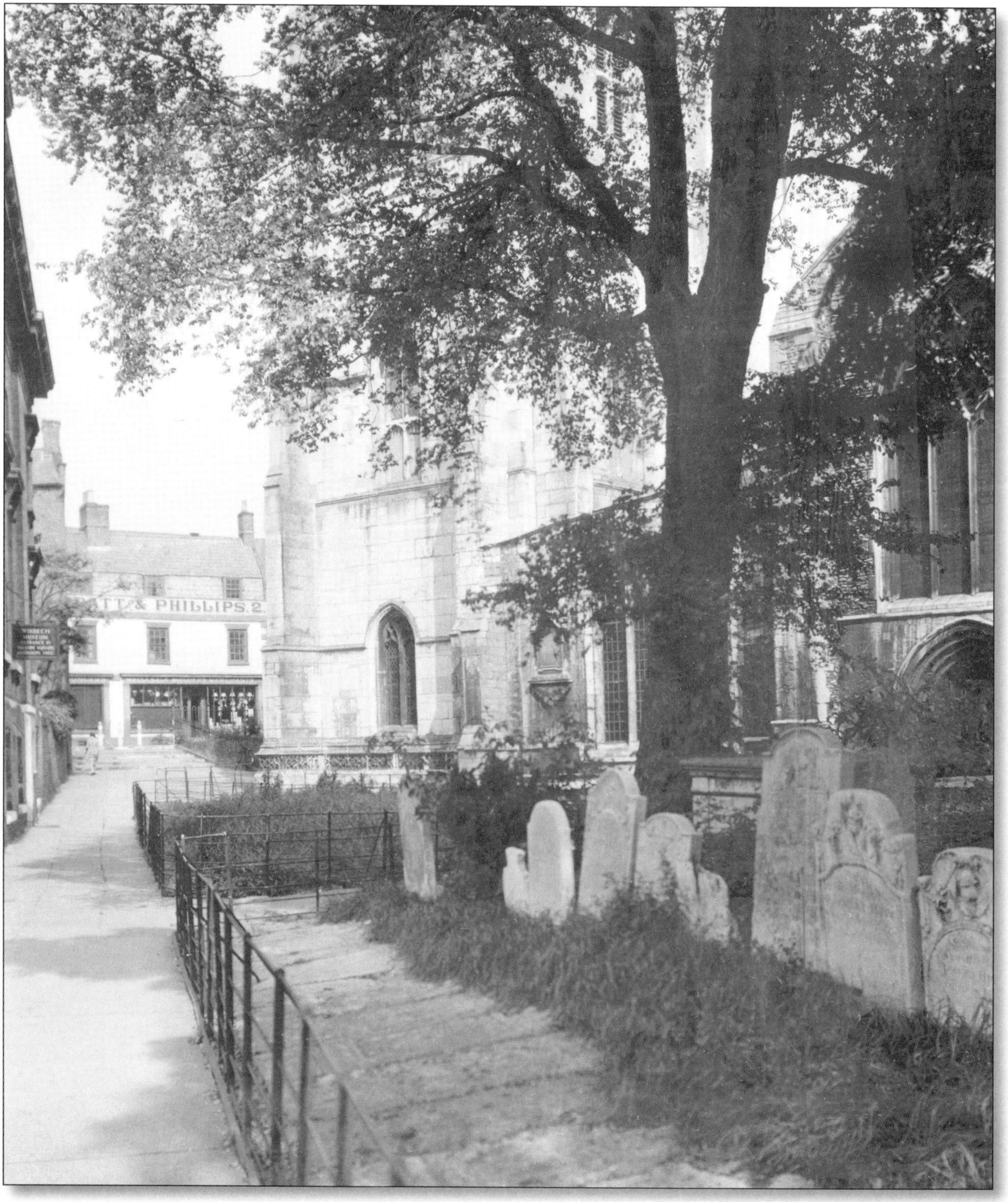

THE CASTLE, CRESCENT AND CHURCH

During its life as a prison, which was particularly lively during the religious upheavals of the 16th century, the castle was host for several prominent Roman Catholic prisoners, including Thomas Watson, Bishop of Lincoln, and John Feckenham, Abbot of Westminster. A political prisoner of note was Robert Catesby who, at the time of the Spanish Armada in 1588, it was thought prudent to detain in Wisbech Castle. Catesby was later to be implicated in the Gunpowder Plot.

During the Civil War, Wisbech allied itself with Parliament and some fortification work was carried out at the Castle. With the coming of the Commonwealth, Church possessions were sold off and John Thurloe, Secretary of State, who promptly cleared the remains of the castle and built the house commonly called Thurloe's Mansion, purchased the Castle Estate. The house was of a similar design to Thorpe Hall near Peterborough, which was constructed about the same time by Oliver St John, the Chief Justice.

After the Restoration, the mansion reverted to the Bishop of Ely who later sublet the premises to local tenants, including the Southwell family, who occupied the house for over 100 years. In 1793, the Bishop obtained an Act of Parliament to sell the estate and two years later Joseph Medworth of Bermondsey purchased it at auction for £2,305. Medworth, who had been born in Wisbech, proceeded to clear the grounds and lay out the row of houses forming the Crescent over the next four or five years. He later completed the circus with the laying out of Union and Ely Places that are divided by Market Street. After the rejection by the Corporation of his scheme to house the Grammar School in the mansion, Medworth dismantled the house and, in about 1816, built the present Regency Villa. When Medworth died, he left a house to each of his seven 'natural children' by his second housekeeper (who also received a house and the rental of the Castle). He left money to his two sons by his first housekeeper.

In 1864, the Castle was purchased by William Peckover and was put to a variety of uses including a school, dental practice and opticians. This last business was owned by Mrs F C D Fendick who, after the death of her husband T Gordon Fendick, the Chief Education Officer of the Isle of Ely, left the building to the county for educational purposes.

Of particular significance, although frequently overlooked, is the Wisbech & Fenland Museum. When built in 1846/7, the museum was one of the first purpose-built museums in the country and holds a surprising and important range of collections dealing with, among other things, the geology, flora and fauna, and social history of the Fens. There is also a library containing over 12,000 volumes. One collection of particular importance is the bequest of the Rev. Chauncey Hare Towshend that includes the original manuscript of 'Great Expectations' by Charles Dickens. The manuscript is on view to the public on the first Saturday of the month.

The Castle may exist in name only; however, the parish church of St Peter & St Paul still remains. This, the oldest building in the town, is a curious mixture of styles, repairs and enlargements. The collapse of the tower, about 1450, into the main body of the church, demolished most of the roof. The central arcade of the aisle was rebuilt in the newer perpendicular style and is quite distinct from the rounded Norman arches of the remaining arcades.

By the 1430s, the long process of repairing the damage to the main body of the church had been accomplished, and it was then that the present massive tower was constructed. The church tower houses ten bells cast by W Dobson of Downham, in 1823, and is the fourth oldest 'peal of ten bells' in the world. They were restored and rehung in a new steel framework in the early 1990s.

In the early part of Queen Victoria's reign, Gothic church improvements became extremely popular. The noted Victorian architect, Sir George Gilbert Scott, designer of the Clarkson Memorial and whose brother, John, later became Vicar of Wisbech, was asked to report on the state of the church. Scott's views were very sympathetic, and involved, among other things, the removal of the two galleries and the restoration of the east window.

Opposite: ST PETER'S CHURCH YARD c1950 W115002

Here, looking past the tower towards Church Terrace, we can see how close the church was to the ancient castle. On the extreme left is the east wing of Wisbech Museum, which was built upon the filled-in moat of the castle. These made-up foundations are the reason for the subsidence that afflicted the Museum shortly after opening, as evidenced by the badly misshapen windows at the front of the building.

ORDNANCE SURVEY MAP

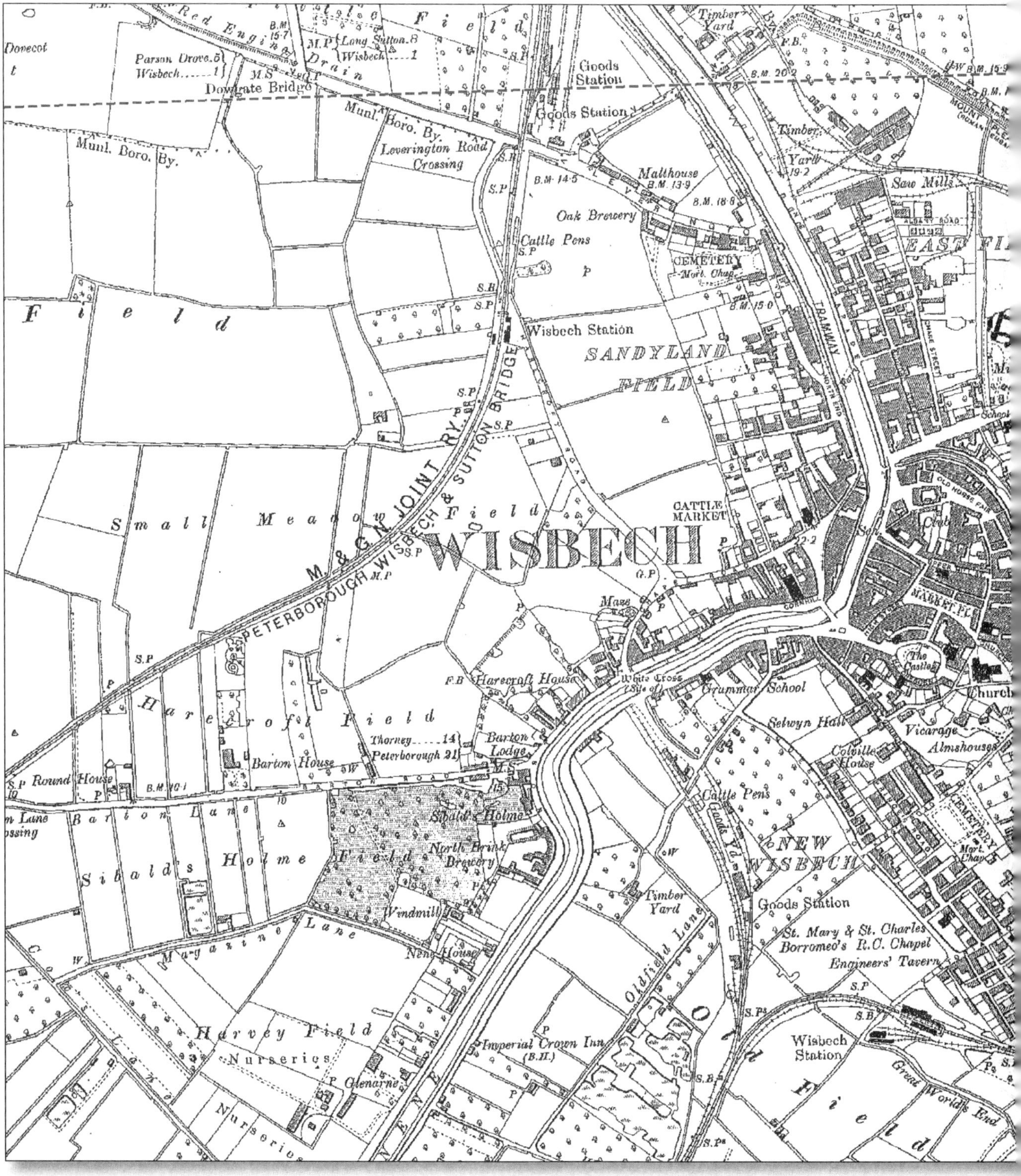

ORDNANCE SURVEY MAP

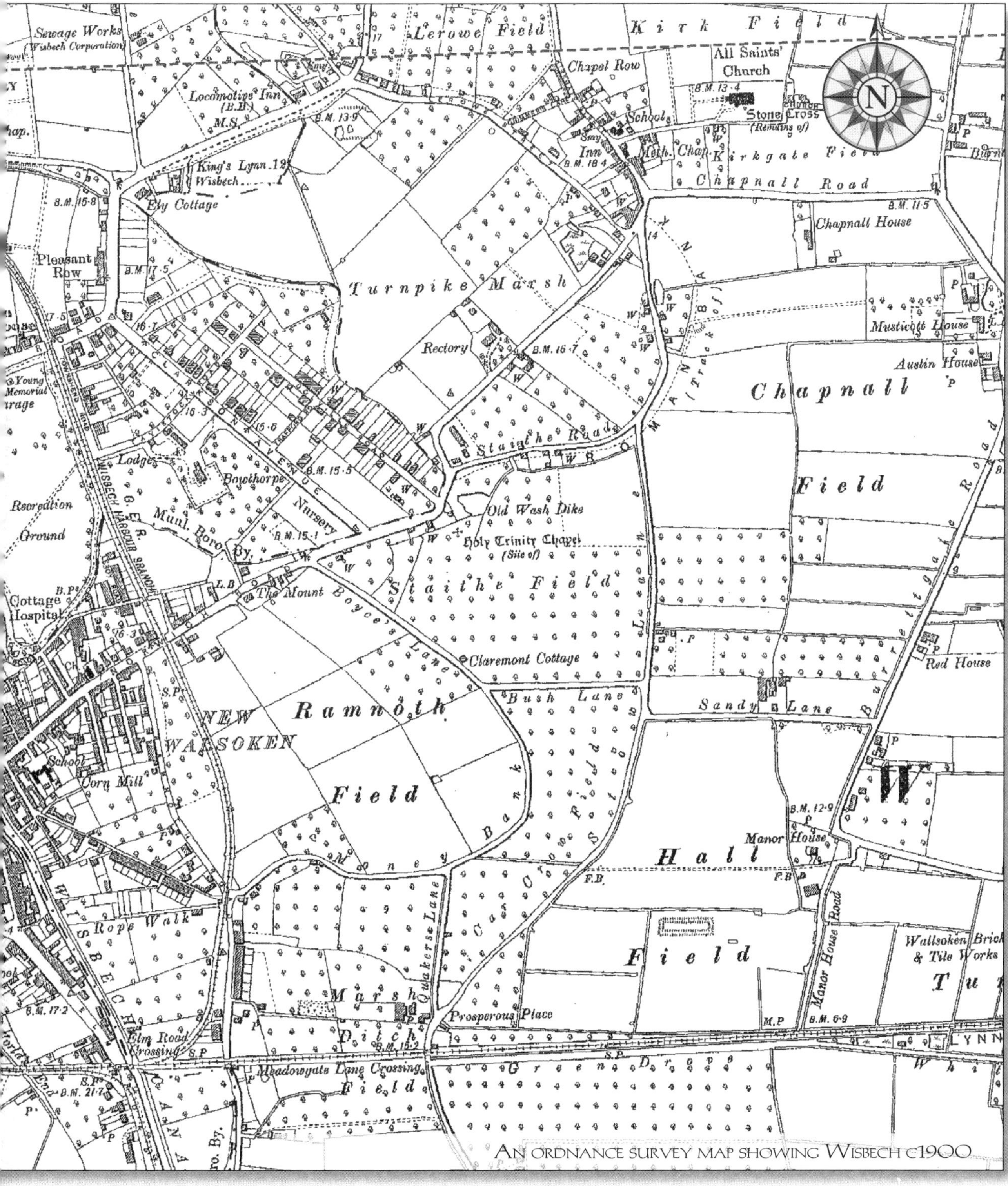

An ordnance survey map showing Wisbech c1900

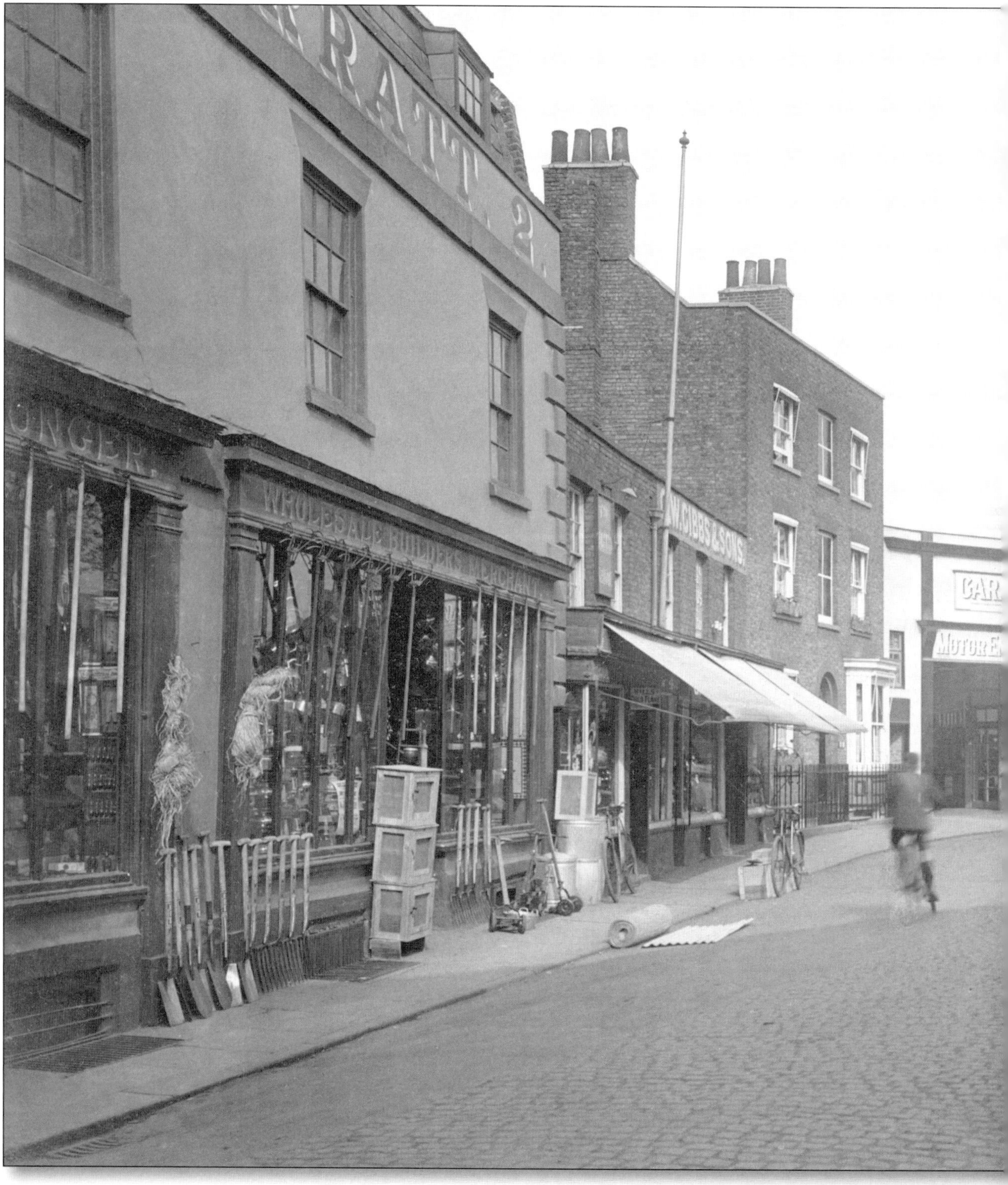
WHOLESALE BUILDERS MERCHANT
W. GIBBS & SONS

THE CANAL, PARK AND ROAD TO KING'S LYNN

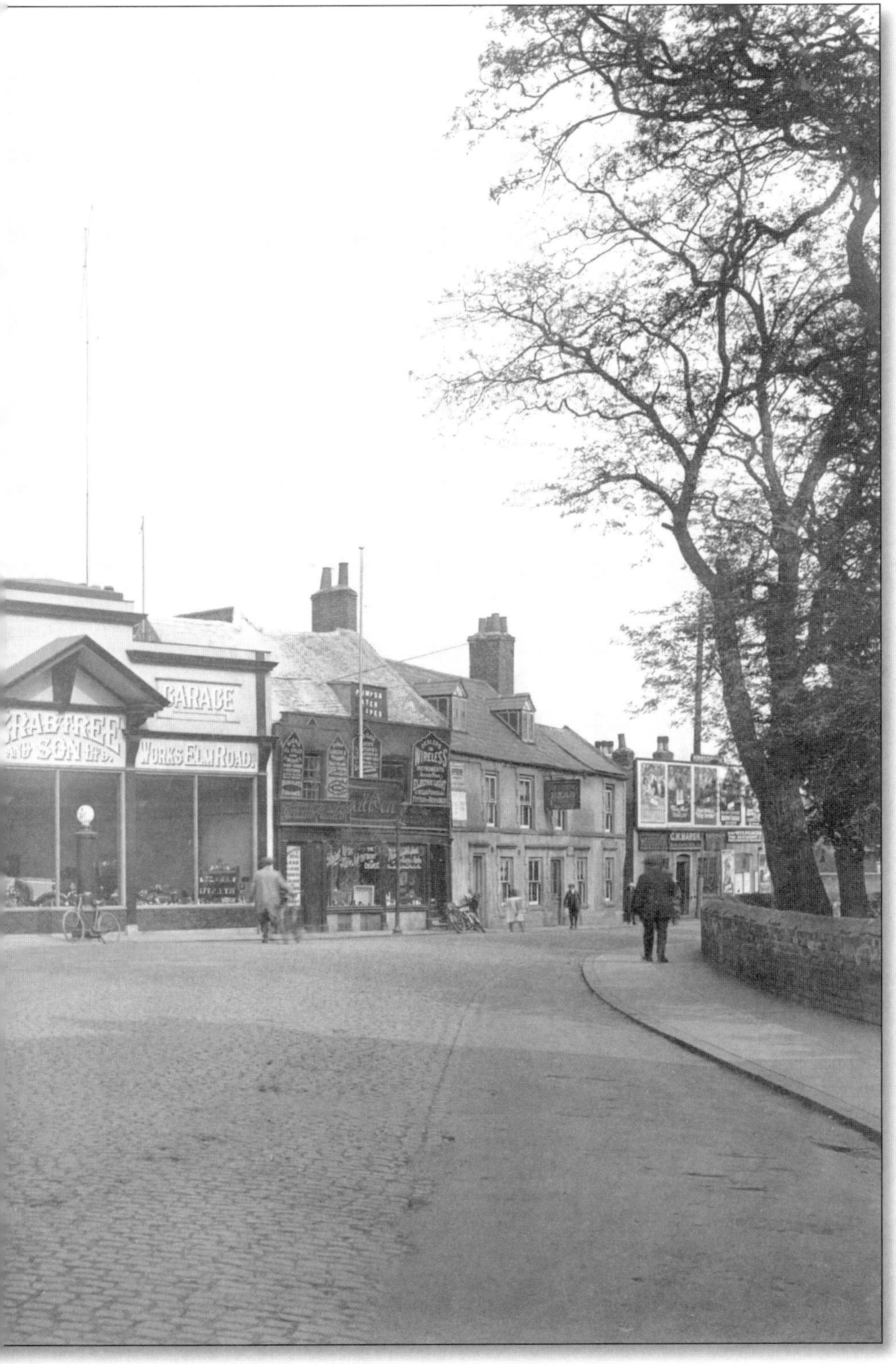

CHURCH STREET 1923
73570

Now known as Church Terrace, this view shows the ironmonger's shop of Mr Barratt, later Barratt & Phillips. Not many modern retailers would display their stock on the pavement today - theft or prosecution for obstruction would surely follow! Further along is G W Gibbs & Sons, bootmakers, who still trade here today. Beyond the fine house, which is now an estate agent's, is the showroom of Crabtree & Son - by 1929 the business had been taken over by W H Johnson & Sons Ltd. Sandwiched between this and the 18th-century Duke's Head Inn, is the shop of Teed & Son, builders' merchants: among other things, they dealt with 'wireless instruments', advised on electric light (no charge!) and fitted and repaired bells.

THE CANAL, PARK AND ROAD TO KING'S LYNN

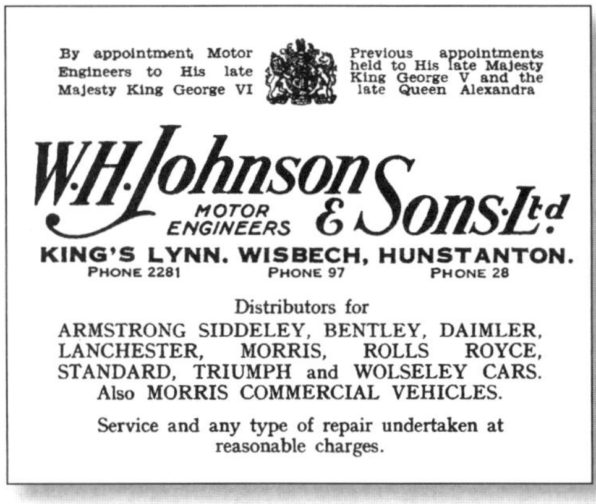

ADVERT FOR W H JOHNSON & SONS

Moving up onto Church Terrace from the depression in which St. Peter's Church is situated, it is plain to see the course of the ancient sea banks that protected the town from the waters of the Well Stream, and later those of the canal. The 'bank', upon which Church Terrace is built, continued down along Norfolk Street, the southern end of which was once known as Timber Market - a reference perhaps to this having been an early unloading place for wood. Near to this point was the site of an ancient ferry that crossed the stream to Walsoken. It is from this that the Ferry Boat Inn, now Whitfield's, took its name.

Until the 1960s, when it was filled-in, the Wisbech Canal ran parallel with these streets as it flowed through the town, before entering the River Nene. Formed under an Act of Parliament, the canal was cut by the Wisbech Canal Company and opened in 1795. The aim of the cut was to re-link the rivers Nene and Ouse, via the Well Creek, and in so doing expand the economic hinterland that could then be serviced by Wisbech port, via the inland waterways.

From the start, the canal only produced modest returns and with the opening of the Wisbech to Upwell Tramway in 1883, its fortunes declined. With little or no income, the maintenance of the canal was neglected and silting-up became a problem. During the Second World War, the Corporation was seeking Parliamentary powers to fill-in the portion of the canal that lay within the Borough, although people living along its course were already helping-out by throwing in their rubbish.

By the 1960s, the canal had been filled-in and a dual carriageway, Churchill Road, was built along its course. With the opening of the Freedom Bridge, by Sir Harry Legge Bourke on 22 January 1971, a road system was laid-out, accessing the new bridge. This system included roundabouts; the largest of which linked the Churchill Road to Lynn Road - the main road-link with King's Lynn, until the 1980s.

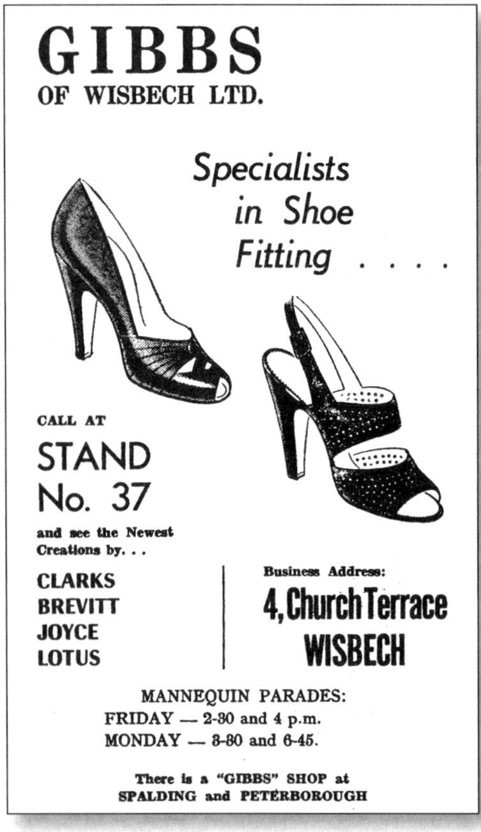

ADVERT FOR GIBBS OF WISBECH LTD 1953

The business is still trading today and the shop has recently been refurbished.

Opposite Top: THE HOPE INN C1955 W115019

The Hope was one of the many inns and pubs that lined the course of the canal, at one time or another. Before the days of refrigerators, patrons often suspended bottles of beer in the canal to keep it cool - one can only hope that the seals were sound!

Opposite Bottom: THE CANAL C1955 W115020

Although a seemingly idyllic view of the canal, what this picture cannot show is the stagnant state of the water, caused by silting and the rubbish thrown in by householders and businesses along the waterway. Lurking behind the Hope Inn is the gasholder that was for many years a dominant landmark in the town. The houses were swept away during the series of 'slum' clearances that began in the 1930s.

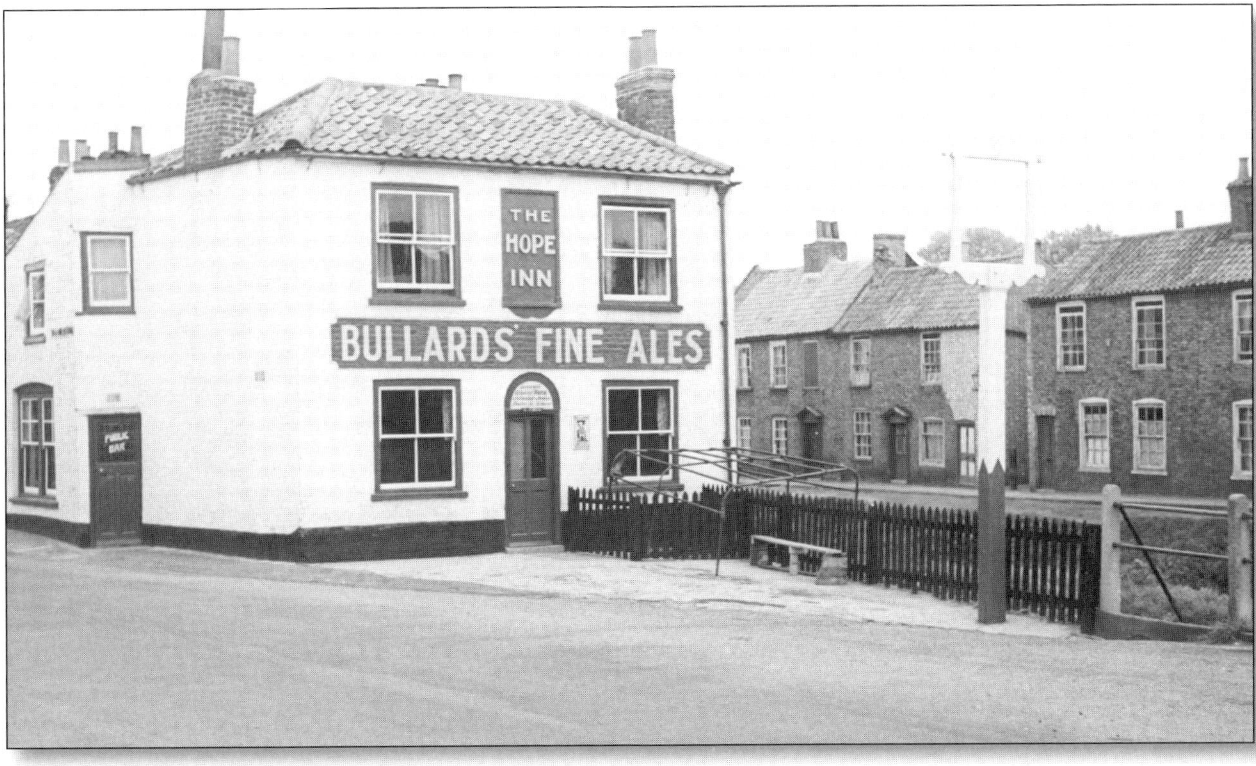
THE
HOPE
INN
BULLARDS' FINE ALES
PUBLIC BAR

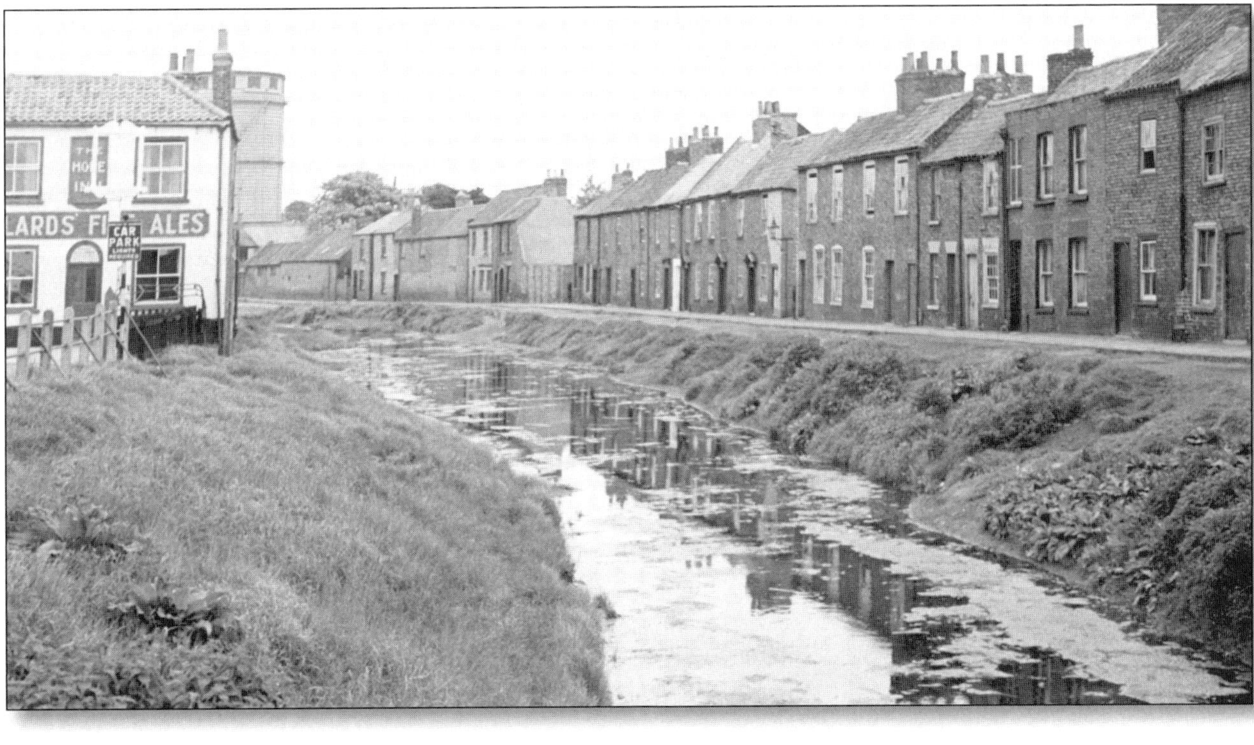
CAR
PARK
ALES

THE CANAL, PARK AND ROAD TO KING'S LYNN

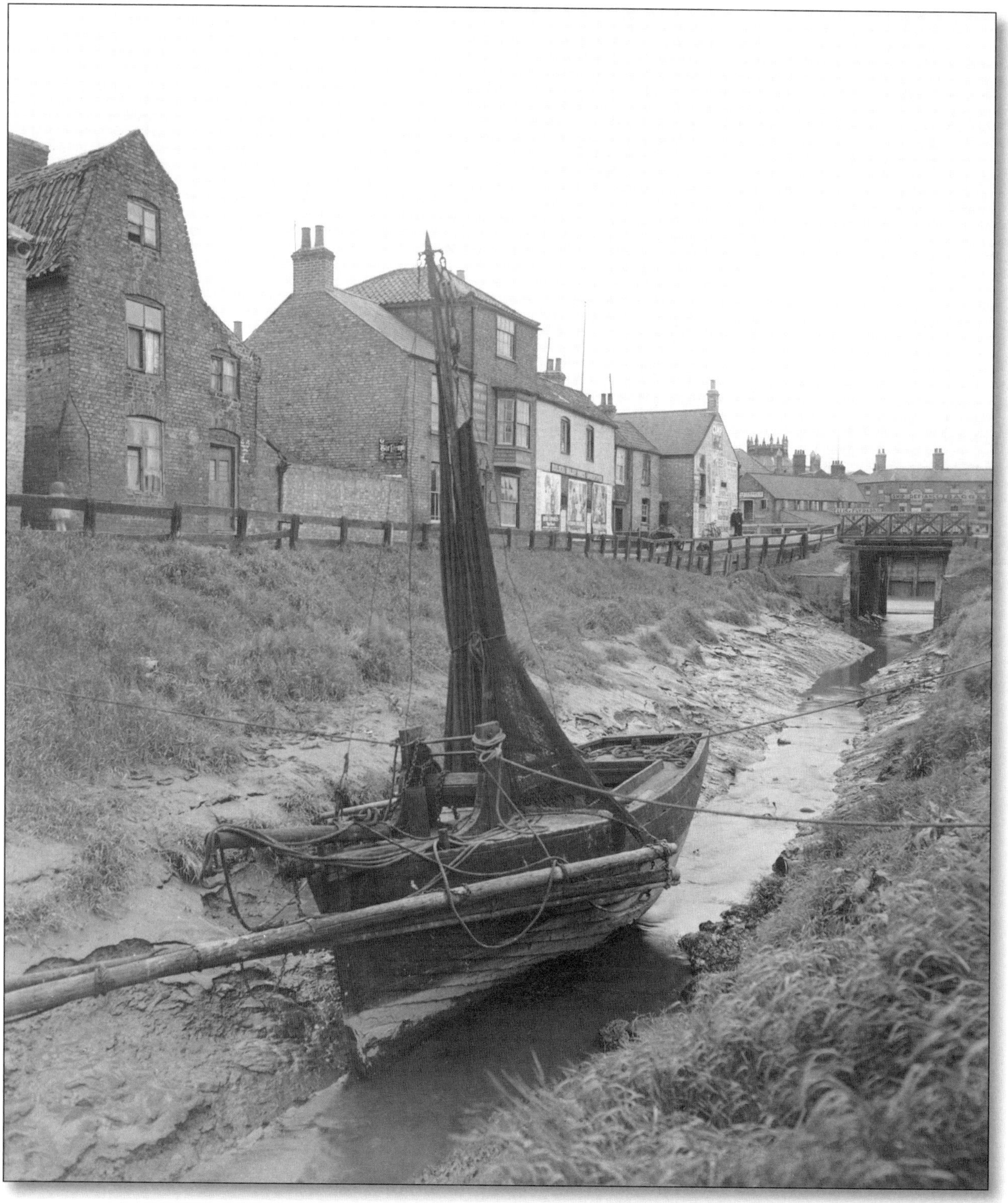

THE CANAL, PARK AND ROAD TO KING'S LYNN

Opposite: THE CANAL 1929 81972

A fishing boat lies in the tidal section of the canal that linked it to the River Nene, which can be seen under Sluice Bridge. The three-storeyed building, to the right of the boat's mast, is the Sun Inn, one of the many canal-side pubs that served the people living in the Horsefair and along the canal.

Below: LYNN ROAD c1955 W115052

P Fitt's fish restaurant, seen here, was subsequently taken over by Frank Retchless, who expanded the business to incorporate the Rutland Arms, after it closed. Nowadays, filling one's car with petrol while still on the highway, and facing the wrong way, would be asking for trouble.

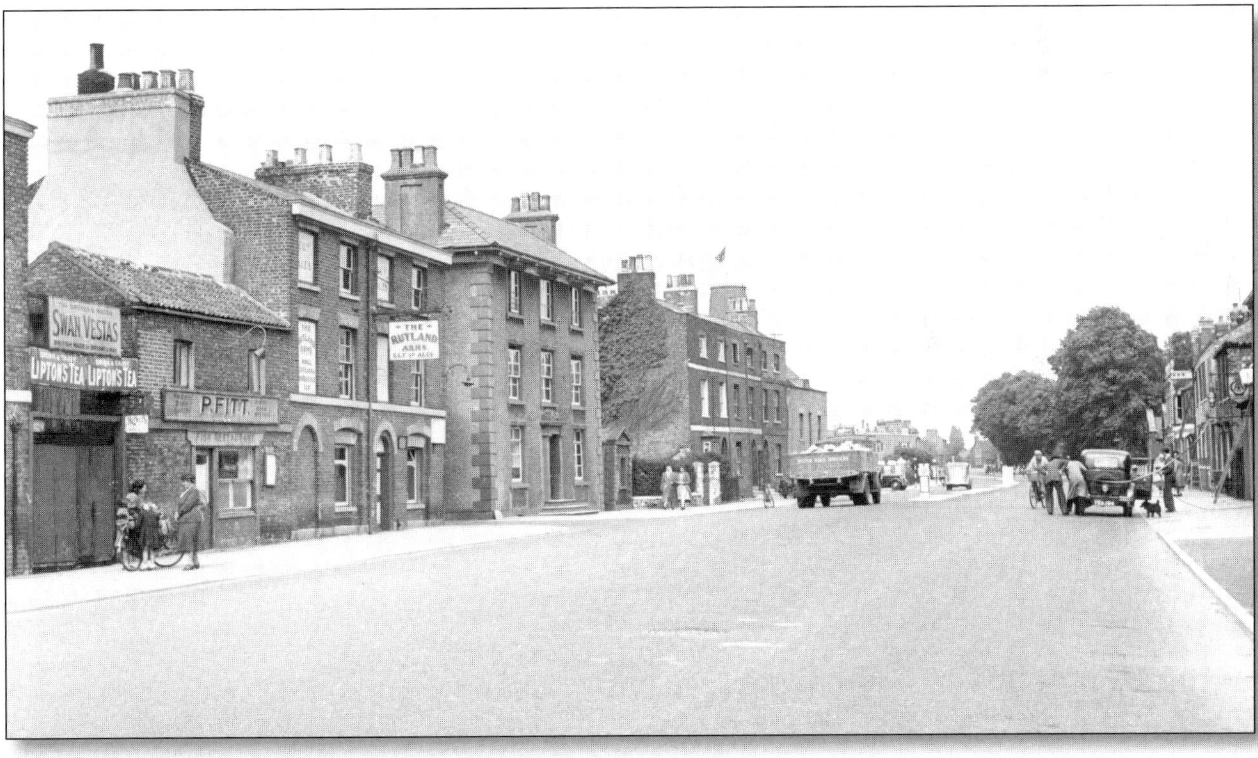

In spite of the Wisbech Bypass, the Lynn Road remains one of Wisbech's busiest thoroughfares. Physically, the wide breadth of the road has been drastically reduced by traffic-calming measures and the laying-out of central islands for the benefit of pedestrians.

Development along this route stems mainly from the mid-19th century and can loosely be attributed to two influences. The north side of the road owes much of its growth to the rise of the industrial areas around the port. To the south, residential developments were stimulated by the opening of the Town Park in 1873.

Despite the removal of two storeys of its converted tower, Leach's Mill - the only remainder of the nine windmills that once stood in the town - is still a dominant feature of Lynn Road. Opposite the mill tower is St Augustine's Church, which was built to serve the new parish - formed in 1870, from portions of Wisbech St Peter and Leverington. The new church was established to minister mainly to the increased population of East Field, which lay between the port and the Lynn Road.

Behind the mill stood the Union Workhouse, an austere and forbidding building; erected after the Poor Law Act of 1834. It continued as a workhouse for a few years after the end of the Second World War II, before being used as a hospital; part of it was employed as a maternity wing until the opening of the Bowthorpe Maternity Hospital, about 1953. The hospital, later renamed the Clarkson Hospital, was closed and demolished in the 1980s.

Further along from St Augustine's, is the Town Park; created after Wisbech Corporation purchased 19 acres from the Ecclesiastical Commissioners for £2,400. With the cost of plants, fencing, gates etc. the cost rose to £3,800, over £1,100 of which was raised by subscription. In November 1869, several members of the Corporation planted trees, and within a few years the park was an important recreation ground for the townspeople. The new amenity also prompted the laying-out of Clarkson Avenue and other streets.

The Park has seen many large public events over the years. In June 1837 the town celebrated Queen Victoria's Jubilee in style with a dinner for 2,000 in the Market Place, followed later in the day by a tea for 3,250 schoolchildren (who all received a jubilee medal); 600 old people were entertained in the Public Hall and a special 'dinner of English fare' was provided for the inmates of the workhouse. In between the Market Place dinner and the children's teas, rustic sports were held in the park. These included: running and hurdling races, a wheelbarrow race, a greased pole competition (although none of the contestants managed to reach the top) and a donkey race, which became quite ridiculous with the spectators having to be forced back to make way for the competitors, although the crowd and donkeys still became entangled.

Later events have included the Charter Celebrations of 1949 (including the second Wisbech Pageant) and the Coronation Celebrations for Queen Elizabeth II in 1953.

Today the Town Park provides an open space that is a welcome antidote to the hurly burly of modern-day living (epitomised by the traffic along the Lynn Road), and should be cherished and developed as a valuable amenity.

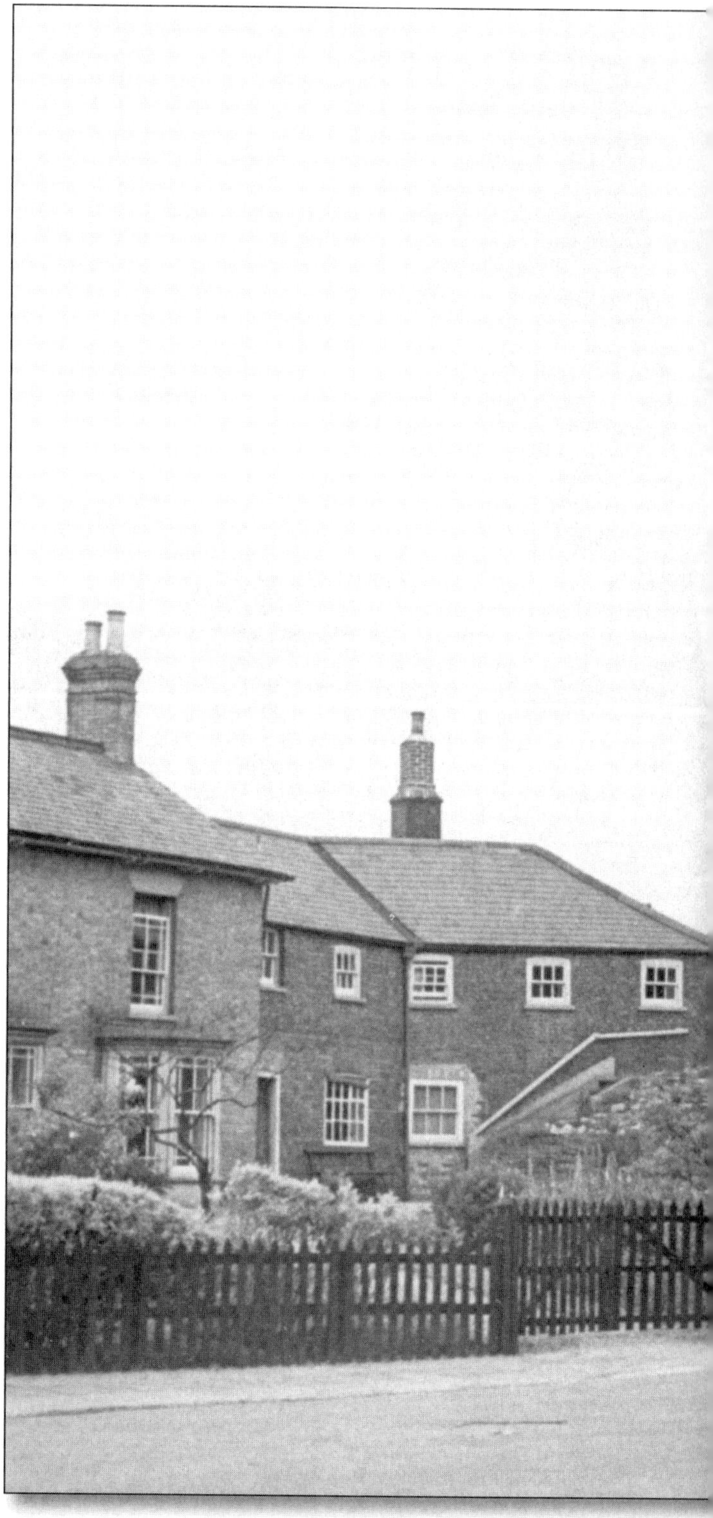

THE CANAL, PARK AND ROAD TO KING'S LYNN

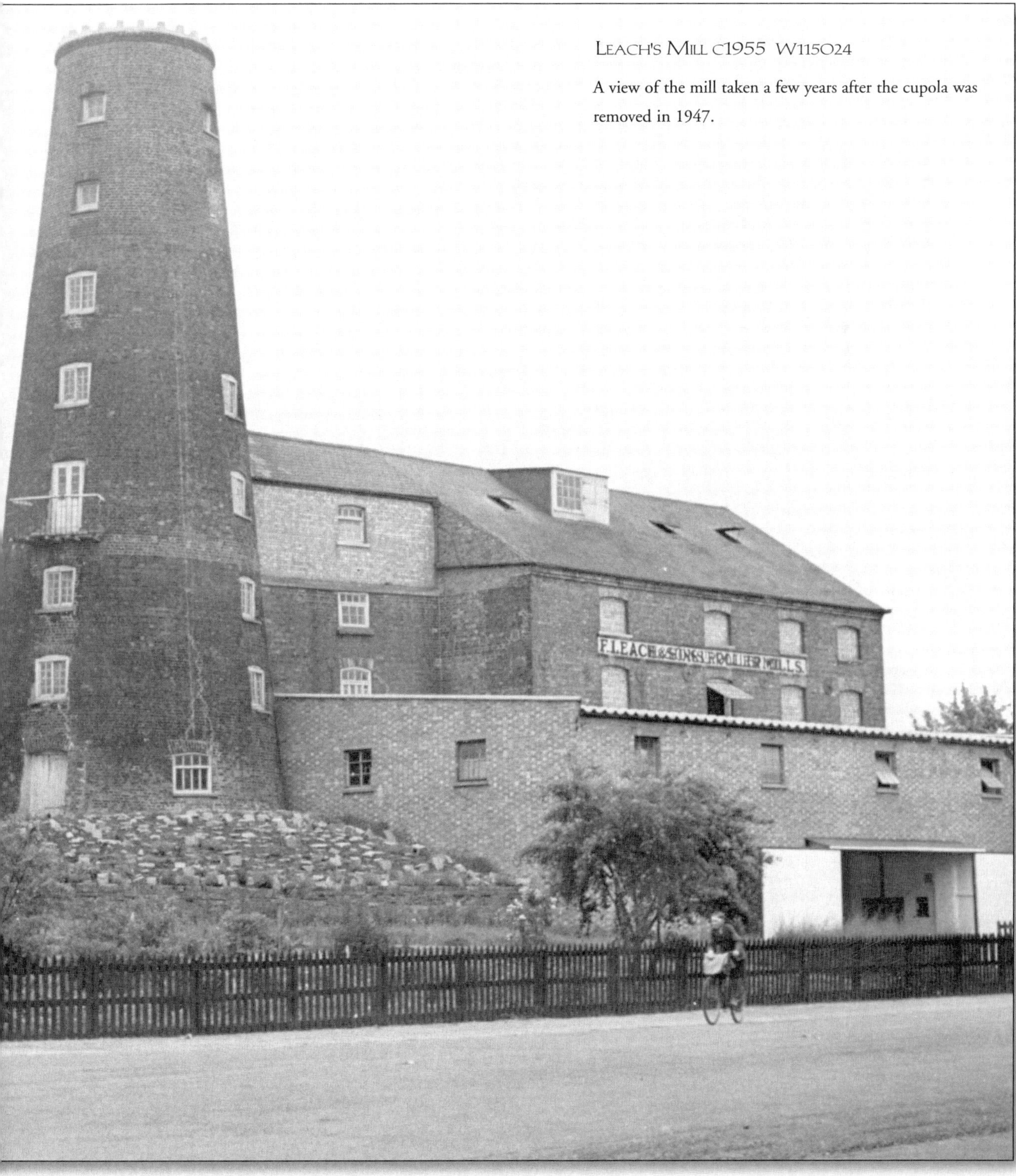

LEACH'S MILL c1955 W115024

A view of the mill taken a few years after the cupola was removed in 1947.

Below: Leach's Mill 1929 81981

Formerly one of the few eight-sailed windmills in the country, the tower is all that remains of the complex of granaries, bakery and mill house. One of the sails from this impressive structure was blown off and landed in the park during Windy Sunday, 24 March 1895, two years later the rest of the sails were removed. The Leach family worked the mill from 1891 until 1965. The tower has been reduced in height for safety reasons and converted into a house.

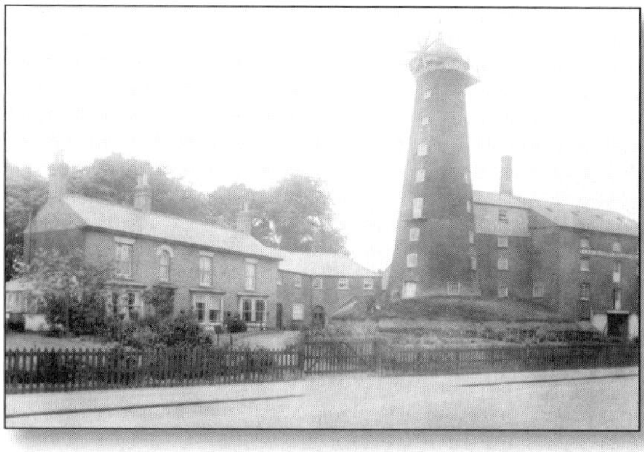

St Augustine's Church 1901 47590

The church was designed by W Bassett Smith of London and built at a cost of £3,320; it was consecrated on 11 May 1869. In 1997, a new parish centre was created when the church was linked to its hall, nearby.

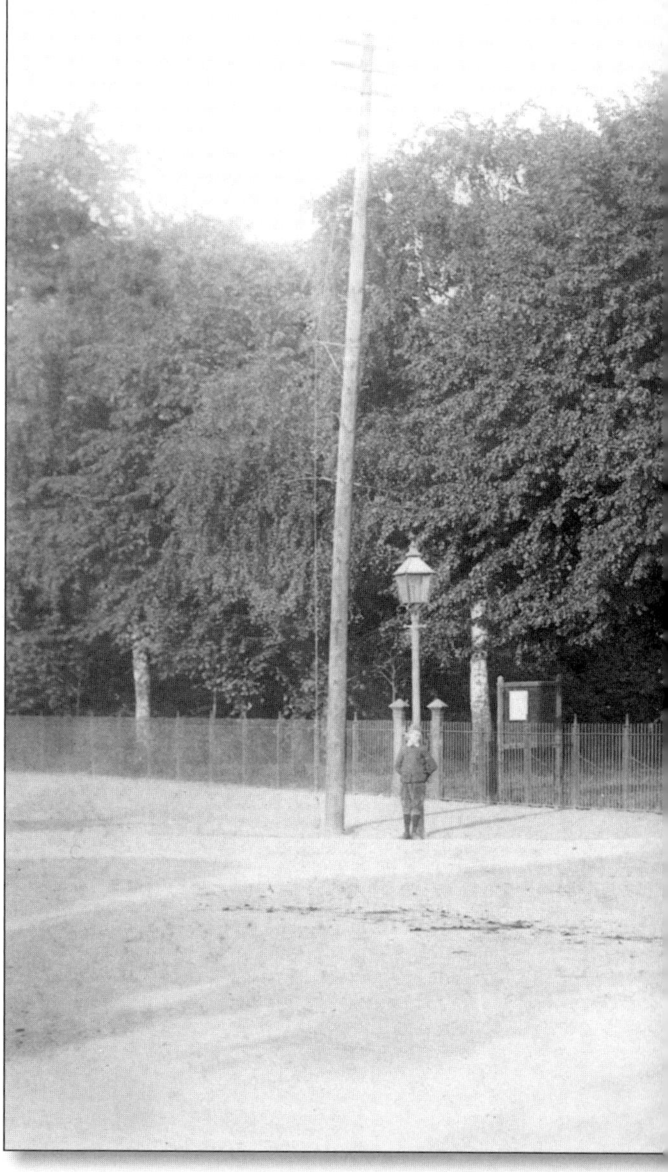

From the end of the 19th century, the fruit industry around Wisbech started to develop in earnest, and the town and district began to gain a reputation as a centre for the production of high quality fruit, such as strawberries, gooseberries, apples, pears, etc. A proportion of this fruit was distributed around the country to be consumed fresh, and the rest was pulped for jam. Opposite the town park is the canning factory of S W Smedley and Co Ltd (now H L Foods) who were pioneers in the canning and frozen food industry. The company was formed by Samuel Wallace Smedley, a fruit merchant from Evesham, on purchasing Keiller's pulp factory on the Lynn Road. In 1925, a new company was formed under the name of Wisbech Produce Canners, and shortly afterwards the company embarked on canning peas. The business expanded and had several factories around the country. In 1937, the Wisbech factory was the first, in England, to produce frozen peas and strawberries. The firm was renamed Smedley's Ltd in 1947 but its fortunes declined after the take-over by Imperial Tobacco in 1968, and the business was eventually taken over by Hillsdown

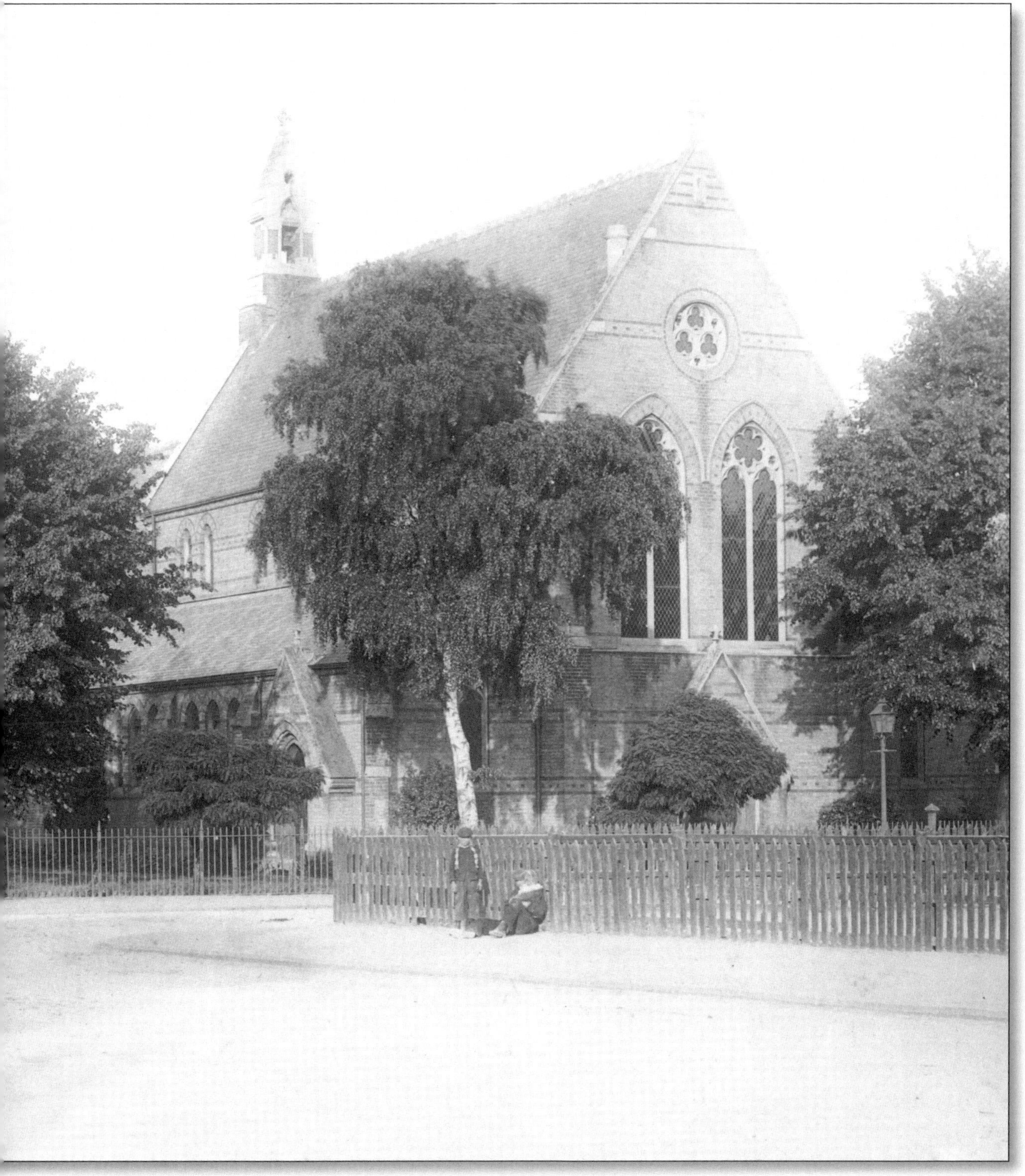

THE CANAL, PARK AND ROAD TO KING'S LYNN

Right: YOUNG'S MEMORIAL 1901 47587

Within the park is the memorial column dedicated to Richard Young (1809-71), a local shipping magnate, Member of Parliament, five times Mayor of Wisbech and Sheriff of London and Middlesex. Designed by J Wallis Chapman, of London, it was inaugurated on 31 October 1872, and cost around £300.

On 11 December 1883, the memorial column was blown over during a gale but was quickly rebuilt, with some modifications. The drinking fountain and enclosed garden have since been removed.

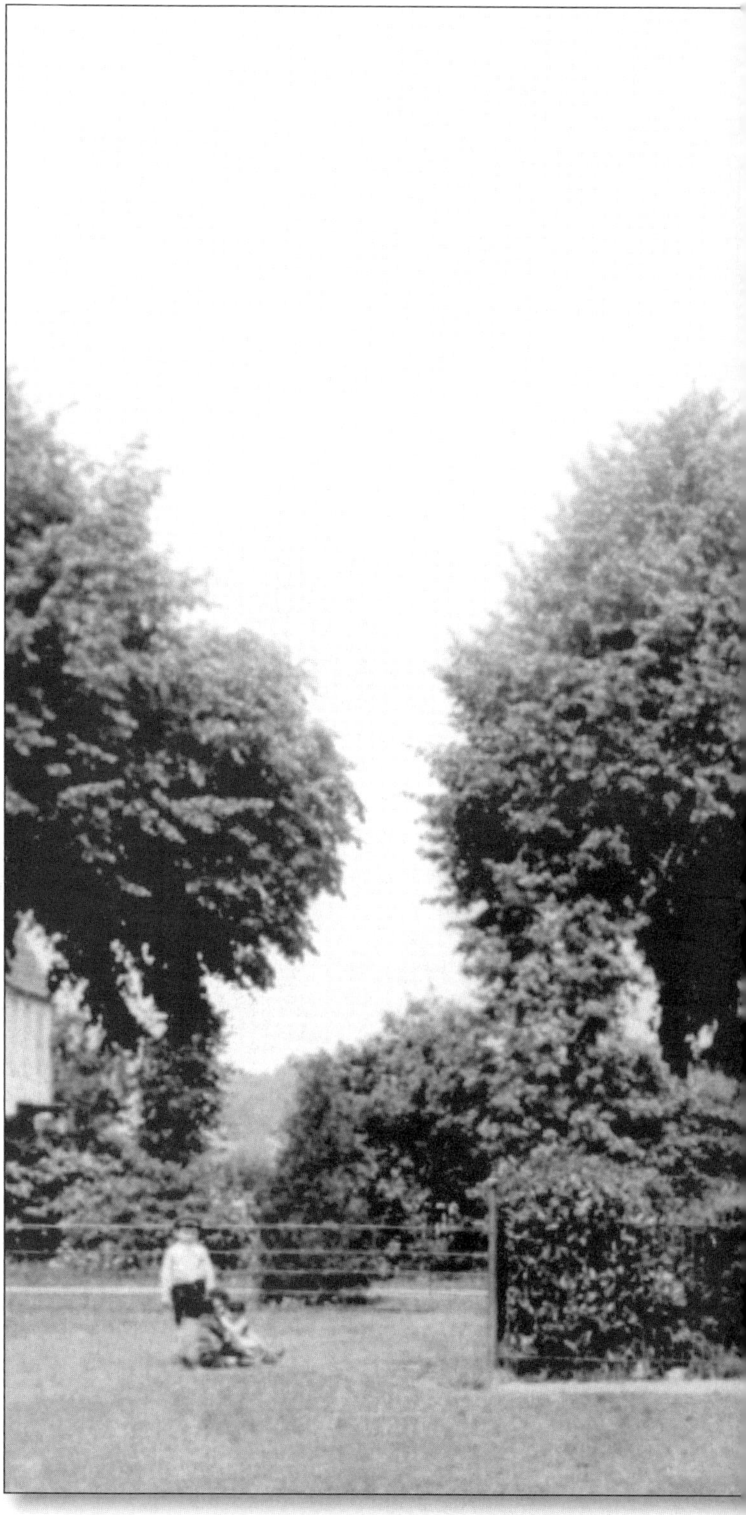

WISBECH CORPORATION CORONATION

Programme

16th May—OPENING OF ST. PETER'S GARDEN
3 p.m. By the Right Reverend the Lord Bishop of Ely

2nd June—UNITED RELIGIOUS SERVICE
9-30 a.m. In the Park (if wet—in the Parish Church)

2-30 p.m. **GRAND CARNIVAL PROCESSION**
With the following Classes:
Tradesmen's Turnouts
Tableaux
Decorated Cars
Decorated Motor Cycles
Decorated Pedal Cycles
Individual Fancy Dress (Adults over 16 years)

The Procession will form up on North Brink and will proceed to the Park via the Bridge, South Brink, Somer's Road, Queen's Road, Victoria Road, West Street, Church Terrace, Market Place, High Street, Bridge Street, Nene Quay and Lynn Road.

3-30 p.m. Approximate time of arrival of Procession in the Park, where judging will take place.
Three prizes per class, subject to a minimum entry of six.
Entry forms obtainable from the Town Clerk's Office.

6-30 p.m. **FANCY DRESS PARADE**
for children aged 4 - 16 years
To take place in the Park
There are prizes for all classes and entries are specially invited from family and school groups.
Details of classes and other particulars may be obtained from the Town Clerk's Office.
(If wet—this Parade will be transferred to the Corn Exchange—by kind permission of Mr. Norman G. Jacobs—and will start at 6 p.m.)

ALSO IN THE PARK:

8-0 p.m. **OLD TIME DANCING**

10-30 p.m. (approx.) **SPECTACULAR TORCHLIGHT DISPLAY**
With marching and counter-marching
followed by
SENSATIONAL FIREWORK DISPLAY
and
FLOODLIT TABLEAU

11-30 p.m. (approx.) to 1-30 a.m. **MODERN DANCING**
(If wet, the evening items will be postponed until the first suitable evening).

PROGRAMME OF EVENTS TO BE HELD IN THE PARK TO CELEBRATE THE CORONATION OF QUEEN ELIZABETH II IN 1953

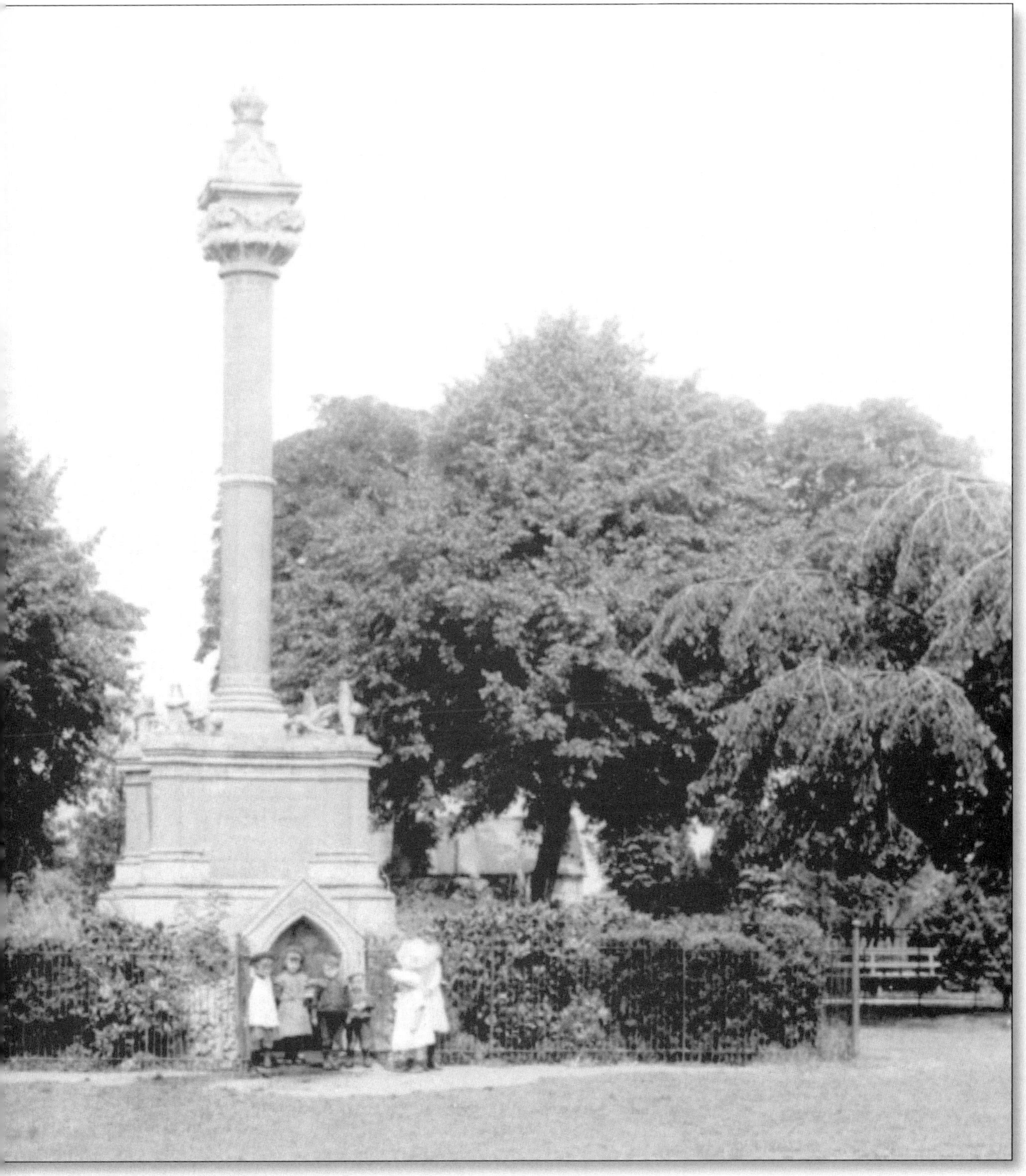

THE CANAL, PARK AND ROAD TO KING'S LYNN

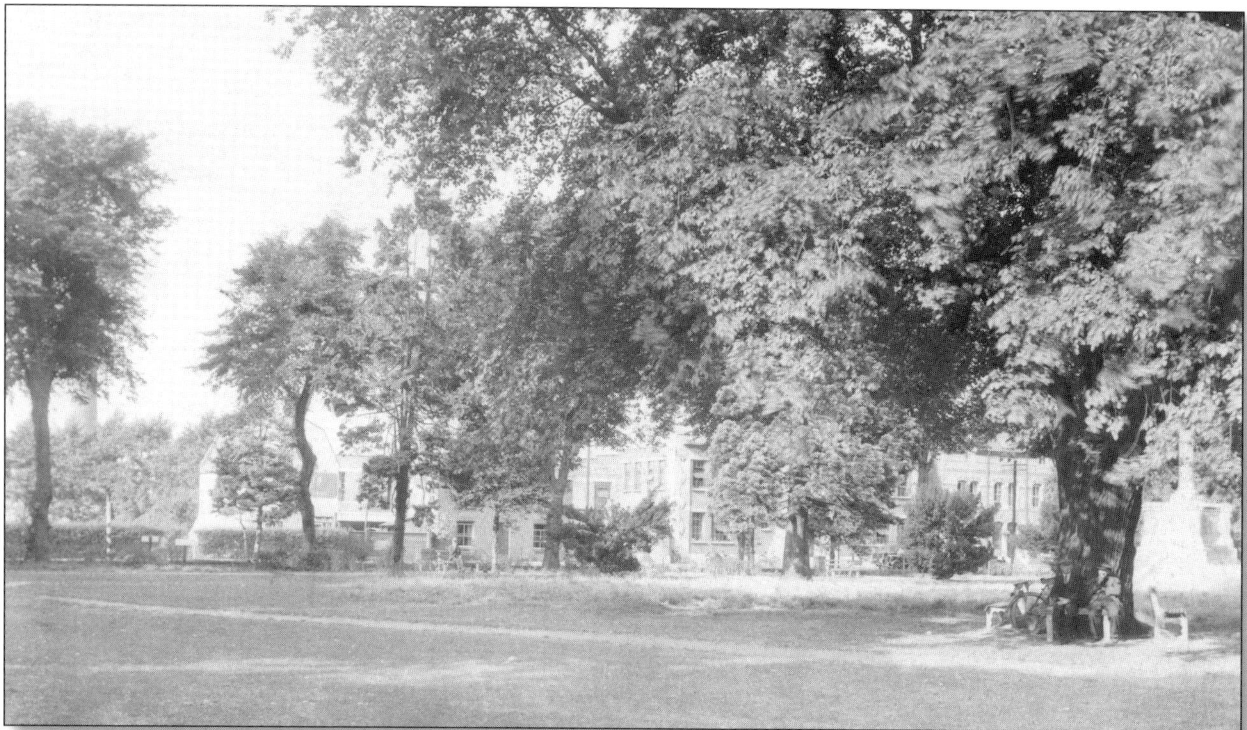

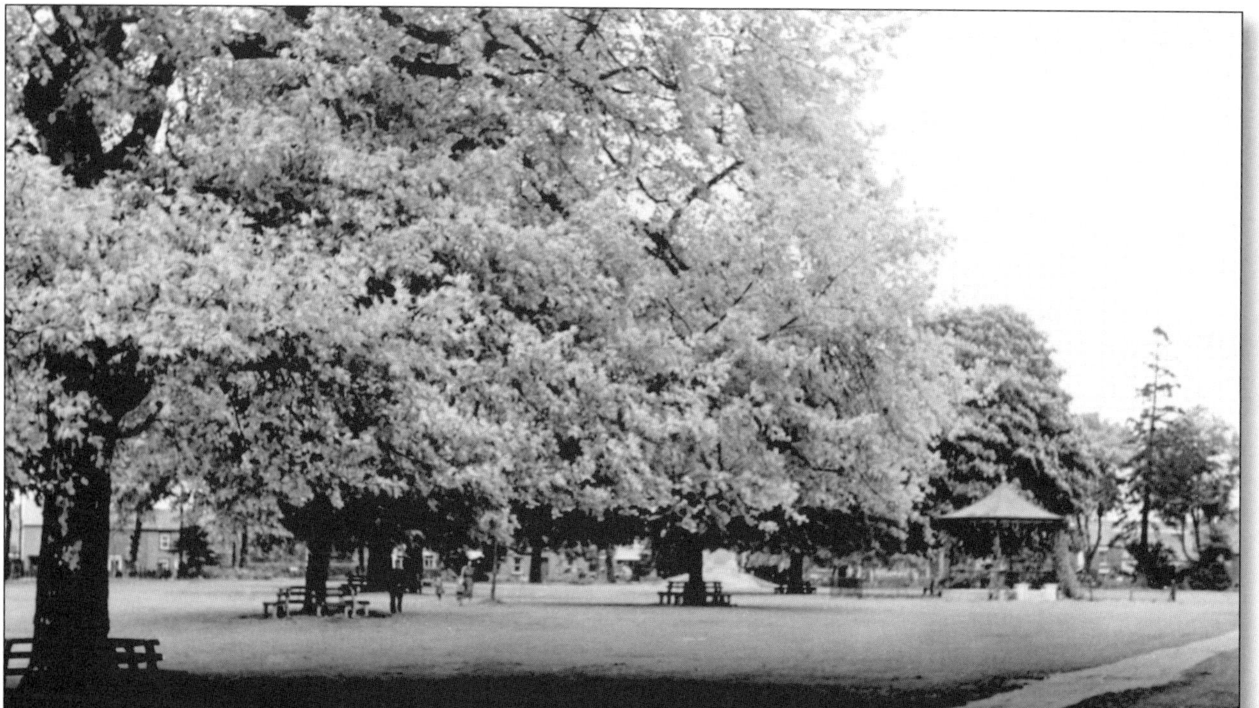

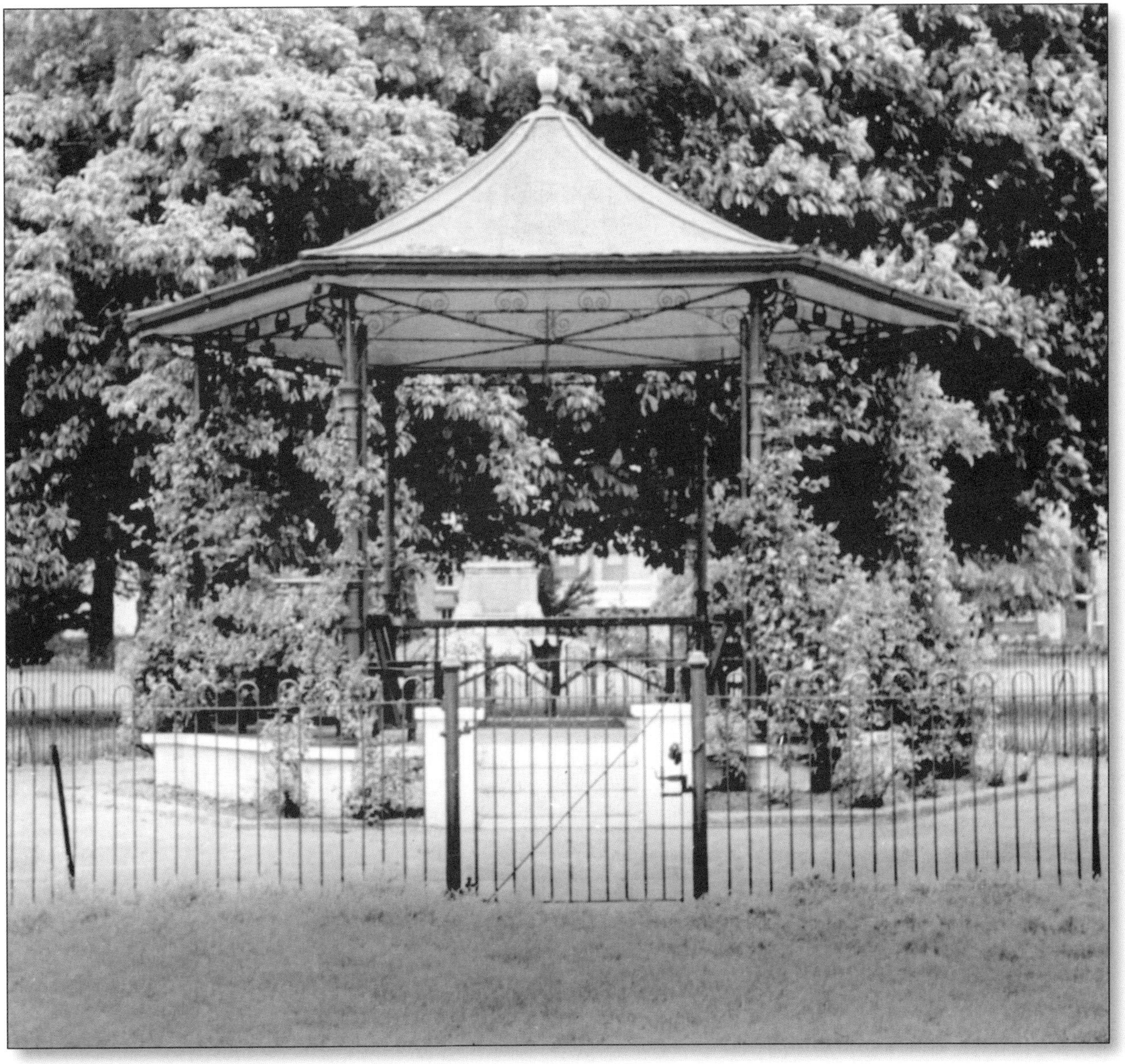

Opposite Top: THE PARK c1950 W115003

Opposite Bottom: THE PARK c1955 W115031

Above: THE PARK BANDSTAND c1955 W115027

Opened on 9 July 1908, the bandstand was built at a cost 'not exceeding £100'. The Corporation, at that time, leased out grazing rights to the park and the then tenant, although not objecting to the bandstand being built, asked for a reduction in rent owing to the loss of pasture - he duly got a rebate of £2 10s.

Names of Subscribers

The following people have kindly supported this book by purchasing limited edition copies prior to publication.

Mary and Gordon Anderson
As a tribute to my Nan, Georgina Andrew
Grace E Ashbee, Wisbech
Mr M D and Mrs D Ashby, Murrow, Wisbech
Mr Simon D Ashby, Murrow, Wisbech
Neville and June Atkinson
The Bailey Family of Wisbech
To M Bailey, Holbeach, Happy Birthday, from Christine, Brian and Laura
Mr and Mrs D W Ball
Pat and Robin Barber, Wisbech
Mr H Barker and Mrs M Barker,Wisbech
Derick and Carole Barsby, Wisbech
To Del and Judy Baxter, Peterborough
Mr J C and Mrs F E Beagles
P A Bennington, Wisbech
In memory of Richard Buxton Beresford
Michael D Bliss, Wisbech
W Bloy, 1925, some are memories
Mr A P and Mrs E F Boughen, Wisbech
Doris and George Boulton, Wisbech
The Briers Family, Wisbech
David John Brown, Wisbech
John Edward Brown, Wisbech
The Bunning Family
Brian Henry Burton
In memory of Gordon Burton of Wisbech
Margaret Butters
The Cable Family, Wisbech
BBC Cambridgeshire
Mr Fred W Clarke, Wisbech
Colin Clarke, Wisbech
Pam and Philip Clarke, Christmas 2005
Mr and Mrs Fred Clements of Wisbech
Paul and Carol Clifton, Wisbech 2005
Amy Rebecca Clingo, Walsoken, 30/04/05
Mr Alan Christopher and Mrs Joy Coates
Mr Jonathan Francis Coates and Family
Mr Paul Julian Coates and Family
Terry and Mary Cobb, Wisbech
Margaret and Anthony Edward Coleman
The Coleman Family, Wisbech
Barry and Ethel Cooper
Mrs Janet Cox, Mr John Patrick Cox
The Crawford Family, Wisbech
Mike Crawley, Wisbech
Celia and Robin Crawshaw
Peter R Crofts, Wisbech
Gof and Lil Crook of Rickmansworth
To Lorraine from Dad
To Samantha from Dad
To Ryan from Dad
To my darling Christine, with all my love David
James Anton De Leuce
Peter and Cherry Dennis, Wisbech
The Didwell Family, Wisbech
Bunard, Happy 80th Birthday, love Dilly
Basil and Elsie Dorks, Parson Drove
The Gedney Family in Murrow, Wisbech
Trevor and Janice Dyke, Wisbech
In memory of Mr A J A Eatherton, Wisbech
Stephen Ellinor
Leslie R W Elsey, Wisbech
In memory of Florence and Robert Esgate
For Barry Esgate
Mr W F and Mrs G M Farr, Wisbech
Sidney Ernest Feltell
T A and A M Fowler
Michael J Fowler
In memory of Sam Frisby, Wisbech
The Fulcher Family, Wisbech
Doug and Wendy Fullbrook
Colin V Sharman and Shirley E W Fuller
Mr K M Fysh
Mrs Gwen Garner (née Woodrow)
Martin Gibson
In memory of my husband, Stan Gray, from Doris
George Henry Green
Precious memories of Mr Bryan Green
Ralph and Joy Green, Wisbech

The Harley Family, Wisbech
In Memory of Brother Mike, George and Di Henson
Stephen Hobley, Wisbech
Caroline and Steve Holdsworth
Peter and Bridget Holmes
For Audrey Howard
The Howard Family, Wisbech
The Wisbech Hunters
Mr H and Mrs M Hutchesson, Tydd St Giles
Beryl Jackson
Mr A O and Mrs J O Janse Van Rensburg
Rita and Michael Jeffery, Wisbech 2005
For Jean Jeffree
Mr and Mrs S J E King, Wisbech
Mr V G Knight and Mrs M A Knight, Wisbech
The Knight Family, Wisbech St Mary
To John Knott on his 65th Birthday from Carmen and Tony
The Kowalewsky Family
The Lancaster Family, Wisbech
Mr F Long, Maurala, Front Road, Murrow, Cambs
In memory of Clarice Longland, Wisbech
Tony Longland, Wisbech
In Memory of Alan Lynn, My Father
Mr R S and Mrs G A Manning, Wisbech
Ian Markillie and Family, In memory of Bill
Esther Marshall
Katrina Mason, Gorefield
Mr J I McDonald and Mrs M A McDonald
Jane and Graham McQuade
Ron and Pam Merrison, Wisbech
David G Moules
Pamela, Francis Mulqueen and Family
In Memory of the Newman Family, Wisbech
Kenneth A Newman, Wisbech
George Nicholas
Avis and Anthony Norris, Wisbech St Mary
Patricia L North, Wisbech
Peter and Tina Nunn, Leverington, Wisbech
The O'Connor Family, Wisbech
The Oliver Family
R B and S R Page, Wisbech
Mr F and Mrs D Pattrick
Mr G Peeling, Wisbech
Matthew Perks
Rita and Philip Perry, Wisbech
To Pauline and Peter, Christmas 2005
Richard Lee Plumb
Raymond F Popeley
Mr L H Radford
Mr J L and Mrs E L Richardson, Wisbech
To our Wisbech friends, Marion and Rocco
Mr J W and Mrs G J Ross, Wisbech
Brother Robin Schooling, Old Memories, Pat
The Shales Family, Wisbech
Anthony George Simpson
Bernard A Smith, Wisbech
Pauline and Hubert Smith
Mr D Snow and Mrs C A Snow
The Stallan Family, Wisbech
Mr Bill Stannard and Mrs Liz Stannard, Wisbech
The Stroulger Family, Wisbech
Mr B C and Mrs A I Taylor
Jimmy Ed Thomas, March 26 1955 - April 7 1986
R W Thomas, Christmas 2005
Michael Charles Thorpe, June Thorpe
To Geoffrey from Dad (D R Threadgill)
To Graham from Dad (D R Threadgill)
A tribute to my ancestors - D R Threadgill
Elaine C Tuck, Wisbech
Anthony Twitchett, Happy 70th Birthday from your grandchildren
The Wager Family, Wisbech
Shaun and Tracy Wales, Walsoken, Wisbech
Frank Waling, Wisbech St Mary
Mr J K and Mrs L K Warren, Wisbech
Mr L R and Mrs B Warren, Gorefield
Mr B C and Mrs C M Warren, Wisbech St Mary
Mr and Mrs M R Watson
Anthony Rex White
To Harry, love from the White Family
Gary Whitehurst, Outwell
Ron Williams, Wisbech
Maureen Wilson
Mrs H G Wood, Wisbech
Douglas Woodrow
Heather Woods
Councillor Trevor Wright, Wisbech
Miss Ellery Yale-Wood

Index

Bridge 22-23
Bridge and Monument 20
Bridge and River 20-21
Bridge Street 39
Canal 75, 76
Castle 60-61
Church Street 72-73
Clarkson Memorial .. 14-15, 33, 34-35, 36-37, 38-39
Corn Exchange 30-31
Cornhill and the Town Hall 32
Docks and Timber Yards 21
Ely Place Baptist Chapel 59
High Street 40-41, 42-43
The Hope Inn 75
Leach's Mill 78-79, 80
Lynn Road 77
Market 2, 52-53
Market Place........ 12-13, 46-47, 48-49, 50-51, 54-55, 56-57
Memorial 58
Museum 62
Nene Quay 22
Nene Quay and Bridge 11
North Brink 24-25, 26
Octagon Church 28-29
Parish Church 10, 63
Park 84
Park Bandstand 85
Peckover House 26-27
River and North Brink 26
River Nene 16-17, 23, 26
South Brink 32
St Augustine's Church 80-81
St Peter's Church 64-65, 66-67, 68
The Rose & Crown Hotel 49
View from North Brink 18-19
Young's Memorial 82-83

Frith Products & Services

Francis Frith would doubtless be pleased to know that the pioneering publishing venture he started in 1860 still continues today. Over a hundred and forty years later, The Francis Frith Collection continues in the same innovative tradition and is now one of the foremost publishers of vintage photographs in the world. Some of the current activities include:

Interior Decoration

Today Frith's photographs can be seen framed and as giant wall murals in thousands of pubs, restaurants, hotels, banks, retail stores and other public buildings throughout the country. In every case they enhance the unique local atmosphere of the places they depict and provide reminders of gentler days in an increasingly busy and frenetic world.

Product Promotions

Frith products are used by many major companies to promote the sales of their own products or to reinforce their own history and heritage. Frith promotions have been used by Hovis bread, Courage beers, Scots Porage Oats, Colman's mustard, Cadbury's foods, Mellow Birds coffee, Dunhill pipe tobacco, Guinness, and Bulmer's Cider.

Genealogy and Family History

As the interest in family history and roots grows world-wide, more and more people are turning to Frith's photographs of Great Britain for images of the towns, villages and streets where their ancestors lived; and, of course, photographs of the churches and chapels where their ancestors were christened, married and buried are an essential part of every genealogy tree and family album.

Frith Products

All Frith photographs are available Framed or just as Mounted Prints and Posters (size 23 x 16 inches). These may be ordered from the address below. From time to time other products - Address Books, Calendars, Table Mats, etc - are available.

The Internet

Already ninety thousand Frith photographs can be viewed and purchased on the internet through the Frith websites and a myriad of partner sites.

For more detailed information on Frith companies and products, look at these sites:

www.francisfrith.co.uk
www.francisfrith.com
(for North American visitors)

See the complete list of Frith Books at:
www.francisfrith.co.uk
This web site is regularly updated with the latest list of publications from The Francis Frith Collection. If you wish to buy books relating to another part of the country that your local bookshop does not stock, you may purchase on-line.

For further information, trade, or author enquiries please contact us at the address below:
The Francis Frith Collection, Frith's Barn, Teffont, Salisbury, Wiltshire, England SP3 5QP.
Tel: +44 (0)1722 716 376 Fax: +44 (0)1722 716 881 Email: sales@francisfrith.co.uk

See Frith books on the internet at www.francisfrith.co.uk

FREE PRINT OF YOUR CHOICE

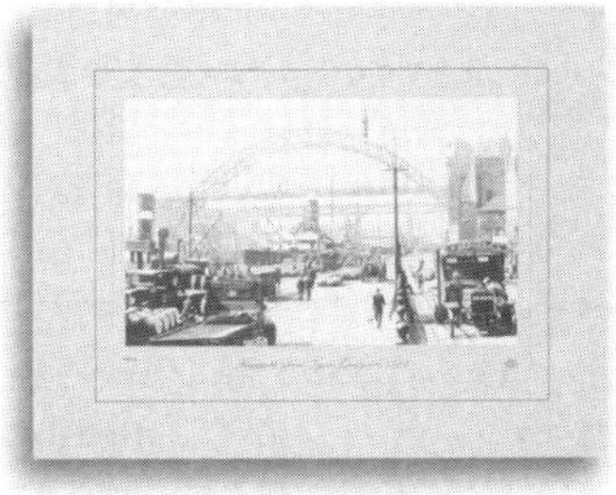

Mounted Print
Overall size 14 x 11 inches (355 x 280mm)

Choose any Frith photograph in this book. Please note: photographs with a reference number starting with a "Z" are not Frith photographs and cannot be supplied under this offer.
Simply complete the Voucher opposite and return it with your remittance for £2.25 (to cover postage and handling) and we will print the photograph of your choice in SEPIA (size 11 x 8 inches) and supply it in a cream mount with a burgundy rule line (overall size 14 x 11 inches).
Offer valid for delivery to one UK address only.

PLUS: **Order additional Mounted Prints at HALF PRICE - £7.49 each** (normally £14.99)
If you would like to order more Frith prints from this book, possibly as gifts for friends and family, you can buy them at half price (with no additional postage and handling costs).

PLUS: **Have your Mounted Prints framed**
For an extra £14.95 per print you can have your mounted print(s) framed in an elegant polished wood and gilt moulding, overall size 16 x 13 inches (no additional postage and handling required).

> **IMPORTANT!**
>
> **These special prices are only available if you use this form to order. You must use the ORIGINAL VOUCHER on this page (no copies permitted). We can only despatch to one UK address. This offer cannot be combined with any other offer.**

Send completed Voucher form to:
The Francis Frith Collection, Frith's Barn, Teffont, Salisbury, Wiltshire SP3 5QP

CHOOSE A PHOTOGRAPH FROM THIS BOOK

Voucher *for FREE and Reduced Price Frith Prints*

Please do not photocopy this voucher. Only the original is valid, so please fill it in, cut it out and return it to us with your order.

Picture ref no	Page no	Qty	Mounted @ £7.49	Framed + £14.95	Total Cost £
		1	Free of charge*	£	£
			£7.49	£	£
			£7.49	£	£
			£7.49	£	£
			£7.49	£	£
			£7.49	£	£
			* Post & handling		£2.25
			Total Order Cost		£

Please allow 28 days for delivery.
Offer available to one UK address only

Title of this book ....
I enclose a cheque/postal order for £ ....
made payable to 'The Francis Frith Collection'

OR please debit my Mastercard / Visa / Maestro card, details below

Card Number

Issue No (Maestro only) Valid from (Maestro)

Expires Signature

Name Mr/Mrs/Ms ....
Address ....
....
....
.... Postcode ....
Daytime Tel No ....
Email ....

ISBN 1-84589-031-0 Valid to 31/12/08

Free Print - see overleaf

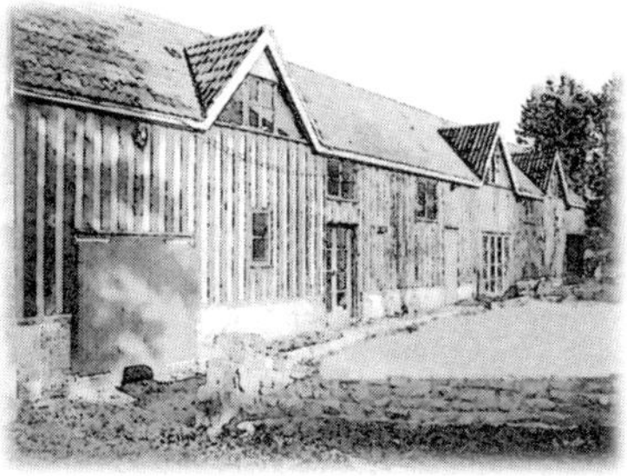

Can you help us with information about any of the Frith photographs in this book?

We are gradually compiling an historical record for each of the photographs in the Frith archive. It is always fascinating to find out the names of the people shown in the pictures, as well as insights into the shops, buildings and other features depicted.

If you recognize anyone in the photographs in this book, or if you have information not already included in the author's caption, do let us know. We would love to hear from you, and will try to publish it in future books or articles.

Our production team

Frith books are produced by a small dedicated team at offices in the converted Grade II listed 18th-century barn at Teffont near Salisbury, illustrated above. Most have worked with the Frith Collection for many years. All have in common one quality: they have a passion for the Frith Collection. The team is constantly expanding, but currently includes:

Andrew Alsop, Paul Baron, Jason Buck, John Buck, Heather Crisp, David Davies, Natalie Davis, Louis du Mont, Isobel Hall, Chris Hardwick, Lucy Hart, Julian Hight, Peter Horne, James Kinnear, Karen Kinnear, Tina Leary, Stuart Login, Sue Molloy, Miles Murray, Sarah Roberts, Kate Rotondetto, Dean Scource, Eliza Sackett, Terence Sackett, Sandra Sampson, Adrian Sanders, Sandra Sanger, Julia Skinner, Lewis Taylor, Shelley Tolcher, Lorraine Tuck, Miranda Tunnicliffe, Will Tunnicliffe, David Turner and Ricky Williams.